To Dr. Herman,

Thanks for all you did
to make this Summit
happen,

Michael Jem
April, 96

THE POLITICS
OF MEANING

THE
POLITICS
OF
MEANING

Restoring Hope and Possibility

in an Age of Cynicism

MICHAEL LERNER

Addison-Wesley Publishing Company

Reading, Massachusetts Menlo Park, California New York
Don Mills, Ontario Harlow, England Amsterdam Bonn
Sydney Singapore Tokyo Madrid San Juan
Paris Seoul Milan Mexico City Taipei

Library of Congress Cataloging-in-Publication Data
Lerner, Michael, 1943–
    The politics of meaning : restoring hope and possibility in an age
of cynicism / Michael Lerner.
      p. cm.
    Includes index.
    ISBN 0-201-47966-4
    1. Life.   2. Meaning (Philosophy)   3. Conduct of life.
4. Cynicism.   I. Title.
BD431.L384   1996
306'.0973'09049—dc20   95-49765
                                              CIP

Jacket design by Suzanne Heiser
Text design by Richard Oriolo
Set in 11 point Sabon by G & S Typesetters

1 2 3 4 5 6 7 8 9-MA-0099989796
First printing, April 1996

Addison-Wesley books are available at special discounts for bulk purchases by corporations, institutions, and other organizations. For more information, please contact the Corporate, Government, and Special Sales Department, Addison-Wesley Publishing Company, One Jacob Way, Reading, MA 01867, 1-800-238-9682.

To Peter Gabel

Peter Gabel is the president of New College of California and associate editor of *Tikkun* magazine, and cofounded with me the Institute for Labor and Mental Health in Oakland, California. We spent two decades working together as psychotherapists and social theorists, analyzing the psychodynamics of American society. We critiqued one-dimensional New Age philosophies, much of contemporary psychoanalytic theory, political correctness on the Left, and the conventional social and political theory that predominates in academia and in the media. It is sometimes difficult for me to remember which of the ideas in this book came from which of us. Peter's brilliance and insight were invaluable in the development of many of these ideas, and he might reasonably have been listed as a coauthor.

Contents

Acknowledgments

M ost of the ideas in this book derive from the Bible and from all that I have learned from the biblically based religious traditions, from my study and practice of psychoanalysis, and from various progressive political movements of the past centuries, particularly feminism and ecological theory. I have avoided footnotes because I hope the book will be useful to people who would feel intimidated by a more scholarly discussion of many of these issues. Yet I am well aware that my perspective, like all intellectual work, is deeply dependent on thousands of thinkers who went before me and on whose shoulders I stand. It is also dependent on the efforts of millions of people who have been engaged through the generations in the often thankless task of healing and repairing this world. Their experience comprises the "unwritten Torah" that I have learned by listening to their distilled wisdom as passed down through the thousands of social change activists, psychotherapists, theologians, spiritual renewalists, ecologists, social theorists, and teachers whom I have met over my thirty-two years of involvement in healing work.

I particularly wish to acknowledge the contribution to my thinking of Abraham Joshua Heschel, z"l (of blessed memory), my teacher at the Jewish Theological Seminary; Richard Lichtman, the chair of my doctoral committee in philosophy at the University of California; and the inspirational writings of Robert Bellah, Jessica Benjamin, Victor Frankl, Emanuel Levinas, Michael Sandel, Charles Taylor, and Wilhelm Reich. I appreciate the research done on this manuscript by Sarah Tobias; the editing by Alice Chasan; and the input and advice I received from Michael Bader, Tzvi Blanchard, Sam Bowles, Lynn Chancer, Herbert Gintis, Abby Layton, Lee Shore, Nanette Schore, Andrew Samuels, Sharon Welch, and Laurie Zoloth-Dorfman. The support of *Tikkun* staffers Pearl Gluck, Mark Levine, Beth Levy, and Martha Mendelsohn freed me to do some of this writing, and is gratefully acknowledged.

Henning Gutmann, my editor at Addison-Wesley, contributed ideas, perspective, and valuable editorial advice. I am grateful for his insights and support.

I also wish to acknowledge Elliot Liebow and the National Institute of Mental Health for supporting the work of the Institute for Labor and Mental Health, where some of the research underlying this book was done, as well as Nan Fink, not only for her generosity in creating *Tikkun* magazine and her wisdom in helping to sustain it during the years she was associated with it, but also for her remarkable ability to embody in her own being an ethos of caring and love.

I wish to thank my sister, Trish Vradenburg, whose humor has enthralled readers and television viewers for several decades, and whose brilliance, liveliness, and wit continue to inspire and delight me. Her love and loyalty are a further inspiration.

Finally, I wish to thank my son Akiba, whose presence in my life has been the primary experience making me capable of sustaining hopefulness and optimism. His warmth, genius, and ability to love and play have convinced me of the possibilities of human life that remain for the rest of us. His being testifies to the possibility of what we could be, and thus has given me the strength to more fully embrace the most hopeful aspects of Judaism and of a progressive politics of meaning.

THE POLITICS
OF MEANING

Introduction

Most Americans hunger for meaning and purpose in life. Yet we are caught within a web of cynicism that makes us question whether there could be any higher purpose besides material self-interest and looking out for number one. We see around us the destructive consequences of the dominant ethos of selfishness and materialism. People treat one another as objects to be manipulated rather than as beings who have a fundamental worth that ought to be respected and even cherished. Many of our cultural and economic institutions teach us to look at the world from a narrow, results-oriented, materialist perspective. In the process we lose touch with the awe and wonder we experienced as children at the grandeur of the universe. We get rewarded for the degree to which we have been able to put our own interests above those of our neighbors and friends, but then find ourselves in a world filled with mutual distrust and loneliness.

At the same time that we are caught in cynicism, however, we are desperate for hope. We hunger to be recognized by others, to be cherished for our own sakes and not for what we have accomplished or possess, and to be acknowledged as people who care about something higher and more important than our own self-interest. We hunger also for communities of meaning that can transcend the individualism and selfishness that we see around us and that will provide an ethical and spiritual framework that gives our lives some higher purpose. Some of us find those communities of meaning in a religious or nationalist framework, others in social change movements, still others in the framework of shared intellectual or artistic activity. These arenas may differ from one another in political, religious, or philosophical dogma, but they all promise something in common to their participants—that our fundamental value as human beings will be recognized and cherished within this context, and that our desire for connection to a community and to higher meaning for our lives will be nourished. It is this sense of the intrinsic worth of human beings and of our connection to something higher to which biblical religions refer when speaking of human beings as created in the image of God.

The "politics of meaning" that I call for in this book seeks to translate this ancient biblical truth into a contemporary language that can also be grasped by a nonreligious person. I am calling for a "politics of the image of God," an attempt to reconstruct the world in a way that really takes seriously the uniqueness and preciousness of every human being and our connection to a higher ethical and spiritual purpose that gives meaning to our lives.

There are millions of people *already* involved in seeking to build lives that are more ethically and spiritually grounded and meaningful. They do not have to be convinced that this endeavor is important. What this book seeks to do is to help them recognize one another, and recognize that their desire for ethical and spiritual lives need not be isolated from their "real-world" activities, but rather could become the basis for reshaping that "real world." The powerful desire of so many of us to escape the distorting impact of the materialism and selfishness of daily life could become a powerful motivating force for changing the way we organize our world, so that we no longer have to escape from it. That is part of the task of a politics of meaning.

The Hunger for Meaning

The idea of a politics of meaning emerged from the work that a group of psychiatrists, psychologists, social workers, family therapists, union activists, and social theorists pioneered in Oakland, California, starting in 1976. Our aim was to better understand the psychodynamics of middle-income working people, and also to try to understand why so many of them were moving to the political Right. We set up a Stress Clinic that was explicitly *not* psychotherapy-oriented, and worked extensively with the labor movement and various corporations to attract a range of people who might never have dreamt of going to therapy. Within our Stress Clinic we created occupational stress groups and family support groups aimed at training people to deal with the problems that any mentally healthy person would likely face at work or in family life.

What we learned from the thousands of people who participated in these groups challenged many of the beliefs that prevailed among us, and, more generally, in the liberal culture from which we researchers had come. We had thought of ourselves as psychologically sophisticated when we started this work, but we quickly learned that our assumptions about middle-income Americans were mistaken, prejudiced, and elitist. For example, most of us imagined that most Americans are motivated primarily by material self-interest. So we were surprised to discover that these middle Americans often experience more stress from feeling that they are wasting their lives doing meaningless work than from feeling that they are not making enough money.

We found middle-income people deeply unhappy because they hunger to serve the common good and to contribute something with their talents and energies, yet find that their actual work gives them little opportunity to do so. They often turn to demands for more money as a compensation for a life that otherwise feels frustrating and empty. In the Left and among many academics it has been almost a rule of reason to believe that what people *really* care about is their own material well-being, and that believing anything else is just some kind of populist romanticization. But we uncovered a far deeper desire—the desire to have meaningful work, work that people believe would contribute to some higher purpose than self-advancement.

True enough, many people told us that it is just common sense to try to get as much money as possible—precisely because most have given up on ever finding a work situation in which they can use their talents for some higher purpose. And yet what we learned was that many of these people hate living in a world governed by a money-oriented ethos, even as they simultaneously believe that it is impossible to change such a world.

Too often, people blame themselves. They internalize the dominant view of society—that they live in a society based on merit. In this meritocracy, whatever they get is what they deserve. Ironically, many of the working people we interviewed know that merit is often not the major factor for advancement at their own workplaces. They frequently told stories of supervisors who know less than those whom they supervise, or of favoritism in promotions based on personal relationships. Similarly, many of our interviewees understand that most of those people in the one percent of the population that owns forty percent of the wealth in the United States have not earned that wealth, but rather inherited much of it, or at least enough to give them a competitive edge in "making it."

Yet so deep is the collective belief in the meritocracy, that these very same people whom we interviewed have often adopted the meritocratic framework to explain their own lives. They believe that if they lack satisfaction in their personal lives, it must be due to some inadequacy in themselves. Most people have developed a complex personal story of how they screwed things up. It explains why they have been unable to find work that would more adequately fulfill their need for meaning and purpose, and why they have failed to build lives in which they receive greater recognition and caring from others.

Naturally, most people do not present this hunger for meaning as the first thing that they tell you about their lives. On the contrary, precisely because they have bought the meritocratic fantasy that their frustrated need for meaning is solely their own fault, they are at first reluctant to reveal how deeply unhappy they are.

At first, most of the people we talked to wanted to assure us, as they assured their coworkers and friends, that everything was fine, that they were handling things well, that they never let stress really get to them, and that their lives were good. (This is the kind of report that many pollsters discover when they ask superficial questions.) But what we found as we continued to talk to people over some time (in eight- to twelve-week group sessions) is that once people got past their initial defensiveness and desire to present themselves as "together," they began to tell real stories about their lives that presented a very different and more troubling picture.

We talked to bus drivers and telephone operators, to corporate middle managers and to government employees, to auto workers and to machinists, to electronics workers in Silicon Valley and to teachers in public and private schools, to hospital orderlies and doctors, to technicians and nurses, to social workers and college professors, to lawyers and to architects, to secretaries and to postal workers, to computer experts and to scientists, to policemen and to insurance salespeople, to restaurant workers and to service employees, to engineers and to people who work in the media.

We found thousands of Americans—from every walk of life, ethnic and religious background, political persuasion and lifestyle—filled with lives of pain and self-blame, and turning to the political Right because the Right spoke about the collapse of families, the difficulty of teaching good values to children, the fear of crime, and the absence of spirituality in their lives. The Right seemed to understand their hunger for community and connection.

Even people who originally seemed the most unconcerned about connection with others, people who acted withdrawn or even hostile at the workplace or in the occupational stress groups we ran, often ended up revealing a hunger for community, recognition, and higher purpose. We learned the hidden sources of some daily behavior that might easily indicate a seeming desire for emotional distance from others, or a seeming indifference or hostility or anger. Such behavior is produced by the frustration of a deep yearning for connection with others, a pessimism about one's ability to ever get one's needs met, and a deep shame about one's own imagined failures.

This same frustration accounts for most of the violence, destructiveness, and other irrational behavior we see in daily life. We typically blame much of the anger and frustration in people on individual pathology, for which the prescribed remedy is psychotherapy or psychotropic drugs. But what we are reluctant to see is how frequently the *deprivation of meaning* in daily life is at the root of many of our individual and social problems.

Even people who at first seemed totally immersed in the pursuit of accumulating goods were, we soon discovered, more complex. They were often using those goods to soothe their pain over the disappointment they experienced at not having been able to find a world in which their hunger for deeper meaning could be satisfied. Some had grown cynical and angry. But few had been totally successful in repressing all memory of a time in their life when they had hungered for something different and more fulfilling. Similarly, even those people who had had a "meaning-overdose" through childhood exposure to oppressive religious, nationalistic, or conformist communities, and had become militantly anti-meaning in their adult lives, sometimes let slip their own hunger for something more than their own cynicism could deliver. Underneath some of the most militant meaning-deniers we could sometimes encounter a person who once had really wanted meaning, had found distorted versions of it, and had recoiled in anger but had not necessarily fully repressed the initial desire. Sometimes we could feel the pain of the meaning-deniers as intensely as the pain we discovered more easily in so many others.

Pain? The term has been so overused in recent decades, and has become so much a part of the psychobabble of our society, that some people think it is merely a slogan or a convenient way to avoid careful thinking. But in my work as a psychotherapist working with these middle-income people, I listened to the stories of thousands of ordinary Americans and their families, and learned of lives filled with loneliness, isolation, and a persistent feeling that no one could be trusted.

Not surprisingly, this way of looking at the world makes people feel terrible about themselves. A great deal of their energy is spent trying to repress these feelings and cheer themselves up, to forget the humiliations that they have experienced at work or at home and in personal relationships where they feel underappreciated and have to prove their worth to others. Most people feel that they are seen as they truly are by very few others, and that they are valued by others only for what others can get from them.

The Effects of Selfishness

The ethos of cynicism and selfishness plays through our personal lives, often in destructive ways. When we look at one another from the standpoint of what we can get, as though the main purpose of others in our world is to be potential satisfiers of our needs, the world becomes filled with insecurity in human relationships. As we increasingly look for the best possible deal in our personal lives, it becomes more difficult to be sure that our friend, partner, or spouse will not someday find a better deal in a relationship somewhere else, and we may be abandoned. Not all relationships are like this, but a growing number of people report feeling insecure in their relationships and unsure that these will last, in large part because such people realize that at some point they may be less marketable.

Seeing others primarily in terms of what they can do to satisfy our needs makes us think that many people are expendable. No wonder, then, that a growing minority of people are willing to turn their backs on the poor and the most oppressed. Corporate elites have no trouble closing down offices or factories, in the process throwing hundreds or sometimes thousands of people out of work, if doing so improves the corporation's profit margin. We used to live in a society in which we felt a greater sense of solidarity with one another, and hence were less willing to let others be left to their own fates. But today, more of us are narrowing our circle of caring to our immediate family and friends. Sectors of the population that are unlikely to become a productive part of the competitive market system are dismissed as economic basket cases, and on these grounds we are told that it is appropriate to turn our backs on them and no longer worry about whether they have adequate food, shelter, clothing, or health care.

All this turning away from one another is terrible for our souls. When we live in a world in which ethical and spiritual goals have been excluded and ridiculed, we find the human spirit shrinking, with disastrous consequences. Selfishness and cynicism are bad for our physical and psychological health.

Few of us actually think of ourselves as selfish. After all, we care about our immediate family and close friends, and sometimes sacrifice our own desires for them. However, in advanced industrial societies today, the circle of people for whom we are willing to make sacrifices or whose interests really concern us has narrowed in recent years.

We might think of ourselves and of societies on a continuum. On one end of the continuum, people approximate the extreme of caring only for themselves. On the other end, people begin to approach the biblical ideal: seeing every single human being as created in the image of God, and hence as infinitely precious and deserving of our caring and respect. On this end of the spectrum, we find people who concern themselves with improving the lot of immigrants and the homeless, for example, because they recognize these others as fundamentally connected to all of us.

We live in a world in which more and more people find it difficult to recognize others as fundamentally deserving of our love and our caring. Flooded by messages that tell us that caring for others is likely to be self-destructive, we find it increasingly difficult to give much attention to the needs of others, unless we can see how caring will be of advantage to us as well.

We learn that everyone else is just out for personal gain, and that we would be foolish to behave otherwise. We assume that no one is going to be there for us when we need help, so there is no point in taking risks for the sake of others.

Yet this cynicism about the possibility of solidarity and community with others actually makes us more powerless than we need to be. Cynicism disempowers, and powerlessness corrupts. Powerlessness makes us feel that we are going to get hurt by others who will overpower us and take advantage of us, unless we do it to them first. As a result, we are often ungenerous to others, whom we see as our competitors. We fear that to trust them will make us more vulnerable to manipulation and defeat of our own interests. But when this fear becomes widely shared, we find it impossible to mobilize people to defend one another's interests, leaving each of us with considerably less power than we might have had.

Mutual distrust and the resulting erosion of community and solidarity make it easier, for example, for corporations to threaten to move their resources to another continent where they can make better profits and face fewer restrictions on environmentally destructive processes. If the ethos of selfishness and cynicism had not already disempowered most Americans, we would stand up together to insist on corporate responsibility to those whose lives would be hurt when a plant closed or significantly cut back its employees. Similarly, we would be making efforts to improve the negotiating power and incomes of people in other countries, so that employees abroad were no longer working for subsistence wages, and strengthening the power of governments in Third World countries to demand environmental responsibility. If we could see ourselves in alliance with others, both here and around the world, we would feel more powerful, and would be in a better position to put constraints on irresponsible corporate decision-making.

Instead, because most of us doubt the possibility of people standing strongly in solidarity with one another, we rarely think we can change much about the big picture of the economy or the realities of social and political life. We know that our economic system is producing a worldwide ecological crisis by consuming the earth's resources at a rate that outpaces its regenerative capacities. But we pretend not to know—and support one another in collective denial. Indeed, we often end up trying to make sure that we personally will find a way out of the immediate problems caused by corporate irresponsibility and social disintegration. We imagine that we personally can get the new skills or find the jobs or make the investments that will ensure that we personally will not get hurt. Perhaps we can even find an angle that will allow us to benefit personally from the globalization of the market. And because everyone is thinking this way, there is no social force to stand up to corporations as they reduce the number of people they employ, globalize their investments, and use their political clout to oppose environmental sanity.

Once we give up on the possibility of building an economic world based on the principle that we are all in it together, it is easy to understand why more and more Americans respond to demagogues on the Right who appeal to narrow self-interest and tell us that it is okay to abandon the poor and the oppressed and to focus solely on our own immediate material well-being. The powerful impact of the Newt Gingrich–style right wing on American politics depends on most Americans coming to believe that we cannot afford to continue to care for others. So we try to close our ears to the pain and upset being caused by our cutbacks in social services, health care, supplemental food assistance, and other programs for the poor. Some of us move to the suburbs, build walls around our communities, and imagine that we can keep out of our lives the problems we see all around us.

Even those who do not build physical walls increasingly build emotional walls, so that we find it easier to avert our glance from the eyes of the homeless and hungry that populate our cities, and easier to shut our ears to the cries of pain of others. But the better we are at closing ourselves off from others' pain, the more isolated we become. And we feel ourselves surrounded by others who have cut themselves off from truly caring about us. All the more reason to fear that no one will take care of us when we really need them— a fear that motivates many people to be ruthlessly engaged in looking out for number one, regardless of the consequences for others.

Does Economics Come First?

To some readers, this may seem like a peculiar moment to be raising spiritual and ethical concerns. As economic competition increases and jobs get transferred to Third World countries, they argue, the world becomes a nastier place, not a place more open to sustaining loving relationships and spiritual development. Economic realities, they argue, must be given priority. Or, in the words of that great social theorist James Carville, "it's the economy, stupid."

The politics of meaning is, in part, a rejection of this reductionist view of human desires and needs. In my view, it's not just the economy! But I do not deny that people also want economic security. On the contrary, it is my view that the growing economic fears of Americans are central to the insecurity and pain they face. Yet these fears are intrinsically connected to our shared beliefs that we can't count on each other either to stand up to corporate power or to provide adequate caring to those of us who will be hurt when corporations downsize and disinvest. If there were a different ethical and spiritual connection between people, there would be a different economic reality.

The economic and meaning crises are not two different ones—they are two different dimensions of the same crisis. One cannot first deal with the economy and then later worry about meaning issues, one cannot argue that the economy by itself causes the disruption of communities, and one cannot argue that these are two separately existing crises that together constitute the problem. The economic and meaning issues are too closely linked. It is my contention that when we understand the meaning dimension of the economic crisis, we will be in a stronger position to deal with it, and that the failure of the Left is in part a product of its inability to understand that meaning dimension. For that reason, I have not spent time in this book reviewing the facts of corporate power and the way that the globalization of the economy is undermining our lives.

Instead, in this book I want to highlight what is missing from all these analyses: a deep understanding of the meaning dimension of the problem. Economic realities are not mere natural facts but are constituted partly by the way we see ourselves. When working people decide to act powerfully and challenge corporations and insist on greater rights for workers, that experience becomes part of the new economic reality. Conversely, when people feel powerless to stop the deindustrialization of America and the transfer of jobs abroad, that sense of powerlessness helps constitute a different economic reality. So economic reality cannot be understood apart from the level of solidarity and the framework of meaning that exists in the society. If we had a different framework of meaning today, for example, it would be possible to redistribute work such that everyone had a thirty-hour week and those who are today unemployed or underemployed would be fully employed. That this change does not happen issues from the level of solidarity and the degree to which people might be willing to share work—reduce their workload, but also somewhat reduce their income. How much people are open to this idea is not an economic fact, but a "meaning-fact"—a fact that could be shaped by the degree to which people come to see their own needs and their own self-interest as requiring that they live in a society with a new sensitivity to the well-being of others. It is the contention of this book that such a sensitivity is both possible and absolutely necessary. And that is why meaning cannot be given lower priority than economics.

To seriously confront the loss of jobs on a global scale, we Americans would have to expand our circle of caring to include people throughout the world. We would have to worry about their standard of living, their ability to stand up for themselves, and their ability to prevent ecologically destructive production.

Some people argue that it is simply economic reality that makes us narrow our circle of caring when we are facing economic uncertainties. Americans cannot be expected to pay attention to ethical and spiritual arguments that would induce us to care for others at a time when we are worried about our own economic survival, can we?

Yet, throughout American history, it has been precisely the hard times that have led us to band together and become more aware of common interests and shared purposes. If that is not happening today, it is not because of some economic condition, but rather because the dominant individualism has led us to be so distrustful of others, so certain that all others are worried about only themselves, that we find it hard to imagine getting together with others to solve common problems. When we saw ourselves as part of some large community of caring, as during the Depression of the 1930s, we were willing to redistribute societal resources to take care of those most hurt by economic downturns. Today, Western societies have far greater wealth, but we often feel we can less afford to take care of those in need. This is not a change in economic facts, but a change in the degree to which people feel isolated and unable to believe that we could be part of some larger "we" in which we all cared for one another.

Extending the circle of caring is precisely the opposite of the dynamic prevalent in American society today. The flow of social energy tends toward smaller and smaller circles of caring; many of us imagine that we can build a good life by limiting our caring to the smallest possible arena—our immediate families. Yet much of what we want most in the world—loving relationships, mutual recognition, friendships based on loyalty and commitment, physical and emotional safety, a sense of purpose and meaning for our lives—cannot be sustained in a world that is continually narrowing the circles of caring, because this very process of narrowing creates an ethos of selfishness that undermines loving relationships.

Some Americans imagine that the way we can best deal with the globalization of capital and the downsizing of American corporations is to protect ourselves by paying less taxes, cutting government programs, and insulating ourselves from the impact of these cuts by retreating to walled suburban enclaves. Yet in order to do this, we have to develop qualities of insensitivity to the fate of others that actually undermine our natural instinct to care for others. The qualities of soul and psyche that make it possible for us to narrow our circle of caring *are* the very qualities that make it possible for us to treat other human beings and their needs as largely irrelevant to us, except insofar as they are able to satisfy our own needs and desires.

"Well," some people might say, "I'm willing to pay that price rather than have to spend my time worrying about the fate of others, particularly given that I don't believe I can do much for anyone else anyway." Yet the cost of developing this attitude is increasing showing up all around us in unexpected and hurtful ways. People who have taught themselves to see others instrumentally (that is, in terms of what these others can do for them) will manifest this same instrumental consciousness when they deal with friends and family members and intimate relationships. The more this attitude takes hold, the more we come to feel surrounded by a world of people who are just out for themselves; the result shows up in broken families and relationships, and in a growing sense of isolation even among people whose families remain intact. The ethos of selfishness that we thought we might leave behind at work, or in our disregard for the fate of others around the world or in our inner cities, leaps over the tallest walls of our gilded suburban ghettos and infects the most intimate details of our lives.

At this moment in American history, elites of wealth and power have managed to convince many middle-income Americans that they ought to identify with the interests of the wealthy and powerful instead of with those of the less fortunate. (Sample arguments include the following: "Perhaps you'll make it someday"; "Why identify with the losers?"; "You can make a personal transition to the world ahead if you watch out for yourself, but that won't work if you have to spend your energies and resources watching out for everyone else.")

The politics of meaning is, in part, a strategy to help change this thinking and renew an alliance between middle-income people and the poor. It is not necessarily aimed *against* the rich, but rather against the ethos of selfishness and materialism that has allowed many people to accept cuts in social service programs as the price for cutting their own taxes and those of the rich. This renewed alliance will be easier to build when people fully understand that the very same selfishness that allows them to shut their ears to the needs of the poor, or to the impact of American economic policies on the well-being of many people in the Third World, is what allows their wives or husbands, boyfriends or girlfriends, children or neighbors, to act in selfish or insensitive ways. Similarly, when people fully understand that the deepening ecological crisis cannot be separated from the ethos of selfishness, and that, as they narrow their circles of caring, they make it more likely that they personally will face a widening array of environmental catastrophes, it will be easier to build a transformative social change movement. The politics of meaning helps people understand why it is in their interest to reverse the flow of energy and expand rather than contract their circles of caring. In short, it is becoming harder and harder for most of us to have the kinds of personal lives we want—blessed with loving friendships, health, and strong family ties—in a world that is dominated by escalating levels of selfishness and cynicism.

Yet, it is sometimes hard to see other people as really deserving of our love and caring when we have so deeply internalized a materialistic and reductionist account of what it means to be a human being. Ever since the rise of market societies helped displace spiritually based conceptions of human life, Western thought has been shaped by the view that human beings are isolated monads whose highest goal is individual fulfillment in a universe designed for this self-indulgent purpose. The egocentricism and arrogance of many strains of contemporary Western thought reflect and help perpetuate a social reality in which human beings are separated from one another and from the larger spiritual reality of the universe. We each have come to see ourselves as the center of reality, and then to wonder how we could ever connect with others or be part of a real community.

Not surprisingly, this way of construing reality generates a great deal of cynicism about our ability to connect with one another or to build a society based on trust and caring. The disenchanting of the world has led us to regard humans as little more than complex machines, perhaps only marginally more clever than the fancy line of new computers soon to arrive on the market, and which are primarily interested in maximizing their own self-interest (often at our expense). Though philosophers can argue that there is no necessary connection between reductionism and disrespect, it turns out that the more people see one another in these materialistic terms, the less they feel compelled by sentiments of sympathy and solidarity in the actual world in which we live. The de-meaning of the world is closely associated (in fact, if not in theory) with the demeaning of other human beings. Hence, reclaiming our sense of the holy, and revitalizing our ability to see others as embodiments of a miraculous spiritual energy whose grandeur is reflected throughout the universe, may be important elements in the process by which we reverse the inward flow of caring energy and begin to expand our circles of caring.

To begin to see reality in this expansive way requires a fundamental rethinking of the underpinnings of our intellectual life. That rethinking is already underway in many areas of contemporary thought, and its success in reaffirming our hunger for meaning will play an important role in building the preconditions for the possibility of healing our world.

A spiritual sensibility encourages us to see ourselves as part of the fundamental unity of all being. If the thrust of the market ethos has been to foster a competitive individualism, a major thrust of many traditional religious and spiritual sensibilities has been to help us see our connection with all other human beings.

Of course, I am well aware of the ways in which religious traditions and spiritual communities have come to demean those who did not share their specific religious or spiritual visions. There are those who have used religion or spirituality as yet another instrument of domination and control, in order to advance their own interests or the interests of a particular group of coreligionists. In fact, it was precisely in reaction to the use of religion to serve the interests of powerful elites, and the resulting sanctification of inequalities of power and wealth, that many people abandoned religion and embraced the promise of individual fulfillment in the competitive secular market. Yet today, most of the major Western religious and spiritual traditions are undergoing a renewal process that is reclaiming their own deepest underlying spiritual truths, even at the cost of overtly struggling against existing religious hierarchies that still use religion or manipulate spiritual language to maintain their own power. This renewal process has created a burgeoning spirituality that cuts across particular religious differences and recognizes a fundamental commonality among all human beings.

Care for the Soul: The Oneness of All Being

The politics of meaning is a modest attempt to apply some of the ancient wisdom of the human race to our contemporary reality, wisdom that has too often been ignored, denied, or even denigrated. In particular, this book attempts to draw out into secular language and concepts the implications of a powerful message that has been communicated by many religious and spiritual traditions: that it is our estrangement from the oneness of all being (or, in religious terms, from the God who is one) that is the source of our greatest illusion, estrangement and misunderstanding of ourselves. It is this separation or estrangement from the oneness of all being that leads to idolatry—our tendency to absolutize or worship some part of the universe or some configuration of reality at a particular moment as though it were the ultimate reality, rather than what it is, a split-off part of the whole. Instead of seeing current tendencies towards extreme individualism and selfishness as the flourishing of an unchanging and unchangeable "human nature," the politics of meaning recognizes that the current way in which people relate to one another is only a manifestation of this particular moment in history when market societies shape our views of what is natural. It is not the absolute, and the world could be very different.

The fundamental aspiration of many spiritual movements today is to help us overcome the false pride and egotism that comes from conceptualizing ourselves as the center of the universe and acting from the arrogant assumption that the world was made to serve our individual needs. This egotistical arrogance has led us to the brink of ecological disaster. A similar arrogance underlies our belief that one country (or one race or one religion, for example) has the right to impose its needs on the rest of humanity, to appropriate a disproportionate amount of the world's resources and wealth, or to impose its agenda on everyone else. One need not be associated with any particular religious tradition to recognize that this form of arrogance has created unnecessary pain throughout human history—and that we as human beings need to change those institutions that embody this distorting consciousness. This consciousness fails to recognize that we live in a globally interconnected world, and that the destruction of the web of life in one part of the planet or in one urban neighborhood will have dramatic consequences for all of us in the not-too-long run.

Ecological theory alerts us to the planetary need for a whole new relationship to the earth. Instead of responding to the world with awe and wonder, we have looked at this planet as a resource to be exploited without limit. Yet, the argument that future generations may suffer from our profligate disregard for the consequences of our ecological irresponsibility has little impact on the individual who has learned to worry only about his or her own needs. It is only by helping such people see that their own needs for love and caring will not be met in a world based on selfishness, cynicism, and materialism, that they might even begin to open themselves to the wisdom of the spiritual inheritance of the human race. That is why a politics-of-meaning movement places so much focus on showing people why their deepest psychological needs require an ethical and spiritual transformation of the world.

In the process, we need to build millions of little moments of caring on an individual level. Indeed, as talk of a politics of meaning becomes more widespread, many people will feel it easier to publicly acknowledge their own spiritual and ethical aspirations and will allow themselves to give more space to their highest vision in their personal interactions with others. A politics of meaning is as much about these millions of small acts as it is about any larger change. The two necessarily go hand in hand.

Ultimately, one of the best ways to take care of our souls is to build a society that supports rather than undermines our highest moral and spiritual intuitions and inclinations. Yet, building that society can never be divided from the daily practices through which we live out our ethical and spiritual lives, both in the way we treat others around us, and in the way we nourish the God within us. Our task is complicated by the fact that attempts to reaffirm the spiritual dimension of reality are sometimes received with a cynical rejection of spiritual categories, or a dismissal of everyone who thinks about such issues as New Age flakes or religious nutcases. This cynicism is rooted in a deep belief that nothing about our social world could be fundamentally transformed, so any aspects of human reality that might be involved in a transformation (such as what some of us refer to as our soul) are irrelevant when explaining human reality.

There is a profound difference between this cynicism and a methodological skepticism which rightly asks for some reason to believe that the world can be different. Much of this book is a response to the skeptic. But it will never satisfy the cynic, who holds with religious intensity the view that nothing fundamental can be changed. Pointing to the terrible crimes that have been committed in the name of social change, and relying on the disappointments most of us have felt when we gave ourselves to social movements or religious or spiritual traditions that promised transformation but actually reproduced some of the distortions of the past, the cynical wisdom of our age insists that to be sophisticated is to know in advance that no attempts to change the world could possibly work, and that anyone who thinks otherwise is necessarily a fool, or dangerous.

Yet, I insist on the possibility of possibility. In place of a world based on cynicism and the frenetic pursuit of narrow, material self-interest, I believe that it is possible to move toward an expanded concept of self-interest that recognizes that our most fundamental survival needs can best be achieved in a world that attends to ethical and spiritual concerns. The selfishness I critique is a misplaced, short-term self-interest that actually runs counter to our own best long-term self-interest.

Envisioning a world that is far more responsive to our ethical and spiritual needs does not mean embracing a naive optimism that is oblivious to the inevitable pain and suffering in human life. We need not deny the "shadow" side of human beings, nor the pain that is associated with disease, nor the distress that accompanies death, in order to envision a world that is far more capable of addressing our hunger for meaning and purpose than are contemporary market-driven societies. Anyone who has witnessed the violence of the twentieth century will rightly resist any theory of human reality that seems to deny the role of cruelty and evil. But this recognition ought not stop us in our quest to develop the psychological, social, and spiritual tools that might allow us to take steps toward decreasing the pain in this world.

Psychoanalytic research teaches that the past exercises a tyranny over the present, and that we humans face a long and difficult process of undoing our social and psychological inheritance. We therefore should be very cautious and skeptical about those people who think that we can leap from the present into some totally transformed reality, and we should oppose those who, in the name of making such a leap, justify means that are hurtful or disrespectful of the sanctity of other human beings. But we should simultaneously reject the cynic who ontologizes Evil, thinking that the current level of cruelty and pain in the universe is somehow built into the structure of necessity. It may take many generations to undo the legacy of cruelty, but cruelty is not Cruelty, a reality that can never be changed.

I reject Pollyanish New Age notions that the sting of death can be eliminated or that we can create a world in which life's disappointments (such as the heartbreak of rejection by a friend or potential partner) can be totally transcended. Nor do I expect that we will soon see a world in which jealousy and anxiety have become historic relics. Nevertheless, our world could contain far less cruelty, pain, and frustration.

The Political Aspect

The politics of meaning is *not* politics in the conventional sense. It is not about the struggle for power between parties to see who gets to govern. Politics is about our public life together. Our public life is not only about government. The way we organize our economic life, the way we organize our health care and our child care and our physical environment, the kinds of housing and neighborhoods we create, the way we socialize with one another, the way we structure our intellectual and cultural and recreational activities—all these are part of our public life. These elements comprise what Vaclav Havel, the courageous anticommunist leader of the Czech Republic, taught us to call "civil society." Havel's success at overthrowing communism added plausibility to the view that the struggle to refashion civil society may be the most important focus for contemporary politics.

Many who oppose a progressive politics of meaning will represent it as nothing more than an extension of the same big-government policies that have discredited liberals in the eyes of some Americans. Nothing could be further from the truth. Much of the work of building the kind of society that we seek will be done on the individual and community level. What will be most decisive will be the millions of little steps that we take in our personal lives, in our interactions with others, in what we insist upon in the world of work and as consumers, and in voluntary activities that we engage in together to reshape our society. Conventional electoral politics can sometimes be an adjunct in this process, because it gives an opportunity to highlight our perspective to people who may not hear about it otherwise, but it must not be the central arena for a politics of meaning.

Feminism is an apt model for the kind of transformative movement that a politics of meaning seeks to generate. The women's movement is *not* primarily about changing laws or governmental programs. Its primary focus has been on changing the way that women are treated and talked about, and the way that women see themselves and are seen by men in the workplace, the media, the kitchen, the bedroom—in every human interaction and every aspect of culture. To help achieve these goals, feminists have become involved in legislative and legal battles. But reducing feminism to a liberal attempt to introduce new entitlements or rights, or to a strategy for legitimizing liberal big-government programs, would miss its primary significance. A politics of meaning is politics in this sense—an attempt to change many aspects of life, which *also* involves changes in the relatively narrow sphere we ordinarily call politics. But a politics of meaning is as much about changing how we deal with one another in our daily lives as it is about social policies or narrowly defined legislative programs.

People who may never want to have anything to do with politics in the conventional electoral sense may easily find an important place for themselves in a movement to change the way we lead our lives together. This is a very different notion of politics, one that fits a movement whose goal is to nurture our souls, not to grab power.

On Personal Flaws

When some of the ideas presented in this book were first noticed by the media in 1993, it was in the context of Hillary Rodham Clinton's adoption of my terminology (though not the substance of my ideas). The media rushed to declare me "the guru of the White House," and a spate of articles appeared that totally ignored or misrepresented the content of the ideas. Right-wing radio commentators and newspaper columnists, in particular, were incensed, because intuitively they understood that the growth of right-wing support benefited immensely from liberals and progressives staying away from ethical and spiritual concerns. These critics therefore had to demean me and the idea of a politics of meaning, to pretend that the phrase was nothing but a cover for tired old liberal thinking, or merely a jumble of New Agey catchphrases, or perhaps a product of a demonic or evil mind.

In his book, *See, I Told You So,* Rush Limbaugh devoted a chapter ("To Your Health, Hillary, or Understanding the Politics of Meaning") to a rather vicious personal attack on me. Limbaugh led a journalistic feeding frenzy in which I, rather than the politics of meaning, became the focus. Even the mainstream media joined in this process, for reasons that I explore in the epilogue. The media never provided the public with an accurate summary or a serious analysis of my ideas.

In fact, I have no wish to be anyone's guru. I do not hold myself up as a model for others, nor as an embodiment of the ideals in which I believe. I know that I am as flawed a human being as any other on this planet. Switching a discussion of the politics of meaning to a discussion of the personality or activities of Michael Lerner (or of any other person who becomes a spokesperson for these ideas) is merely a device to avoid engaging the ideas, a distortion of focus.

If our world needs to be healed, it will be done by "wounded healers," people who themselves are in need of healing. Once we realize this, we have every right to insist that the media stop carping about the personal inadequacies of political figures and refocus instead on the content of their ideas. What an elevating notion this would be for a society that reduces ideas to personalities, and then, quite predictably, manages to find the many flaws in those who propose social change.

It will be flawed human beings who become part of the movement to change our world, and those who become spokespeople for these ideas will not be perfectly realized spiritual gurus, but rather ordinary human beings with all our normal limitations. The insistence in American politics that our leaders be on a higher moral plane than everyone else has not led to a new level of morality in politics. Instead it has ensured that our leaders are liars, since they are forced to pretend that they have magically avoided the seductions and distortions that have helped morally flaw the rest of us.

If only those people who have already achieved a higher moral level have any right to articulate moral vision, we will never get beyond our current ethical morass. Therefore, it makes more sense to show compassion toward one another's flaws, even as we give one another support to overcome them. We will not be shocked to find people who articulate ideals and who cannot fully embody them, or who have selfish aims or egotistical needs. In fact, we will expect this, and try to find compassionate ways to support people to move beyond these contradictions so that they can move toward a better embodiment of our ideals. Most of us pursue a combination of self-interested goals and higher goals. A politics of meaning aims to strengthen our most idealistic side, but not to induce guilt about our self-interested side. Nor should we allow the forces of cynicism to convince us to scale down our vision so that it merely describes our current reality with all its defects. That is the essence of idolatry— to let *what is* define *what could and ought to be.*

The flip side of recognizing that our healers and our leaders will be "wounded healers" is to refuse to give up our own critical capacities or subordinate them to some guru or supposedly perfectly realized human being. Some spiritual movements elevate their leaders onto a pedestal and encourage their adherents to suspend their critical intelligence. But a politics of meaning movement would reject such an idealized conception of leadership for two reasons: first, because we know that everyone living in an ethically and spiritually distorted age will necessarily inherit some of those distortions; and second, because we consider every human being to embody the divine image, and therefore seek to encourage people to develop their own insights and intuitions rather than to subordinate their ideas to someone allegedly on a higher moral or spiritual plane.

In today's world, people feel so badly about themselves and live in so much pain that they are often ready to grab on to gurus or to anyone with prepackaged answers. The 1994 takeover of Congress by a conservative coalition, headed by Newt Gingrich and responsive to Rush Limbaugh and the Christian Coalition; the increasing popularity of anti-immigrant or punish-the-poor legislation; and the reemergence of fascistic or xenophobic nationalist forces in Europe—these events should sound a wake-up call, alerting us to the lengths to which people will go to express their despair with lives that feel emptied of meaning and economically threatened.

Pat Buchanan's electoral strength in the 1996 primaries is a further indication of the kind of leader to which many people will respond as America's moral and spiritual crisis deepens. Buchanan mixes his economic populism with a powerful appeal to the feeling of so many Americans that they are not being adequately recognized or appreciated, and that the little corners of meaning that they have developed in their lives are being swept away. In the same breath Buchanan talks about the need to give voice to the powerless—whether those unable to stop corporate downsizing or the fetus about to be aborted. Though pundits reduce Buchanan's popularity to his economic populism, they are unable to explain why the same critique of corporate irresponsibility and trade agreements generated so little support when articulated by Democrats or progressive labor and environmental groups. From my perspective, it is Buchanan's powerful manipulation of unmet psychological, ethical, and spiritual needs, mixed with his economic populism, that makes his politics worrisome and a potential vehicle for reactionary, racist, homophobic, anti-Semitic, and xenophobic ideas. All the more reason, then, why we who do not wish to see this country move further in that direction need to develop an alternative worldview that could counter the appeal of the Right.

The politics of meaning put forward in this book is one attempt to provide this alternative.

1

—m—

Is There Really a Spiritual Crisis? And What Does It Have to Do with Politics?

....

It is no news to most Americans that our society is in the midst of an ethical and spiritual crisis. It manifests itself in crime and violence, the breakdown of families, the seemingly never-ending revelations of corruption in government, the spread of alcoholism and drug abuse, the destruction of our planet's ecological life-support system. Yet more and more Americans are coming to believe that these problems cannot be solved by scientific progress, nor by a new governmental program, nor by a set of earnest young technocrats with Ivy League degrees and fancy new language or advanced computer techniques. Many Americans have come to believe that the problems are deeper, more fundamental, and are rooted in the way that our society approaches reality.

The Meaning of Meaning

As a teenager I had the great fortune to make the acquaintance of one of the twentieth century's most impressive theologians, Abraham Joshua Heschel, who was later to be my teacher at the Jewish Theological Seminary of America. Heschel taught me that the quest for meaning is the central hunger in advanced industrial societies. What people search for, however, is not a meaning that is merely personal, but rather a meaning that transcends the "me" dimension and addresses the ultimate relevance of human being. The self is in need of a meaning which it cannot furnish by itself.

Some people dismiss questions of ultimate meaning as themselves meaningless. Basing their views on what they believe to be a more "scientific" approach to the world, they insist that only words or sentences have meaning. Any attempt to find larger meanings, they insist, are based on now-discredited metaphysical systems that could not possibly be verified by scientific knowledge. These skeptics insist that our interest in meaning is nothing more than the intellectual expression of a vague longing for wholeness or unity that ought not to command our respect or attention.

But such dismissals are really only pseudo-science.

Every attempt to restrict meaning in this way is itself based on a metaphysical foundation. Those who dismiss questions about ultimate meaning as meaningless are simply relying on an alternative framework of meaning whose epistemological foundation is no stronger. They have no recourse but to appeal to their own framework of meaning (for example, that the only claims which are really meaningful are those that can be verified through some form of empirical observation) or appeal to "common sense" (namely, the dominant framework of meaning in their own society).

There are others who question the desire for meaning because they think that human beings can never be motivated by a purpose higher than material self-interest. To these reductionists, the fundamental motivating forces that drive human beings are food, sex, power, and individual or species survival. Freud used the term "id" to discuss the basic energy force in human beings; all of our higher activities, he thought, derived their energy from this id energy.

It would be pointless for me to deny the importance of our primary desires, or for that matter, to deny the importance of air, water, or any of the other essentials for physical survival. Yet those of us who are meaning-theorists focus on another key issue: understanding the distinctive and specifically human dimension of "human being." It is the desire for meaningful connection—not only to other human beings, but to a transcendent purpose in the universe—that plays the central role in shaping human reality. It is this desire for meaningful connection that characterizes the distinctively human id energy.

This desire for transcendent purpose is partially but never fully achieved in our relationships to others. Conversely, it is the frustration of that drive for meaning that helps explain much of the accumulated anger and cruelty that we see around us in daily life. We experience this frustration inside ourselves in the form of irrational angers, jealousies, hunger for power or fame, and many other seemingly inexplicable feelings that are sometimes labeled "the shadow" or dark side of human life.

There are societal and psychological obstacles to our pursuit of meaning. But meaning is neither a psychological nor a social construct; it is an ontological, metaphysical or spiritual one. Meaning cannot be fully supplied by an existential choice (as in, "I choose to make the meaning of my life the amount of power I can accumulate"), nor can it be fully supplied by service to society or humanity, though the existential choice and the service to humanity may be *part* of the process.

Because the search for meaning is the sine qua non of human existence, as central to the reality of what humans do as any description of our struggle for food or power, we are continually led back to the realm of the spiritual and the religious. Abraham Joshua Heschel provides us with an account of this aspect of human reality in his book, *Who Is Man:* "Animals are content when their needs are satisfied; humans insist not only on being satisfied but also on being able to satisfy, on being a need not simply on having needs . . . [I]t is a most significant fact that . . . life is not meaningful to us unless it is serving an end beyond itself, unless it is of value to someone else."

Our quest for meaning is an effort to understand human life in terms larger than the self, an attempt to find the ultimate relevance of human being. And, according to Heschel, that quest leads us quickly to discovering that human life is meaningful because human beings are called upon by the ultimate reality of the universe. To be human is to be commanded. To embody the divine spirit—to be made in the image of God—is to be a creature who has received a message and a command, to be partners with the divine in the healing and repair of this world. Or, in secular language, to be human is to recognize a categorical obligation to an objective moral task of world repair.

This book, however, is not a book about the best way to find meaning in one's personal or social life. There are a wide variety of religious and spiritual traditions, and I have no intention of arguing here for any particular approach. Though I belong to a particular faith community, Judaism, I hope for a world in which many different faith communities, as well as those who find meaning in various secular worldviews, can live together in harmony and mutual respect.

I do *not* want a world in which either government or civil society forces or even subtly inculcates in us a particular approach to meaning. We have so much more to learn about building and discovering meaning. What we need now is to develop a democratic ethos of mutual tolerance and humility when it comes to public discussion of this or other ethical and spiritual issues.

I am seeking in this book to focus on the ways in which our current social and psychological condition blocks the pursuit of meaning, and on what can be done to eliminate those blocks. But it would be a deep mistake to conclude that meaning can be achieved solely through a reordering of society, or through some psychotherapy or psychic healing. The social and psychological healing that we need is only a necessary—not a sufficient—condition for satisfying our needs for meaning. The healing called for in this book is not a substitute for religions, spiritual practices, or inner caring for our souls. This is not a self-help book, but an appeal to reorganize our society as well as our personal lives to make them less an impediment to and more congruent with our highest ideals.

A Crisis of Spirit

In contemporary public life we are taught that human beings are fundamentally motivated by material self-interest, and that the physical and social worlds have no room for spiritual notions or non-material human needs. People, we are told, are fundamentally selfish. They look out for themselves and they do not really care about anyone else, except as a way to advance themselves. People want to accumulate material goods and bodily pleasures without end, and all human actions are aimed at achieving those ends.

Cynicism about ideals and other people's motives is one of the major correlates of this worldview. According to the dominant thinking of our age, those who pursue higher ideals beyond self-interest, who let ethical vision determine their life choices, must either be dissembling or deeply disturbed. In either case, the rest of us should keep our distance, because such people are either consciously trying to manipulate us or unconsciously seeking power and likely to hurt us in the process. This cynicism permeates daily life, undermining people's ability to trust others or to pursue ethical or spiritual vision, and making it extremely difficult to convey to the next generation the shared ethical values and spiritual experience of the human race.

Yet, more and more people are coming to see that this cynical way of thinking and doing things is itself irrational and self-destructive. Religions, spiritual traditions, art and literature preserve for us the collective memory of a different way of ordering the world, a way that validated our desire for community, human connection, mutual recognition, and a sense of higher purpose to our life. Although most of what we are taught in this society leads us to dismiss all of this spiritual heritage as irrational and outdated, many people intuitively know that a world that has been stripped of these dimensions is a poorer, less fulfilling place.

Unconsciously, we lament the disenchantment of the world and the reduction of our experience to forms that fit contemporary materialism and selfishness. Many people intuit that treating the world and other human beings as resources to be exploited may lead Western societies to the brink of social and ecological disaster. If we continue to tolerate this way of thinking in our public lives, it is *not* because we believe that things are going well in the larger society, but because we have come to believe that we are too powerless to change anything as large as the dominant way things are done.

No wonder, then, that many Americans have fought to preserve a private sphere in their personal lives where they can retain a very different sense of what is real and what is important. Some of those who describe themselves as conservative are really people who wish to protect themselves from more government, because they see government as the wedge that introduces this materialism and self-ishness into public life. Part of what these conservatives are trying to protect themselves from is the dominant paradigm of material-ism and self-interest which has such disastrous consequences in public life.

Many liberals write these people off, but those who wish to cre-ate a progressive politics of meaning understand that many conser-vatives share with us a profound distaste for the alienation that permeates our society. Some conservatives imagine that if they can get away from the public realm, they might be able to preserve a personal life that offers a more humane way of relating to other human beings. Sophisticated liberals who ridicule the conservative nostalgia for an earlier America may be correct to note its evocation of highly romanticized visions of the past—visions that obscure the real class divisions, the racism, and the sexism of the small towns whose demise conservatives bemoan. But such liberals miss the quite legitimate desire underlying this romanticization: a desire for a less alienating world in which selfishness and materialism would not rule the day.

Yet attempts to find greater humanity by escaping from the alienation of the larger society can themselves become new sources of alienation. Our focus on personal fulfillment leads some of us to turn our backs on the plight of the less fortunate and to see them as the problem that must be escaped. People build gated communities in suburbia, hoping to keep out all that has become inhumane and destructive in our larger society. But these gates also sever our con-nections with other, often poorer, people. Hoping to escape crime, many of us symbolically shut the gates on that part of ourselves that once responded to the plight of others. The very act of shutting ourselves off from others mimics the inhumanity of the larger society that we have sought to escape.

In our personal lives, we know that human beings are not isolated, independent creatures whose sole concern is to improve their own material comforts. We understand that we all exist in relationships with others, and that relationship is fundamental to what it means to be human. We were born in physical connection to our mother, and survived because of the care given to us by our biological parents or other caring adults. It was this caring that sustained us. Every human being is born with an intrinsic need for recognition from others, and it is in and through this recognition that we become ourselves. We desire a spiritually deep and emotionally real connection based on a recognition of who we are (not only as unique beings, but as beings who share a common tie to the spiritual reality of the universe).

Unfortunately, the people who surround us, beginning with our parents, are often so emotionally buried within their own painful lives that it is hard for them to see us clearly. All too often, the recognition that they give us depends on our willingness and ability to perform within their predetermined categories, responding to their needs for us to fit their already existing picture of the world.

These early experiences begin a long process of encounters with others in which we are continually being forced to develop a false self and to deny our own deep need for recognition, in order to achieve the forms of pseudo-recognition that are more readily available. In the words of psychologist Peter Gabel, we are "systematically misrecognized": first by parents, then by teachers, and ultimately by most of the others whom we meet in daily life. We encounter these others through a false self developed out of despair that our real self will never be recognized or confirmed. We are surrounded by a world filled with people who are desperate to be recognized, yet who simultaneously accept a depressive stance in which they imagine that no one will ever really see them as they are. They have come to believe that their own isolation or loneliness is the "reality" to which they must adjust. It is this psychological dynamic that underlies our willingness to deaden ourselves to our world and give rote compliance to its demands.

The most fundamental demand of the contemporary world is that we give up our ethical and spiritual sensitivity, or at least marginalize those sensitivities by keeping them out of the so-called real world. We first learn to do this in our families. Here we learn to repress our intuition that something is deeply wrong with the way we are being misrecognized and encouraged to develop a false self. Most significantly, we continue learning to be ethically unconscious in schools, where we learn to separate "knowledge" from our own ethical and spiritual intuitions (the latter often dismissed as "merely subjective"). We spend twelve years submitting ourselves to supposedly objective criteria, learning to jump through endless hoops that define intelligence and competence in ways that separate them from ethical and spiritual awareness. When we graduate from high school, we are prepared to function in a world that is deeply cynical about the possibility of relationships that are loving and caring.

All this "learning" must be unlearned if we are to reconnect with the deepest truths of the human experience. Recognizing ourselves as spiritually and emotionally connected—to one another and to some transcendent aspect of existence—and understanding these connections as fundamental, are not new ideas. They emerge from the experience of the human race through most of history. They are part of the common wisdom of many indigenous peoples and form the basis of many of the world's religious traditions. Yet in the past few hundred years, this knowledge of spiritual and ethical truth—this fundamental need that we have, to recognize and be recognized as beings who embody this higher energy and who fundamentally deserve respect and caring—has been excluded from our public lives and has been under assault even in our private lives.

The rise of market societies in the West has produced a dominant worldview that ridicules spiritual and ethical realities, insisting that there is nothing more important than material self-interest. Love is reduced to sexual gratification plus a desire for protection, or for mutual economic or political interest. Friendship is seen as a temporary opportunity for mutual self-advancement. Ethics is dismissed as an attempt to dress up personal preferences or group interests, and impose them on others. Spirituality is seen as an escape route for people who are too mushy-headed to face reality.

Ironically, this materialist outlook was originally considered to be liberating, and it probably was. The new emphasis on the lone individual was an important advance, because it freed people from coercive communities that used the language of ethical and spiritual awareness, of community and caring, in order to force people to conform and submit to domination and inequality. Though individualism today has taken extreme and destructive forms, it has served in the past as a very important counterweight to a wide variety of oppressive religious communities that have lost their connection to the spiritual truths they claimed to embody.

Up until about four hundred years ago, most people in the West lived in traditional or feudal societies dominated by ruling elites, usually allied with the Roman Catholic Church. Whenever anybody challenged the existing patriarchal system, with its stratified, unequal distribution of wealth and power, he or she was told that the way things were had been sanctified by God—and how dare this person challenge the spiritual and ethical order of the world? It is not surprising that many people eventually rebelled against this hierarchical framework.

Leading the rebellion were the merchants, traders, shopkeepers, bankers, and independent professionals of the social middle class (collectively referred to as "the bourgeoisie"), who felt most resentful of the older feudal order. These people resented the degree to which the church had set limits on their own economic activities. For example, the church often set a "fair price," a "fair profit," and a "fair wage" in ways that impeded the creation of a free market. The traders and shopkeepers did not want the larger society to limit the profits they could make or to demand that they be responsible for the well-being of their workers. So the bourgeoisie began to challenge the very notion of a spiritual or ethical order.

It was not difficult for the bourgeoisie to win support among the populace. For many centuries, the language of spirituality and ethics had been a cover for the selfishness and materialism of feudal lords and ladies, who danced in chivalric splendor while the vast majority of the population struggled to feed themselves from that part of their harvest not paid to the lord of the estate.

The newly emerging middle classes jettisoned the language of spirituality and ethics—and replaced it with a new theory of reality and a new theory of knowledge.

What was real, these merchants argued, was that which could be presented to the senses and actually touched, tasted, seen, or experienced through our physical bodies. Anything that could not be presented to the senses for verification, such as any belief in a spiritual realm or in an afterlife, was literally "non-sense." So total was the eventual victory of this new way of looking at the world, that today the word "nonsense" has come to mean "having no foundation and hence no claim on our attention."

This revolutionary argument was grounded in two presuppositions. First, the new middle class spoke, quite appropriately, about the importance of a this-worldly focus. But such a focus did not necessarily exclude spiritual reality (indeed, from my standpoint, it is precisely in this world and on this earth-plane that we so desperately need to reconnect to the spiritual dimension of reality). Second, the argument assumed that reality consisted only of that which could be observed through the senses. That assumption excluded the possibility of spiritual and ethical reality. The philosophical heirs of this new way of looking at reality (often referred to as "empiricism," a view that insists that all that can be known must be related in complex ways to our experience of the world) found themselves reducing ethical judgments to nothing more than personal feelings.

Why did the empiricist view catch on? For two reasons: first, it responded to people's anger toward feudal and religious systems that had been using spirituality and moral judgments to subjugate them. By the late medieval period, there was growing recognition of the corruptness of a church that accumulated riches for itself while ignoring the plight of the poor, and of a feudal aristocracy that was morally obtuse and ruthless in its attempts to keep power. There was growing frustration with the conventional moral wisdom that urged people to stay in their preordained social positions and never try to better themselves. If moral and spiritual language had led to this kind of a world, many people reasoned, then perhaps it was time to reject that whole way of thinking.

Second, the traders and shopkeepers meanwhile had been able to bring better living and greater material abundance to some, and they promised much more once all constraints were removed. Indeed, they promised a world in which, once the feudal aristocracy was abandoned and the church taken out of public life, everyone would have an equal opportunity to advance, to change his or her position in life, and to acquire all the material wealth he or she desired.

If the defenders of spirituality and ethics had been perceived to be seriously committed to love, caring, spiritual sensitivity, and moral vitality, the battle for the primacy of sense data would have taken much longer. It was not the case that people had tasted a genuinely spiritual and ethical order and then rejected it in favor of a preference for material satisfaction. Rather, by the middle of the eighteenth century, growing numbers of people felt that the language of spirituality and ethics had indeed proved "meaningless," because little in their experience gave it any meaning. As a result, there was a growing tendency to dismiss as "nonsense" many of the spiritual vocabularies of the past.

A materialist worldview emerged that validated only that which could be experienced by the senses. And in place of any ethical concerns of the community, this new social order insisted that the ultimate reality was the pleasure and satisfaction of each individual. The lone individual became the center of the universe, and if we built families or communities, it was only because the lone individual had found it in his or her interest to do so. All connections between human beings hereafter would be based on contract: free individuals choosing to make a connection with others. The sole goal of the state, in this scheme, was to ensure that there was a realm of free contracts in which no one would interfere.

Marxist historians who correctly note the aspects of class struggle in the rise of capitalism usually miss the crucial dimension of meaning. In its historical context, the rejection of patriarchal, hierarchical, and oppressive communities of meaning was actually an affirmation of our needs for meaning. It was a radical attempt to subvert the existing official system of meaning, which had been perceived as a total sham.

The new order lionized the individual and taught that our individual happiness and fulfillment was to be the ultimate criterion of value, quite apart from our connection to others. However, it is clear to me that the more we see ourselves and our fates as separate from our fellow human beings, the more difficult it becomes to sustain the belief that our individual lives have ultimate meaning or purpose.

Paradoxically, the Marxists and other leftists who attacked the absence of social justice in the bourgeois world nevertheless bought into its epistemology and ontology. They constructed a narrow view of human liberation based on class struggle because the only human needs that they thought could be frustrated in the contemporary world were those material economic needs or individual autonomy needs that were presumed by a rigidly empiricist social science. So both the bourgeois and those who claimed to be revolutionaries effectively agreed on a way of looking at reality that ignored the dimension of meaning.

The Denial of Meaning: Spiritual Impoverishment

Marxists used to say that the fundamental contradiction of capitalism is its inability to provide for the material needs of the working class. From my standpoint, however, the critical contradiction is not the economic but rather the spiritual and ethical impoverishment caused by the prevailing organization of society. Middle-income Americans today have far more material goods and economic benefits than we had in the past, but we feel less secure, less connected, and less fulfilled. We feel far more vulnerable to economic danger because we recognize that we can count less on one another to help out when times get rough. Ripped from the network of connectedness, unable to see the ways in which we need one another, assured that our only hope lies in fostering our interests even at the expense of everyone else, we perceive ourselves as alone and desperate to hang on to whatever flimsy reeds of connection remain.

We live in a society that encourages us to treat one another as means to achieve our own personal satisfaction, and rewards us for our ability to accumulate wealth and power over others. Not surprisingly, we find ourselves surrounded by people who are self-absorbed and indifferent to our well-being. Far from producing happiness, our society universalizes cultural and psychological misery, because people actually do *need* one another, not just when we can get something out of being there. Living in this society—in which we are deprived of mutual recognition, in which loving relationships and trusting friendships are increasingly difficult to sustain, in which the idea of caring about others seems increasingly utopian, and in which it is rare to find work that contributes to the common good—can be just as painful as living in a society without adequate food or shelter.

The loss of meaning causes deep pain. Yet we are surrounded by media and other interpreters of public values and social norms who not only deny the possibility of meaning, but also insist that we hide this kind of pain from ourselves and one another.

On the one hand, we are encouraged to interpret our pain as a personal problem, one that we have brought on ourselves by not being more psychologically healthy. The disintegration of trust and connection among people, the instability in families and friendships, the sense that people are out only for themselves, and the feeling that our work serves no higher purpose and is thus frustrating and alienating—all are experienced as personal problems.

The psychologically healthier among us are able to acknowledge to ourselves some of this unhappiness, even though we have no social categories that help us understand our problem as anything more than a personal defect. So we rush off to psychiatrists, psychologists, social workers, marriage and family counselors, spiritual healers, seminar leaders, growth groups, astrologers, soothsayers, and anyone else who promises to fix our personal problem with good advice or experiential learning. And in fact, although these various healing activities are predicated on the assumption that our problem is merely personal and subjective, they often *do* help. Why? Because the actual process of being able to discuss our "private" issues with someone else, and the experience of being listened to and cared about, provide us with human contact and connection that partially satisfy our deep need for connection to others. Though this is only one aspect of the crisis of meaning, it is often the one in which the crisis is most immediately apparent in our lives.

When tens of millions of people are in internal pain, deeply involved in self-blame, and unable to understand the social realities that have caused, contributed to, or exacerbated that pain, a series of social crises is likely to emerge. People will act out their inner pain in a wide variety of ways, depending on their own experiences as children, their own psychological makeup, their economic situation, their cultural assumptions, and the support mechanisms available to them. Some will become deeply depressed, withdrawing energy from their lives and feeling despair about ever achieving anything that makes any sense. Others will become deeply angry, approaching all of life's tasks with resentment or bitterness that sours their relationships with others. Still others will act out in more socially destructive ways: divorce or rapid disintegration of friendships and loyalties, drug or alcohol abuse, sexual abuse in families, drive-by shootings, and other seemingly incomprehensible acts of violence or cruelty.

While the crisis of meaning is typically ruled out of public discussion, its consequences in these publicly observable social crises cannot be ignored. But to keep ourselves from knowing the relationship of these problems to any deeper underlying social crisis, our society insists that the problems be analyzed and dealt with in isolation from one another. We therefore will pour millions of dollars into research to see what genetic factors might predispose someone to crime or to drug or alcohol abuse. But we will not ask, "What are people trying to escape when they deaden their consciousness through drugs or alcohol?" This kind of a question would open the gates for a more systematic critique of society than the proponents of this research care to take on.

Similarly, while we will pour billions of dollars into building more jails and putting more police on the streets, we are afraid to face honestly the breakdown of human connections, the dissolution of moral and spiritual bonds, and the resulting pain and inner frustrations that have engendered the escalation of violence and crime in Western societies.

Public Values Shape Private Life

It is increasingly difficult to protect private life from the encroach-ment of the dominant materialistic, self-interested way of thinking. The hard-nosed realism that is fostered by the media and encour-aged by the bottom-line consciousness of the market undermines our confidence in the seemingly softer realities of caring and love, making us wonder whether we are merely being romantic when we talk about experiences of love or caring in families, friendships and relationships, or when we take ethics or spiritual life seriously. Ulti-mately, our belief becomes self-fulfilling. The more we assume that the world really is dominated by materialism and selfishness, the more we begin to act in our personal lives in ways that reinforce these assumptions.

The pollution of private life by public materialism and self-ishness is hard to resist. Those of us who are rewarded all day for thinking about how to get the most from others while giving the least, and who learn to see others as people to be manipulated and controlled, rarely have the capacity to transform ourselves in a few hours of private life in the evenings and on weekends. We cannot take off these attitudes when we come home from work as if these were so many dirty clothes. Instead, this way of thinking persists and shapes how we treat others. Increasingly, we deal with friends, lovers, even family members the same way we have learned to think about people in general—namely, by assessing them according to how well they meet our needs.

Under this market framework, people always seem to be look-ing for a better deal elsewhere (for example, a spouse who is more attentive, attractive, financially successful, charming, intelligent, youthful, or able to help advance one's career; a friend who is more helpful or has better contacts or connections). Attracted by the new possibility, they will often drop a relationship of many years. And if the new possibility doesn't work, people can always go on to some-thing else, because an expanding market in relationships presents endless possibilities. Since most of us have learned that it is com-mon sense in our society to look out for number one, we imagine that looking at others in this way is what everyone else is doing, too. This utilitarian way of thinking makes it more difficult to sustain belief in the possibility of a moral universe, and encourages us to believe that we are wasting our time or hurting our chances should we act in a loyal and trusting way.

Yet, simultaneously, we feel increasingly insecure as we begin to recognize that we constantly may meet others whose interest in us grows out of their ability to use us for some selfish end. Now, it would be foolish to exaggerate by claiming that these nasty interactions are all that ever happens in our world. Most of us, if we reflect for a moment, can remember some wonderful experiences of meeting people who have encountered us as we really are and who have wanted nothing more than to be in our presence. Nevertheless, the world feels increasingly dangerous as more and more of us recall far too many disturbing encounters in which we have found ourselves being used or manipulated by people whom we originally had trusted. As a result, our general level of personal fear has grown dramatically in the past few decades.

Our insecurity is intensified when we see that major corporations are laying off long-term workers and that we ourselves may someday be on the unemployment line. But even when economic issues are not at stake, the ruthless mentality surrounding them makes us feel terrified and insecure.

It becomes extremely difficult to teach children ethical values in this context. Kids infer that their parents' lives are dominated by the fear or "healthy suspicion" of others. The primary message that is communicated from generation to generation, then, is that everyone is out for himself or herself, leaving little place for alternative messages about love or caring.

The Right Grabs the Ethical and Spiritual Issues

Most Americans hate the way that the ethos of selfishness works in their lives, and yet they are skeptical about the possibility of changing it. They understand that the instability in family life, reflected in the dramatic growth of divorce, and their decreasing ability to count on friends to really be there for them, are tied to the general moral deterioration of our society. The Right has made its major comeback in American politics over the past thirty years by representing itself as the force that cares about the crisis in families, the deterioration of values, and the spiritual vacuity and the pain that middle-class Americans have been facing in their daily lives.

The Right has managed to position itself as the political force that cares about God, spirituality, and the ethical crisis. But the spiritual energy of the universe, and God's manifestations in the world, are not prepackaged in ways that automatically make them part of a right-wing or left-wing discourse. In fact, both the Right and the Left have a tendency toward deep cynicism that interferes with their ability to really understand and integrate into their politics the fundamental spiritual unity of all being.

The Right cleverly positions itself as the defender of spirituality. Nevertheless, in the world of work where most of us spend most of our waking hours, the Right champions the ethos of materialism and selfishness. It unashamedly adheres to eighteenth-century philosopher Adam Smith's view that our collective well-being is best served when everyone pursues his or her own narrow self-interest without regard to the well-being of others.

The Right defends those very economic and political institutions that are most committed to the ethos of selfishness and the bottom-line mentality of a competitive marketplace. The Right is the champion, for example, of the National Rifle Association's campaign to defend the manufacture of weapons that have been central in the escalation of the violence in the society. It is the champion of corporations that are major polluters. It is the champion of the tobacco industry and the alcohol industry, whose products have demonstrably negative impact on health. Moreover, the Right argues that, in our economic life, it serves the common good if all of us sink our energies into advancing our own personal and selfish interests.

The Right does not directly address any negative aspects of the selfishness and materialism that dominate our society, because to do so would necessarily introduce significant changes in the way we organize our economic lives together. Instead, the Right blames the ethos of selfishness and materialism on various scapegoats who are seen as having introduced selfishness and self-centeredness into a community that would otherwise have been nurturing, ethical, and mutually supportive.

Throughout most of the past four hundred years in the West, the primary scapegoat blamed for undermining community and caring has been the Jews. Because Jews had long been a major target of economic and political oppression in feudal societies, Jews were more unequivocal than most in embracing the "equal opportunities" pledge of the free market and in unambiguously rejecting the ties and limitations of premarket societies. In contrast, many non-Jews experienced the market as a mixed blessing. They welcomed the new opportunities for individual advancement but simultaneously feared the loss of traditional social solidarity, which provided some security against the market's inevitable upturns and downturns.

When economic conditions worsened, it was easy for ruling elites to turn against the Jews whatever popular anger might otherwise have been directed at the elites. Building upon hundreds of years of Christians demeaning Jews, right-wing nationalists in many countries have been able to portray the Jews as the force most responsible for the dissolution of communal solidarity and mutual care. After all, the Jews have seemed to be least ambivalent toward the market system, most effective in using it for their own self-advancement, and most unresponsive to nostalgia for the more communal past.

Similar dynamics apply to the current anger that the Right has mobilized against various minority groups in the United States. Historically, the role of the demeaned Other—blamed for disruptions of safety, security, and morality—has been assigned first and foremost to African-Americans, and subsequently to feminists ("uppity women"), homosexuals, communists (and more recently, liberals), Jews, various immigrants, and other minorities. By deflecting onto these demeaned Others the anger that people might reasonably have expressed toward an economic and social system that rewards selfishness, the Right has managed to play both sides of the street. On the one side, it defends the economic and social system that proudly proclaims its commitment to me-firstism and promises that if everyone just looks out for himself or herself, the result will be a good world for all. On the other side, it articulates the pain that people feel when this ethos of selfishness permeates private life, and finds other groups to blame for this pain.

Of course, some of the appeal of the Right is not to spiritual sensitivity but to baser feelings. I do not doubt that there is a hard core of racists, sexists, homophobes and anti-Semites who form the backbone of the American Right. Yet this extreme group does not represent more than twenty percent of the American electorate. I am more concerned in this book with the thirty to forty percent of voters who sometimes swing to the Right, but who are not always at home there. These are the people who are attracted to the Right, despite its various racist and sexist distortions, because they feel it addresses their hunger for meaning. That hunger grows even stronger when fear of economic dislocation intensifies for many Americans their anger at living in a society where no one will be there for them. This group may in the future become an important constituency for a progressive politics of meaning.

But in the last half decade of the 1990s, faced with a world in which everyone seems to be pursuing his or her own special interests, many people are attracted to the Right's vision of a community in which all divisiveness is subordinated to the authority of family or nation. Such people would accept this kind of authority in order to escape the deceptions and pressures and dog-eat-dog realities of the market, in hopes of finding a community that is harmonious and has shared values. What they see on the Left is an assemblage of groups, each squabbling with the other for greater recognition— a rerun of the divisiveness and self-centeredness that people have to contend with every day in the world of work.

However, the most important reason that the Right has been so successful in recent American politics is that it makes people feel better about themselves and their lives. It addresses some of the central manifestations of the crisis of meaning—as reflected in family problems, rising crime, and the general decline of values and community—and it tells people that these are not caused by their own personal failures, but because there is something deeply wrong in the larger culture. This kind of analysis reduces self-blame; it allows people to stop punishing themselves for what is wrong in their lives. People respond with deep gratitude for this message, which the Right has effectively translated into political support for a legislative and social agenda that few of its adherents have ever thought out nor care about very much. People vote for the Right because they feel understood and cared for by it. They trust the Right—but not because it has managed to win the national policy debate, of which, in most cases, its adherents know very little.

These dynamics are evident in the powerful success of right-wing radio talk-show hosts who reframe people's personal pain in racist, sexist, or homophobic directions. The radio hosts provide a simple and powerful answer: "The reason you are being denied recognition, love, and meaning is that the liberals have given these scarce commodities to someone else, and they've set up society in such a way that these others will get what you badly need. It's only if we can dismantle government and the programs that they've created to benefit these special interests that you, the American majority, have any chance of getting the caring you deserve but which these liberals and their various client groups are withholding from you."

This message resonates deeply with many Americans because it captures a real truth: people do *not* receive the recognition they deserve or the meaning that they need in order to build satisfying lives. The Right unfairly blames this lack on liberal programs, on feminism, or on allegedly selfish groups pursuing their narrow self-interest. Affirmative action, for example, is now popularly cast as a selfishness program that unfairly favors groups who, in any event, are too focused on their own needs and not adequately sensitive to the needs of the larger community. The Right will continue to get away with this kind of distortion until liberals and progressives can understand that the resentment people feel is legitimate: they really *are* in pain, they really *do not get recognized* in this society, and they *have a right to be angry*. Until the Left can validate this anger and articulate this pain by speaking the language of a progressive politics of meaning, liberals will surely continue to decline in popularity.

The Left's Failure of Empathy:
The Fight to Be Most Oppressed

Because liberals and progressives have a narrow conception of human needs, the only kind of oppression that seems real to them is the denial of economic security or political rights. By this logic, any group can present itself as oppressed if it can show itself to be suffering from economic deprivation or denial of equal rights by other groups in the society. Since oppression becomes an entitlement on the Left—the entitlement to have one's needs given special attention—a fierce battle continually is being waged about who is suffering most from the deprivation of economic and/or political rights.

Unfortunately, most people in advanced industrial societies get cut out of the group whose interests and needs are worthy of the Left's attention, because they are unable to show that they are victims of economic or rights deprivation. There is a subtle form of Marxist economic determinism at work here in many people who think that they despise Marxism, or who would be astounded to be called Marxists: namely, the assumption that oppression is only really legitimate if it involves the denial of economic or political rights.

This limited perspective undermines the ability of liberals, progressives, cultural radicals, or the Left (as understood in its widest context), to reach out to people whose lives are not primarily characterized by the denial of political rights or economic well-being. To the contrary, the Left seems to be giving them a very strong negative message: "Your suffering, whatever it is (and we can hardly believe it is real, given that nice house you partly own or that nice stereo you spend too much time listening to) is certainly less important than the suffering of others."

Ironically, this tendency to ignore the real pain of middle-income people is a central reason why the Left has been unable to deliver very much for the poor and the most oppressed. Most middle-income people perceive this constant insistence on the centrality of "the most oppressed" as a clear statement that the Left doesn't care about them. This message comes through even in the more subtle form it assumes in Democratic Party and liberal circles, namely, "Of course we care about alienation and families and the ethical and spiritual crisis, but we first must attend to the suffering of the poor and the most oppressed, and after we have dealt with that we will turn our attention to these other, less pressing problems." And middle-income voters reciprocate by not giving the Left the electoral support it needs in order to be able to deliver social programs for the poor and the oppressed. Thus, the insistence on *first* solving the problems of "the most oppressed" almost always backfires.

Self-Interest and Selfishness

When I criticize selfishness in this book, I do not mean to be suggesting that the ideal is a selfless individual who cares only for others. In a healthy world, each healthy individual strives to maintain her or his own individual well-being while simultaneously recognizing that that well-being depends on the well-being of the larger realities of which she or he is part. What has happened in the modern world is that we are out of balance, and the call to fight against selfishness is a call to restore that balance.

Selfishness, then, is not healthy self-interest. In fact, viewed from the largest perspective, it is detrimental to our self-interest. Selfishness typically arises when we are no longer able to see that our lives are inextricably linked to the well-being of others and to the well-being of the universe. When we lose our understanding of these links to the larger wholes of which we are part, we can act out of sync with the rest of creation. A typical example, though not the only one, is when as individuals or as members of a group or a nation we think that we have a right to consume available physical resources or emotional nurturance in ways that then make it hard for others to get the resources or nurturance they need.

The cure for selfishness is not the obliteration of the ego or the denial of healthy needs. This can lead to equally destructive pathologies, as in totalitarian systems, in which the individual fuses with the group and loses herself or himself. The healthy individual possesses a degree of self-interest, and will fight to preserve her or his own existence, but simultaneously recognizes inextricable ties to others and to the well-being of the planet and the totality of all Being.

We know what it is like when one cell or group of cells in the body begins to advance at the expense of every other cell. We call this cancer. When this same principle becomes accepted or valorized in the larger society, we get a pathological form of self-interest that I refer to in this book as the ethos of selfishness.

I do not wish to associate my critique of pathological self-interest with assaults on pleasure or guilt-inducing suggestions that people are being bad if they are having too much fun or too much self-love. Similarly, the desire for a comfortable standard of living is not necessarily pathological self-interest. Too often, people who are spiritually oriented (and/or work for progressive social change movements) seem to suggest that there is something wrong with people who want material things. In my view, there is nothing intrinsically wrong or selfish or materialistic about wanting material goods. Those desires are perfectly healthy, as long as we can arrange society in such a way that others have equal access to a comparable level of material goods, and as long as people do not become focused on getting those things to the exclusion of ethical or spiritual pursuits.

What a politics of meaning *does* suggest is that we are unlikely to be fulfilled if our lives are built primarily around obtaining material comforts. Human beings require more than that, and to the extent that accumulating goods becomes the only arena in which we can feel meaning and exercise power, other parts of ourselves will feel undernourished and eventually begin to ache.

This is not a question of absolutes but of relative balance. Our contemporary world is badly out of balance. In fact, it is so far out of balance that many people have come to think that it is the mark of sophistication to imagine that this self-destructive selfishness is actually "human nature." But in rectifying the balance, I do not seek to impose an equally unrealistic view of human beings as totally transcending their own self-interest or caring about others without regard to their own needs. The kind of loving and caring society I seek includes an affirmation of the individual, an affirmation of self-love, and an affirmation of our intrinsic need for each other, our need for mutual recognition, and our need to be a need of others. Thus, the insight of the Bible's injunction to "love your neighbor as yourself" is based on a recognition that self-love is also necessary, but never sufficient. Or, to put it in ecological terms, that true self-love necessarily leads us to a concern for the larger wholes of which we are part.

Resistances to Meaning

Often, those who insist most vehemently that a politics of meaning is impossible are those who once tried to follow their highest hopes, and discovered that the world was not easily transformed. The assertion that the world could really be different and could embody the spiritual and ethical values that most of us hold dear is anxiety-provoking because it reminds us of dashed hopes and the sharp pain of disillusionment. We fear deeply that change really cannot happen, so we may insist that anyone who thinks that the world can be moved from selfishness to caring is either a fool or a threat.

Many people have had the experience of living in societies or families in which systems of meaning were used in oppressive ways. If I had been living in a communist country in past decades, or had just emerged from a patriarchal family or from an oppressive religious community, I would also be emphasizing the value of individual freedom. I would find the whole notion of meaning suspicious, because it would remind me of the language used by oppressors to keep me in line with their wishes. Even within American society, there are some people for whom the battle against patriarchal families or oppressive religious communities must take precedence; for them, the critique of individualism and of an excessive focus on rights will be felt as disempowering, because they still need the traditional liberal language to bolster them in their fight.

Our personal experiences differ widely and in complex ways. I know that what I say in this book will hit the mark for some people, but will seem exaggerated for others. For people who are struggling out of more traditional societies and have not lived in a largely unrestrained materialistic, competitive market society, what I say may fail to address their current experience. For example, Professor

Moshe Halbertal of the Hebrew University knew that right-wing nationalists in Israel had appropriated Judaism's system of meaning to justify an oppressive occupation of the West Bank and to impose Orthodox religious restrictions on Israelis' personal lives. He captured this complicated situation well when he commented to communitarian theorist Michael Sandel of Harvard, "To you Americans, community is a dream; to us Israelis it is a trauma."

One of the central features of modern life in the Western world is that each of us belongs to a number of communities, takes on multiple identities, and hence has numerous selves with differing and sometimes contradictory elements. In some of these identities, we may be living according to traditional definitions of self and may be struggling for more autonomy; in others, we may be experiencing the breakdown of traditional societies and the attendant spiritual and ethical crises. Moreover, while we still find ourselves in some communities by virtue of having been born into a particular family, culture, and geographical area, we also have many opportunities in the modern world to choose or create new communities. Indeed, one of the strengths of urban life is the range of opportunities that it affords many of us to be involved in a variety of partially overlapping communities, and to monitor our own levels of involvement.

A progressive politics of meaning is committed to fostering tolerance and mutual respect among these communities. It insists, too, on allowing each of us as individuals to be free to set our own level of involvement, to change that level at various points in our own development, and to respect those periods in our lives when we may choose to have no involvement with any community. In creating the preconditions for a spiritually and ethically sensitive society, the politics of meaning vigorously rejects the use of communal power to impose any particular system of meaning. Similarly, a progressive politics of meaning is firmly committed to the democratic safeguards ensured by the Bill of Rights and by a system of checks and balances for political power such as that established in the U.S. Constitution.

It may seem that I underplay issues of tolerance and democratic safeguards in the rest of this book. This certainly is not because these matters are unimportant, but rather because at this historical moment, these safeguards are far better established in advanced industrial Western societies than are communities of meaning. If this situation were to change, progressives committed to the politics of meaning would be in the forefront of the battle for tolerance and individual freedom.

The greatest current threat to tolerance comes from a political Right committed to demeaning some groups and making them the scapegoats for our anger at not having more meaningful and loving lives. We have all the more reason, then, to develop a progressive politics of meaning as a political alternative that might counter the Right's appeal and recover popular support for the liberal values that we ought not discard.

There is another major source of resistance to meaning-oriented politics that I call "surplus powerlessness": namely, our tendency to see ourselves as more powerless than we really are. Unlike those who tilt toward psychological reductionism, I believe that, in a society in which the top one percent of the population owns forty percent of the wealth, there are bound to be real inequalities of power. These inequalities have been demonstrated by the ways in which the wealthy have successfully used government over the past decades to redistribute wealth away from the poor and toward the extremely rich. So, as opposed to those who think that people are only imagining powerlessness, and that everything would be possible if only people struggled for what they really want, I insist on the reality of relative powerlessness: the fact that most of us are less powerful than we ought to be, and that to change this situation will take considerable and difficult struggle.

On the other hand, as opposed to those who tilt toward a certain vulgar Marxism or economic determinism, and who therefore say that "all we have to do is eliminate inequalities of power and everything will be fixed," and who have no understanding of the internal obstacles to making such a dramatic transformation, I argue that most of us have been subjected to a set of experiences in our childhood and adult lives that makes us feel that we do not deserve to have power. Furthermore, I contend that we have also bought into a set of ideas about the nature of the world that makes us believe that nothing fundamental really can be changed. Consequently, quite apart from our real powerlessness, we also bring a certain amount of surplus powerlessness into each situation, making ourselves far less able to imagine ourselves changing reality than an impartial analysis of our relative powerlessness would yield.

It is this surplus powerlessness that kicks in whenever we imagine challenging the ethos of selfishness, materialism, and cynicism in our contemporary world. This ethos seems so big, so built into the ontological structure of necessity, so much a part of the way the world "really is," on the one hand—and we seem to ourselves so inadequate and ill-prepared to take on such a world-transformative task, on the other hand—that we fall back into cynicism or despair whenever someone tells us that things could be really different. No wonder, then, that we often react with anger and hostility toward people who talk about addressing our meaning-needs. To the extent that we have come to believe that nothing can be fundamentally different, we have made a thousand accommodations with a world of selfishness and materialism.

Powerlessness corrupts.

And surplus powerlessness makes us feel that the only realistic approach is to accept selfishness and materialism as fixed and unchangeable, and then to make whatever personal moves we need to make in order to protect ourselves.

Yet, things have not always been this way, nor will they always be so in the future. There have been times throughout the twentieth century when people took bold steps that transcended their surplus powerlessness. At such moments, they allowed themselves to imagine that other people would be there for them if they took leaps of moral courage. Union organizers, civil rights organizers, antiwar organizers, fighters for social justice, feminists, gay and lesbian organizers, and many others have taken these imaginative leaps—and often they have found that their courage made it possible for others to find *their* courage.

Yet the process is never static. There is a constant struggle going on in our society and inside each of us over how realistic it is to pursue one's highest ideals. Those who wish to preserve the status quo have powerful mechanisms for convincing the rest of us that such struggle is foolish and likely to be self-destructive, such as constant attempts to help us forget past moments when people really were able to transcend their own fears and narrow self-interest, and acted together in powerful ways. Yet there are many potential moments when the power of shared ideals, and the willingness to fight for them, can reemerge and energize people who have previously believed nothing can be changed. At such moments, societies fill with the powerful bond of optimism, idealism, hope, and possibility.

The politics of meaning is a strategy aimed at helping us reconnect with that part of ourselves that knows all this—that knows we all have had moments that gave us a glimpse of how we might transcend our fears and come together in hope, and that knows that all the cynicism is primarily congealed hurt and disappointment about what happened when last we hoped and then lost our hopes (perhaps prematurely). And yet, precisely because these hopes make us feel vulnerable and scared, most people have a high stake in dismissing a politics of meaning, and staying as hard-nosed and "realistic" as they can, even while they wish that someone could move them and others beyond their doubts.

The sad truth, I have learned, is that there is no one else but us—you and me, reader. We have to do this for ourselves. It is we who are going to have to overcome our surplus powerlessness together, imperfect as we all are, and disappointing as we all inevitably will be. And when we recognize this necessity, we can either desperately try to invalidate this message and pretend that we do not understand what "meaning" could possibly mean, or pretend that there are no such things as "meaning-needs," *or* we can face our task and strive to do what we can to reassure one another of our mutual support in the years ahead as we attempt to build a more loving, spiritually alive, and ethically and ecologically sensitive society.

2

What Is a Progressive
Politics of Meaning?

....

A Brief Definition

A progressive politics of meaning is a political effort to accomplish the following five goals:

1. *To create a society that encourages and supports love and intimacy, friendship and community, ethical sensitivity and spiritual awareness among people.*

Our economic, political and social arrangements make this kind of sensitivity and awareness more difficult to obtain and sustain. A politics of meaning does not seek to create a particular meaning system, but it does seek to create social and economic arrangements that will be friendly to meaning-oriented communities rather than harmful to their central concerns. In part, it means challenging the instrumental, utilitarian, mechanistic reductionism of thought and the disenchantment of our social experience. In part, it means creating institutions and economic practices that awaken within us our own ethical and spiritual sensitivity and our desire to treat one another with gentleness and compassion.

By spiritual awareness or sensitivity, I mean this: an awareness of the fundamental unity of all being and of our connectedness to one another and to the universe. When our unity and interconnectedness is fully appreciated, the arrogance and egotism that predominates in politics will dramatically decrease. Virtually every religious and spiritual system aims at this awareness. The politics of meaning does not seek to endorse any particular way of achieving it, but seeks to replace political and economic institutions that undermine this kind of spiritual awareness and that encourage human arrogance and ecological insensitivity.

2. *To change the bottom line.*

In most Western societies, productivity or efficiency is measured by the degree to which any individual or institution or legislation or social practice increases wealth or power. To pay attention to the bottom line is thus defined as paying attention to the degree to which the person or the project in question succeeds in maximizing wealth and power. Other goals are ancillary—acceptable only if they help accomplish (or, at least, do not thwart) the material goal.

A progressive politics of meaning posits a new bottom line. An institution or social practice is to be considered efficient or productive to the extent that it fosters ethically, spiritually, ecologically, and psychologically sensitive and caring human beings who can maintain long-term, loving personal and social relationships. While this new definition of productivity does not reject the importance of material well-being, it subsumes that concern within an expanded view of "the good life": one that insists on the primacy of spiritual harmony, loving relationships, mutual recognition, and work that contributes to the common good.

3. *To create the social, spiritual, and psychological conditions that will encourage us to recognize the uniqueness, sanctity, and*

infinite preciousness of every human being, and to treat them with caring, gentleness, and compassion.

4. *To create a society that gives us adequate time and encouragement to develop our inner lives.*

We seek a society that no longer counterposes the time needed for inner work to develop our spiritual, aesthetic, and psychological sensibilities with the time needed to make ourselves economically secure and successful.

5. *To create a society that encourages us to relate to the world and to one another in awe and joy.*

Instead of rewarding our ability to dominate, manipulate, or control, we seek to build families, communities, and economic and political institutions that encourage our capacity to experience wonder and radical amazement at the grandeur of the universe, and to experience pleasure and celebration of one another as embodiments of the spiritual energy of the universe (or, in religious terms, as creatures made in the image of God).

Large-scale changes of this kind cannot be accomplished quickly. Nevertheless, there are many things we can do in the short run to move our society toward this goal. I discuss these possibilities in greater detail in the last section of this book, but will outline a few of them here.

For example, a program for a progressive politics of meaning in the next few decades would seek:

- Public-school curricula that integrate the teaching of empathy and caring for others, and reward schools according to their success in creating empathic human beings (a goal quite different from that of traditional liberal demands, which have focused on student-teacher ratios or teacher salaries, but have rarely addressed the values being taught).

- Restructured health-care systems, so that medical care more adequately reflects an understanding of how the frustration of people's needs—for meaningful and nonalienating work, mutual recognition, love and caring, and a spiritually and ethically grounded society—may underlie receptivity to disease. Certainly, a progressive politics of meaning would endorse a single-payer universal health-care plan, on the grounds that we are never going to build a society that rejects selfishness while denying equal access to health care. But what distinguishes a politics-of-meaning approach is that it also links physical health to our ethical and spiritual well-being. So, for example, it also maintains that meaningful work—affording workers the opportunity to use their intelligence, creativity, and cooperative ability, and providing space for their spiritual lives—will decrease vulnerability to disease.

- A pro-family agenda that gives families the social supports they need. In addition to the traditional liberal elements (economic viability, flextime, child care, and so on), a politics of meaning approach includes as equally central the psychological and spiritual needs of families. We want to create a society that is safe for love and intimacy—as opposed to contemporary societies that identify sophistication with cynicism, critical intelligence with moral detachment, and maturity with "healthy suspicion of others." Instead, we seek a society that will encourage people to be more caring, sensitive, and empathic to others. So, for example, we want workplaces that encourage cooperation and give all of us an opportunity to use our intelligence and creativity. We want an economy that encourages us to take into account the needs and interests of others. We see these things not primarily as "rights" of the lone individual, but as requisite for shaping societies that nourish loving relationships.

- Annual ethical-impact reports from government and private-sector institutions to assess their effect on the ethical, spiritual, and psychological well-being of our society and on the people who work in and with these institutions.

- Reflection within every profession on activities and attitudes that would be possible if the goals were to serve the common good; to heighten ethical, spiritual, and ecological sensitivity;

and to reward loving and caring behavior. Such reflection, for example, has led some lawyers associated with a politics-of-meaning perspective to envision a second stage of trials, in which the adversary system is suspended and the focus is shifted to healing the problems and pain that the initial trial has uncovered in the community.

Anyone who takes these specific examples and regards them as the sum total of the politics of meaning has missed my point. A progressive politics of meaning leads to a rethinking of every aspect of our public and private lives. However, it resists any attempt to impose one particular lifestyle or one particular approach to spirituality.

Most importantly, a politics of meaning is an invitation to transcend all the internalized messages that tell us that it is unrealistic to base our lives on our highest ideals and to fight for their realization. It is no longer appropriate to fight for instrumental goals that do not really express our vision of the kind of world we actually seek. Doing politics in this limited way turns out to be unrealistic and ineffective, because the political Right advocates its full vision enthusiastically. Progressives, to compete successfully, must present their highest, most compelling vision.

The Destructive Ways in Which People Find Meaning

The primary dynamic of politics in the twentieth century has been the alternation between repressive communities of meaning and the alienation and loneliness produced by market societies. In reaction to the disintegration of existing communities, and with nothing to protect them from the alienation and loneliness produced by market societies, many people have become so hungry for human connection that they have even been willing to join repressive communities to fill that need. Some have turned back to traditional religious communities. Others have been attracted to the vision of community being offered by xenophobic nationalist movements.

Yet, to the extent that these various communities embody patriarchal privilege and class oppression, they frequently generate their own internal opposition. Just as, in the past, liberalism was created in opposition to the repressive nature of feudal societies, so today we find groups of people within these repressive communities who have begun to question the necessity of sacrificing for the community, once they realize that the sacrifices being sought primarily benefit the interests of small male elites. Disillusioned with such communities, these people turn back to the market, happy to be rid of what they have discovered: that their community is not truly a community, and that it does not really operate according to its proclaimed values. By contrast, in the market there is no similar hypocrisy: everybody really does try to maximize his or her own self-interest, and says so.

However, pursuing the market option and its logic of individualism also proves problematic for many people, since most of them *don't* "make it," and the ethos of selfishness sanctified by market-dominated societies soon yields deep unhappiness. So the cycle continues, and once again, people begin to grasp for communities of meaning, however repressive.

If we look at the recent history of Eastern Europe, we have a clear example of this phenomenon. Communism was a repressive community of meaning. As people saw through its empty communitarian rhetoric, they withdrew energy from collective life and buried themselves in alcoholism and despair as the entire economic system slid into ruin. When the Iron Curtain came crashing down in 1989, people imagined that they would find salvation in the competitive market. Indeed, some individuals have begun to enjoy greater prosperity. Yet most people quickly have discovered that their worth in the market is judged solely by how much money they can generate, and most have not done so well. Since the market encourages them to blame themselves for their own failures, they have come to feel ever more miserable. The tremendous pain and havoc created by the introduction of the free market in Russia is a predictable outcome.

In response to this misery, xenophobic nationalists emerge with a solution. They say, "We will value you not for what you accomplish but for who you are. You are really a Russian (Pole, Serb,

Slovak, German, Hungarian, American, . . .), and you deserve respect just for that, and not for anything you have to do." This message is particularly appealing when coupled with a vision of the nation as providing some ultimate meaning to which one can attach oneself.

The nation represents itself as a community in which each person is to be valued and given support simply by virtue of being a member of the nation, regardless of personal achievements. This idea feels wonderful to people who do not have this sense of acceptance in daily life, particularly not in the economic marketplace. Unfortunately, most existing systems of nationalism prop themselves up by demeaning some other group of people, either domestic minorities or external enemies.

The politics of meaning that I advocate in this book seeks to transcend this unhealthy alternation between repressive communities and the alienation of the competitive market. I support the communitarian instinct, but only when blended with a fundamental respect for individual freedoms and a resistance to gender-based, class-based, or racial and ethnic oppression. And I am cautious about anything that resembles forced community. I do not want any New Age orthodoxy or cheerleader for togetherness to force me or anyone else into communities that have obliterated the cherished private space that the community cannot invade.

The Limits of Communitarianism

Communitarianism has much in common with a politics of meaning. Both approaches recognize the need to change society in ways that build a caring and responsive community. But in the form made popular by George Washington University sociology professor Amitai Etzioni, communitarianism differs from a progressive politics of meaning in these three ways:

First, communitarianism has downplayed any criticism of the economic structures that foster selfishness. Like so many conservative movements, its enthusiasm for lecturing the public about individual responsibility is not matched by enthusiasm for challenging the irresponsibility of large corporate institutions and the

competitive market, which have contributed so much to the dissolution of communities.

Second, in its desire to maintain what passes for intellectual
respectability, communitarianism largely avoids the spiritual dimension of our contemporary crisis. Hence, it misses our pervasive hunger for spirituality and meaning, and addresses only our hunger for
community.

Finally, communitarianism does not sufficiently emphasize what
was right about past struggles against oppressive and patriarchal
communities. It is less vehement than a progressive politics of
meaning with regard to the importance of ensuring civil liberties,
insisting on democratic checks and balances, providing private
space for the individual that will not be violated by the community,
and working to overcome patriarchal tendencies to use communitarian language in order to mask male domination.

Are People Ready to Be Part
of a Meaning-Oriented Movement?

There already are millions of people effectively engaged in challenging the de-meaning of the world. But so far, most of these people do
not see themselves as part of a larger meaning-oriented movement.

There already are millions of people involved in the pursuit of
meaning and in challenging the atomistic, meaning-denying, economistic, or reductionist accounts of reality that have dominated
public discourse. These people recognize that there is something
fundamentally wrong with the dominant paradigm in the West, and
they are building a more holistic view of our relationships to one
another and to the natural world.

Some are involved in alternative approaches to health and healing, to nutrition and diet, to exercise and sports. Some are involved
in a worldwide ecological movement which understands that, in order to save the planet, we may need to relate to the world with
greater amounts of spiritual energy (awe, wonder, and radical
amazement). Some are involved in developing spiritual practices, either in connection with religious communities or in connection
with secular approaches to meditation and inner spiritual work.

Many are engaged in creating new relationships between men and women, either through the organized women's movement and the pro-feminist men's movement, or through more personal experiments in creating gentle and caring ways of relating. Many are engaged as teachers, nurses, social workers, and counselors; as rabbis, priests, ministers, and imams; and in other pursuits explicitly dedicated to reconnecting people to one another, to the spiritual energies of our inner selves, and to God's presence in the universe.

Currently, however, most people who are working for meaning operate in relative isolation from one another; they do not share a unified analysis. Some of them are involved in New Age philosophies that I find unpersuasive, or even in right-wing politics. Others resolutely assure one another that they are apolitical and uninterested in social issues. But what all these people *do* share is an ultimate concern with transcending the mechanistic, atomistic, antispiritual, and nonrelational ways of understanding the universe that have so crippled our thinking in the past.

These people already are challenging the dominant discourse, already are discounting what the official spokespeople have been saying. Some of these challengers turn to self-help and inspirational books, creating best-sellers as they grasp (sometimes indiscriminately) at accounts of reality that affirm our unity and innerconnectedness. Some people, to be sure, want nothing more than a personal solution, and will never be interested in any transformative vision that takes them beyond the confines of their own personal situation. But many more people understand that there is something deeply wrong with our world. Their alienation from the meaning-deadening world in which we live turns them toward new paradigms and new ways of conceptualizing reality. These people, who have faced the spiritual impoverishment of our contemporary world, will form the vanguard of social and political change in the twenty-first century.

One subgroup of this coming vanguard includes the millions of people who were ethically engaged with the social change movements of the 1960s and 1970s, but who today live private lives in part because they can see no political organization that plausibly speaks to their sensibilities. The political struggles of this generation of baby boomers awakened millions of Americans to an ethos of caring for others that was manifested in the civil rights movement, the antiwar movement, the women's movement, and the social justice and environmental movements.

Conservatives have correctly pointed out the ways in which these groups sometimes flirted with a countercultural ethos of individual fulfillment and unchecked self-indulgence that often undermined the moral content of the social change movements. There were moments when "liberation" was construed to mean freedom to do whatever one wanted to do, without regard for the consequences to others. To the extent that countercultural and political movements fell into this way of thinking or acting, they were quintessentially mainstream, providing yet another way for the dominant ethos of the market to permeate and shape mass consciousness. I myself and some of my friends sometimes fell into this self-indulgent definition of liberation, and we were deeply mistaken. I have learned from this experience to be more self-critical and also to listen carefully to the criticisms of people who have conservative politics with which I disagree, since they are sometimes correct and can see things that I cannot see. In fact, I believe that my entire generation has learned to approach politics with the humility that we tragically lacked several decades ago.

Indeed, a politics of meaning runs counter to this earlier tendency toward moral relativism and immediate gratification without moral standards. Yet, I must hasten to add that, even in the 1960s and 1970s, there was within these social change movements a countertendency, often explicitly challenging countercultural indulgence, that emphasized social solidarity and caring for others, that rejected moral relativism, and that articulated a powerful moral critique of the alienation and injustice of the contemporary world. Millions of people who went through that experience remain deeply committed to social justice and to building a more humane and loving society. Many of them have despaired that it ever would be possible to achieve those ends, and have become involved in lifestyles that on the surface seem superficially unconcerned about larger issues. Yet, like so many people in the religious world and in the labor movement, they could be mobilized to a new politics of love and caring were they to learn about it and come to believe that it was possible. Having been burnt by past failures, these former activists will not quickly jump into new political movements. Yet, as a meaning-oriented movement gains momentum. many of them will feel a homecoming that reconnects to their deepest hopes.

These are some of the groups from whom the movement for a politics of meaning will draw its initial support. They will become the transformative agents who move these ideas into the mainstream of American society. These people respond out of a real inner need, not from a commitment to an abstract idea, nor out of a sense that someone else ought to be treated differently. These people know that they cannot secure the kind of life they deeply desire, unless much changes in our society—its structure of values, its relationship to spiritual values, and its opportunities for mutual recognition. These are radical needs. Unlike needs for economic well-being or political rights, these cannot be fulfilled inside our society as it currently is constructed. Nor can these be fulfilled by buying off any one group. In that sense, the condition for the fulfillment of our needs for meaning is the condition for the liberation of our entire society from a materialist and individualist ethos.

Today, people involved in the pursuit of meaning do not yet form a coherent movement, and if they did, it seems unlikely that it would be a politically progressive movement. Nevertheless, the problems that have sensitized them to the crisis of meaning will not be solved by any other contemporary political movements. For this reason, I believe that people who recognize the crisis of meaning will provide the basis for a socially transformative movement in the twenty-first century. This movement will be at the center of creating a different kind of politics in America. That such a movement would be progressive is not guaranteed. It depends on whether the crisis of meaning remains the property of the Right, as it has become in the past decades, or whether liberals and progressives allow themselves to move beyond the limits of their current conceptual schemes and seriously begin to address meaningful issues.

One function of bringing these people together through the framework of a politics of meaning is to help them recognize their potential power as a transformative and healing force. At this moment, their potential social power appears invisible even to themselves, and their voices remain marginalized.

Nevertheless, their marginality applies only to the conventional political arena, whereas the strategy of social transformation articulated here is *not* narrowly political in that sense. Changes in consciousness and in the ways people lead their lives will, in the long run, be far more important than who wins this or that election.

Every person engaged in acts of aesthetic and spiritual creativity, every person engaged in acts of mutual recognition that reach beyond the conventions of contemporary isolation, every person engaged in prayer that is spiritually alive, every person who refuses to be cowed by the dominant materialism or ethos of selfishness, every person who rejects technocratic accounts of reality, every person who affirms humor and playfulness and awe and wonder, is herself or himself part of the transformative process that will eventually break through the stranglehold of a meaning-deadening society.

The Immediate Task:
Shifting the Dominant Discourse

Society's dominant discourse shapes not only its politics but the way people think about their personal lives and choices. Just as John F. Kennedy helped legitimize a discourse of idealism that gave impetus to the social movements of the 1960s, so Ronald Reagan managed to legitimize a discourse of selfishness and insensitivity that has had profound social consequences, far beyond his administration's legislative successes.

Shifting society's discourse—from one of selfishness and cynicism to one of idealism and caring—is the first and most important political goal of a politics of meaning in the next several decades. Long before we can reshape American society in any practical way, we must shift the way we think about our social institutions, politics, and economic practices. Therefore, one of the first priorities of a campaign for a politics of meaning will be to challenge the bottom-line assumption that people must always give priority to looking out for number one.

Changing the dominant discourse will change the messages we give to ourselves and to one another. The more we are able to support the part of ourselves that wishes to commit to a higher vision of who we can be, the likelier we are to take the steps in our personal lives that will make that possible. We are likelier to care for our souls and for our own spiritual and moral development when we live in a society where these kinds of concerns are publicly validated rather than ridiculed or marginalized. We are likelier to find ways to repair the psychic damage done by early childhood misrecognition and the forced denial of our desire for meaning when we live in a society which publicly values our ability to care as much as it values our ability to dominate or control.

The ultimate test of a politics-of-meaning movement, however, will always be the degree to which it liberates us to engage in small acts of caring and spiritual sensitivity. The more we engage in such acts, the more we are actually building a politics of meaning rather than just talking about it.

The Big Picture and the Little Picture:
Understanding Recent Politics

There are moments in history when we look around and see other people acting on their highest hopes. At such moments, we feel more hopeful about being able to do the same, and we are spurred to take greater risks in a particular situation or with a particular person we meet.

This was the experience of many people during such natural disasters as the 1994 Los Angeles earthquake, the 1993 Midwestern floods, the 1992 Florida hurricane (Andrew), and the 1989 Santa Cruz earthquake. People working in social change movements often report similar pivotal moments in their lives, as do people involved in religious movements. Moreover, an entire society can feel this way. During World War II, American society seemed to join in a higher moral purpose, and individuals felt freer and more confident to give of themselves to one another. In the late 1960s and early 1970s, tens of millions of people throughout the Western world let themselves share the vision that together they could change the world in fundamental ways. The hopeful spirit captured in John Lennon's song, "Imagine," reflects a historical moment in which people allowed themselves to envision a better world, and were willing to try to make it so.

In short, the big picture affects the little picture. To the extent that we feel ourselves part of the surge of collective energy toward hopefulness and mutual recognition, we act differently in our personal lives, seeking higher levels of connection and pushing limits that we had previously accepted as unchangeable.

Conversely, when our collective fear prevails over our collective hope, when the forces of positive change are in retreat from the public arena and the forces of self-interest predominate, then we despair in our personal lives about the possibility of things being different. As a result, we face particular situations with greater suspicion, and focus on maximizing our personal advantage, meanwhile paying less attention to the consequences for others. This, for example, is the usual mood when political conservatives of both parties dominate Congress, as they have done for much of the 1980s and 1990s.

Society rarely leans all one way or the other. Even in moments when society is leaning most toward selfishness, there is still hopeful and idealistic energy pushing forward; even when things are leaning most toward idealism, there is always some collective energy pushing toward selfishness and materialism. At any given moment, society is somewhere on the continuum between these forces. Often, what counts most is not where we are, but where we perceive the energy is flowing. Is it surging more toward narrowly defined self-interest, or more toward caring, optimism and idealism?

When we take trusting steps toward others, we make it possible for them to do the same toward us. But this path is not easy or linear, because we have been so heavily conditioned by the ethos of selfishness, by past hurts from misrecognition, and by fears (often well founded) that others will not be fully there for us should we choose to make ourselves vulnerable. As a result, we need much patience and compassion for others and for ourselves as we start on this challenging path.

Instead of being shocked at the ways in which each of us tends toward selfishness, pettiness, materialism, manipulation, or distrust of others, we need to recognize that those are precisely the behaviors that get most highly rewarded. Therefore, we should honor people to the extent that they transcend these behaviors, and we should not be surprised to find many wounded and wounding people in our movement, including our own leaders. If our movement can recognize the social realities that make "wounded healers" of all who engage in transformation, we can begin to develop compassion—not only for one another, but also for the many people who are far too scared to allow themselves to hope, and who respond to our movement with scorn, ridicule, or dismissal as irrelevant and unworthy of attention. To the extent that our movement manifests true compassion, not as a sappy, feel-good optimism, but as a reflection of a deep understanding of the nature of reality, we will eventually reach many whose hearts or minds are currently frozen in the conviction that nothing fundamental can be changed.

The Transgressive Nature of Imagining What Could Be

The first commandment of the modern world is, "What Exists Now Is Reality—Thou Shalt Have *No* Other Gods Before It."

To imagine a different reality, then, is to violate the central command upon which the modern world depends. Whenever we violate it, others will be angry at us, in part because we seem to be suggesting that the endless compromises that they have made in their lives were not absolutely necessary. Others may try to make us feel embarrassment or shame, by suggesting that if we are not happy with the way things are, it is probably because we have personally failed to make a good life for ourselves. The implication is that our desire to change things stems from being unwilling to look at how we personally have screwed up our lives.

When greeted with this kind of hostility, it is no wonder that people who are attracted to social change movements often back away. To many of us, it seems so much safer to stick with the alienation that we already know, rather than face new feelings of rejection and messages that tell us we are only making fools of ourselves and showing how "untogether" we are whenever we even think about challenging so-called reality.

Yet many of us retain a part of our consciousness that can also imagine the joy of transgressing the social injunction to "be realistic": of allowing ourselves to play with fantasy and joy, and refusing to allow the goals of whatever current reality existed to set the limits of our thought. This transgressive joy, in fact, has been part of the appeal of various religious, spiritual, and mystical traditions: they, too, give people permission to leave this goal-directed world and to respond to the universe in a more loving and playful way.

Affirming the Life Energy That Permeates Our Being

A politics of meaning may succeed in the not-too-long run because it affirms a part of our being that many people have not fully repressed: our deep desire to be recognized by one another not only for our individuality, but also for that which we have in common— what various religious traditions call the spirit of God, and what secularists call the fundamental dignity of each person. Many people are deeply dissatisfied with a way of human life that is highly competitive, mutually suspicious, and very alienating; we would much prefer a world in which people share common goals and purposes, rooted in a higher ethical and spiritual vision. This desire is so intense in most people that it seems almost physically palpable.

Every pore of our being pulsates with the desire to be recognized by and connected to other human beings, and to the life force that pulsates through the universe. This desire draws us to others and to people, projects, ideas, and social movements that similarly seem to be pulsating with this life force or energy.

The need of this life energy to find expression partly comprises our hunger for meaning. However, not all life energy finds healthy expression in ways that lovingly link us to other human beings in communities of ethical and spiritual meaning and purpose.

When healthy avenues for the expression of our meaning-needs are blocked, our life energy will seek other, sometimes destructive means of expression. Our spiritual energy, banned from the respectable institutions of public life by liberals determined to keep them value-free and "scientific," resurfaces in distorted forms, such as excessive consumerism and the fetishization of sports, sex, drugs, and rock and roll. Because spiritual energy, like other forms of energy, cannot be destroyed, its repression in one area of our lives ensures its emergence in other areas of our lives, sometimes in other forms.

Our hunger for meaning is so pervasive that we are attracted to a wide variety of activities, institutions, and social practices that seem to promise some minimal satisfaction of this need. These entities acknowledge the hunger for meaning, unconsciously appeal to our need for meaning, and simultaneously assault us in ways that make us feel that our orientation toward meaning must be kept within narrowly restricted boundaries. This is the mysterious and opaque part of daily life: it demands repression of our awareness of our need for meaning, and simultaneously gratifies that need in incomplete, distorted forms. I want to focus a little on the ways in which this partial meaning-gratification occurs.

Moving Toward the Life Energy

Tens of millions of people become attracted to anything that is alive and energy-generating in society. Working all day long in mind- and spirit-deadening jobs, many of us have managed to cut ourselves off from our own spiritual and emotional needs. Yet, without acknowledging to ourselves that there is anything desperately wrong in the functioning of our daily lives, we find ourselves drawn to any public arena in which spiritual energy surges and emotions are allowed to seep through.

Let me take a few examples of these energy surges and the ways in which they either are validated or contained in daily life.

HOW THE RIGHT STOLE GOD

It was not the policy positions of the Right that drew millions to Christian sects espousing right-wing ideas, but their religious energy. Listening to television evangelists or attending a prayer service of those in the religious Right is to feel a palpable energy and excitement that simply does not exist in many of the religious denominations with whose politics I agree more.

In some communities of the religious Right, the key to this energy is straightforward: they actually take the teaching of communal caring seriously enough to get themselves involved in the nitty-gritty problems of life. Many of these religious communities encourage their members to visit the sick, to share child-care burdens, and even to give active support when people are unemployed. Members are there to welcome newborns, to pay attention to children as they grow up, and to help single adults meet one another. While this kind of mutual caring is restricted to those who are part of the religious community, those who participate in it find an energy surge in caring for others that is exciting and fulfilling, and that, to many, feels well worth the cost of admission: namely, the willingness to buy into right-wing metaphysical or political assumptions.

In other such communities, an ecstatic religious experience provides a taste of the energy that has been missing throughout so much of one's life. In this context, people do things that express a liveliness and even irrationality, which feel like an act of communal rebellion against the manipulated consciousness that is rewarded in the secular world of work.

The act of singing together in a spirited way, shouting out "amen" to some truth that has been expressed, allowing oneself to move beyond oneself and into a community that allows emotionality and spirituality to be validated as real—all are sufficient to make one feel alive in ways that are never permitted in other corners of public life. Connecting to that life energy is so self-validating that those who stand against it *must* be wrong. No wonder, then, that the typically secular, rational, liberal intellectual often has trouble getting the juices flowing for constituencies that have found some life energy being expressed in the world of right-wing religious experience. It is not that these people have been brainwashed into right-wing ideas. Rather, they have experienced a touch of meaning and purpose, while those who challenge the ideas put forward by right-wing churches articulate their critique in a technocratic and deadening style.

Nevertheless, people have to go back to the world of work after their weekends in Church, and there they find a world still dominated by the ethos of selfishness, and a political Right that refuses to question the individualism and selfishness of the corporate world. All the good communality and mutual care that these right-wing communities sometimes provide is not enough to offset the overwhelming impact of daily economic life.

Yet instead of challenging the selfishness of the world of work, the Christian Right suggests instead that those feeling this pain must surrender themselves to God, and if that surrender is total and real they will find relief from the pain. If the pain persists, the religious Right suggests, there must be one of two reasons: either we as a society have not been sufficiently successful in blocking the selfishness of the demeaned Others, or you as an individual have not been sufficiently serious in surrendering yourself to God.

This surrender to God has great appeal precisely because it does allow a certain degree of transcendence of the self-obsessed dynamics of the contemporary world. Moreover, the process of surrender may often involve an experience in which one's own energy surges to meet the communal energy of others who have already made this kind of life commitment. Compared to the boring and lifeless energy that prevails in some of the more liberal churches, this experience of surrender and connection to others feels self-validating.

From my standpoint, there is a problem with the kind of surrender that the Right encourages. Surrender to God, on the rightist account, seems to be little more than a verbal and mental process, carrying no necessary implications for loving action. Yet the God of the Hebrew Bible, and the Jesus of the New Testament, are very clearly asking for something more: they are asking for people to love their neighbors and act accordingly. Contemporary religious rightists join the long line of religious fanatics throughout history who conveniently have managed to forget this central message of Jewish and Christian teaching. Using as their excuse an insistence that it may be arrogant for human beings to believe they can achieve perfection in this world, the religious rightists seem oblivious to the Biblical demands that people join in the effort to bring love and healing to the world.

For the past several decades Christian rightists have managed to gain the upper hand in the Christian world because they seemed to be taking religious teachings seriously, while religious liberals seemed to lack all serious involvement in the religious dimension of their teachings, and seemed to do little more than invoke Biblical passages as a justification for the standard liberal agenda. More recently, a renewal movement in the Christian world has produced a new group of Christians who are challenging the Right on its own ground, arguing that surrender to God is *not* just an act of the mind, but an act involving a commitment to a life of service emulating the lives of the great saints and others who devoted their lives to the poor and the oppressed. The Christian Evangelical magazine *Sojourners* and organizations like Evangelicals for Social Justice have helped launch the "Cry for Renewal," a document issued by dozens of religiously conservative theologians and ministers who are insisting that religious surrender must involve a new willingness to commit to an ethos of love and caring.

Liberals have contributed to the success of the Right in claiming to be the representatives of spiritual concerns. Many liberals have a gut distrust of religious ideas and automatically assume them to be right-wing, and they have often created an implicit demand on religious people that they leave their religion at the door when entering into liberal political arenas. To the extent that religious liberals have complied, it has been easy for the religious Right to portray them as lacking religious seriousness, and not really caring about serving God.

Yet one of the great moments of liberal politics in the twentieth century was the campaign of Martin Luther King Jr. to challenge American racism. King's civil rights struggle emerged from the black churches, connected to the powerful energies that black Baptists have retained in their religious tradition, and explicitly fostered its political demands as emanations of a larger religious vision.

Liberals will never get this if they attempt to manipulate religion for political ends. God is not a slogan to attach to an advertising campaign for one's politics. The only hope for liberal religions is to reconnect in a spiritually serious way to the deepest sacred energies of their religious tradition. What I argue in *Jewish Renewal: A Path to Healing and Transformation* and what Jim Wallis argues in

The Soul of Politics is that when one does that, one finds at the heart of the spiritual energies a powerful injunction to recognize the God within every other human being, and to build a world consistent with that understanding. It is only from that spiritual base that liberal religions could reconstitute themselves as a serious alternative to right-wing religious movements. People have to be able to feel the energy of a loving and caring community, to experience the passion of commitment that goes far beyond the passive reading of prayers and Biblical quotations, and to find themselves surrounded by the passionate commitment of others who are moved to serve God. When liberal religious communities emanate this kind of spiritual energy, they will be in a position to expose the distortions that the Right has introduced. Until then, the Right will continue to steal God, to speak in the name of divine energy, and to coopt the legitimate hunger people have for a connection to higher purpose.

SPORTS

America's enormous interest in spectator sports is not accompanied by a widespread *participation* in sports. People love sports *as fans*— as people who do not engage in the physical contact of the game but who vicariously participate in an imagined community of meaning and purpose, in which "we" are fighting against some "them." The sense of participation in a community—especially a community that is outside the normal constraints—that acts out its enthusiasm in somewhat outrageous fashion, and that permits people to be irrational, to yell and scream for their team, and to behave in ways that are not controlled is what makes sports so energetically exciting.

Though the form of these "pseudo-communities" (in Peter Gabel's phrase) replicates the competitiveness of the larger market, it is not the competition of "all against all" that Hobbes described, but rather of "a we against a we," in which our "we" gives us a sense of home and place. It is a pseudo-community because the connections last only as long as the game and the victory party, but do not extend to the rest of our lives. Those in our pseudo-community do not worry about us when we are sick or when we have family problems or when we may be out of work. Our momentary high disappears; our life situation remains unchanged and just as alienating as ever. Yet, like every momentary "high," it feels good while it lasts. The hungrier that people are for some form of connection that permits them to experience being part of a "we," the more frenetic is their connection to "the team." With this attachment, people begin to see their own lives as being validated or negated depending on how well their team is doing—hence the fantasy that "we" are winning (or losing) and that "we" are "the best" (or not).

Moreover, sports is the one arena which most closely approximates what the rest of the society claims to be: an arena in which reward is allocated according to merit. How well an athlete's capabilities are developed actually shapes his or her chances for success. By emotionally investing in sports, spectators can covertly (and as it happens, ineffectively and therefore safely) rebel against the lies of the larger competitive market. With this surge of energy, we transcend the emotional deadness of the world of work. For that very reason, sports (along with sex) becomes a major topic of discussion whenever workers are allowed to communicate, and provides important confirmation that they are still alive and have not lost touch with the life energy of the planet.

SEXUALITY

Sexuality as a separate category of human experience may be a reflection of the alienated state of our existence, a reflection in our bodies of the frustration of our hunger for meaning and connection. When people spend huge amounts of time and energy invested in sexual conquests or sexual acrobatics, they are often displacing onto sex their desire for loving connection and for a more fully alive set of human interactions.

It is the deprivation of our need for loving connection that allows for the creation of sexuality as another commodifiable activity, available on the market and separated from meaning and love. In that context, our desire for meaningful human connection often finds expression, though usually in only partial ways, in our experience of sexuality.

Yet even in its alienated form, sexuality testifies to the presence of a life energy pulsating through us that cannot be fully extinguished, even in the most meaning-stultifying realities. Alienated sexuality becomes a living reminder of our hunger to be connected to others.

The psychiatrist Wilhelm Reich was one thinker who partly understood this hunger for meaning and connection. His brilliant account of the rise of fascism in Germany was sensitive to the flows of life energy. Unfortunately, Reich was limited by his mechanistic view of psychoanalytic theory, which reduced this life energy to physical units of energy. Reich translated life-energy needs into sexual energy, and proposed that it was the blocking of sexual expression that prevented the human connection that people sought.

Orthodox Marxists expelled Reich from the Communist Party and orthodox Freudians expelled him from the psychoanalytic movement, so Reich never got the support to test his theory that combating sexual repressiveness might undermine the growth of fascism. But I doubt whether any program based on his rather mechanistic focus on orgiastic potency would have had the political impact he imagined, because that focus was far too narrow and ignored the underlying need that had drawn people to fascism: the desire to be cared for, quite apart from one's achievements in the market or one's ability to perform. It is not more orgasms but more love, recognition, and mutual connection that people seek when they turn to the Right—although the cost of getting connection within a right-wing community is to share an ideology that demeans others and sometimes turns people into haters.

Those who adopted various versions of Reichian ideas in the 1960s imagined that if they could break the sexual taboos of society, and make sex readily available outside the moralistic constraints that had previously deadened it, they could inspire a total cultural revolution that would shatter existing forms of domination. However, they were deeply mistaken.

Separated from our need for genuine recognition and loving connection, and divorced from communities of ethical and spiritual purpose that transcended the individualism of the competitive market, the demand for sexual liberation was quickly assimilated and sold back to people in the form of sexually explicit records and films, in the form of male-chauvinist-dominated communes and alternative lifestyles, and in the form of sexually exploitative transactions between men and women. Women were told, for example, that they were being uptight and repressed if they did not make themselves sexually available, and that such behavior impeded the revolution.

The truly liberating aspects of human sexuality—its potential access to pleasure experienced with and through others, its function as a connecting mechanism, and its close ties to our ability to reproduce human life in all its mystery and grandeur—are denied by contemporary forms of prudery and sexual repressiveness as well as by individualistic or market-driven conceptions of sexual liberation. The marketplace speedily appropriated the countercultural attempt to free sexuality from prudery and the fear of pleasure, and transformed this effort into a powerful mechanism for selling its products. It sublimated our desire for connection into the highly individualistic, materialistic consumption of others.

The appropriation of sexual energy by corporate advertising and mass media is only the latest stage in a distorting process that reduces our hunger for connection to its material expression (the sexual act) and then removes its sacred context in loving and caring relationships so that sexuality can be used to entice us into the salable lifestyles of the marketplace.

In every encounter between a man and a woman, this entire marketization of relationships repeats itself. The dominant culture of mutual sexual consumption encourages each partner to remain distant from any notion of sanctity in human contact; to see the body as a terrain of pleasure, detached from loving commitment or from ethical or spiritual meaning; and to allow the self to be treated as a marketable commodity. Women often sense the diminished pleasure available when sex is detached from commitment. Their protest at this separation stems not only from a recognition of their particular vulnerability to the consequences of meaning-shorn sexuality, but also out of a desire for the fuller pleasure of sex with commitment.

Men often protest that women are sexually repressed if they do not happily accommodate the diminished forms of sexuality that flourish in contemporary culture. Yet many of these men are themselves victims of the deprivation of meaning, to such an extent that they can no longer experience bodily pleasure without experiences of conquest or domination. Their demands for immediate gratification of their alienated sexuality gives them only a small taste of the pleasures that would be available in a world which did not detach sexuality from commitment and loving relationships. It may well be women's greater capacity for pleasure that allows them to say "no," while men often are so alienated from their own bodies that many have no idea how much more delicious and stimulating a meaning-based sexuality can be.

Yet people are legitimately suspicious of anyone who talks of meaning in the sexual sphere. Many religious systems have used meaning not to enhance but to denigrate sexuality, or to firmly restrict its expression in ways that favor men's needs and desires. Here, as in every other sphere in which contemporary society has stripped us of meaning, the solution suggested by a politics of meaning is not to return to patriarchal or oppressive meaning systems, but to renew communities of meaning in ways that incorporate liberal sensibilities without being confined by them.

It is no surprise that ancient Roman culture, expressing the largest system of imperial domination that the world had yet known, articulated the principle that "after sex, everyone is sad." Indeed, in a world of oppression, sexual energy simultaneously reminds us of the potential for genuine human connection and of the frustration of this desire in the world as constituted.

Though it is popular wisdom today to say that rape and other acts of sexual abuse have *nothing* to do with sex and everything to do with power, it would be more apt to say that these are violent, ugly expressions of the pain engendered by a world in which healthy forms of human connection are rarely available. Indeed, the hunger for any kind of power over others may similarly be rooted in the frustration of our hunger for meaningful connection.

Consider, for example, widespread reports of the sexual abuse of children. All too often, we find stories of human beings who are deeply frustrated in their other attempts to make real human contact, and who then proceed to immorally use their superior power to inflict themselves on those least able to defend themselves. In the past decade, as reports of abuse have escalated dramatically (in large part because it has become safe for women to talk about what they endured as children), American society has made a monumental effort to deny the reality of these reports. Focusing on some instances in which memories of abuse may have been implanted by overly zealous therapists, our society now hides behind what it calls "false memory syndrome." Yet the power of these memories, like the memories of all kinds of physical and psychological abuse, is that they testify to the perversions that emerge when healthy forms of loving connection are systematically frustrated.

It may even be a fear of exposure that leads some of the powerful in this society to consider eliminating insurance for long-term psychotherapy in which memories of childhood abuse are sometimes recovered. When long-term psychotherapy served to accommodate people to the existing power relations of the society, it was considered culturally acceptable. But when the women's movement began to reshape therapy to serve the needs of women, and then others began to extend its techniques to reempower other victimized groups, psychotherapy became culturally suspect and subject to ridicule and cynicism.

The desperate attempt to keep out of our consciousness one of the most disgusting aspects of contemporary life, the widespread abuse of children, serves existing power relationships well. It allows us to ignore the obvious question, "Why is it that so many parents find a need to seek sexualized connections with their children or the children of relatives, friends, or neighbors?" Society's defensive reply is, "These *must* be false memories, because there couldn't be so many people in our society who are perverted in this way!" But it would make more sense if we were to understand that much (not all) of the abuse is a perverted expression of the widespread hunger for connection and love in the face of a world that provides systematic disconfirmation and alienation.

I certainly am not excusing this outrageous behavior, nor am I suggesting leniency in dealing with the perpetrators, when I note its origins in our crisis of meaning. I see this behavior on the same continuum with other alienated responses to a legitimate human need for loving connection—a continuum that includes the perverse demands of many men and some women for sex without commitment.

It takes a very rare human being these days to stand up to the entire thrust of the dominant market consciousness and insist that sexuality be reclaimed from objectification and returned to meaning.

MUSIC AND DANCE

Throughout most of human history, music and dance have provided ways for people to be together, to harmonize voice and body with others, to communally celebrate the universe and human experience, and to rejoice in one another and in the pleasure of life. It is only since the rise of market societies in the past several hundred years that music has been split off, has become a separable commodity, and has been sold back to us as a scarce pleasure to be purchased.

Even with commodification, there have been cultural and religious traditions that have kept music alive to its fullest spiritual purposes, suggesting to us in nonverbal ways that the transcendent has surrounded and permeated our being, and that we are so much more than we can express in language. The celebratory and spiritual dimension to music has never fully been repressed, even at the height of its appropriation into the commodity market.

In recent decades, music has also become the locus of an only partially articulated rebellion against the spirit- and energy-deadening aspects of contemporary culture. The musical scene that erupted in the 1960s and that continues in various incarnations in the 1990s (such as, until the death of Jerry Garcia, the Grateful Dead) has radically critiqued the one-dimensionality of the manipulated consciousness produced by the dominant corporate-oriented, bottom-line focused, homogenized culture that has triumphed in most Western societies.

What music and dance often enact without language is the contemporary expression of the inner struggle between that part of us that is most distrustful of others and most insistent on our need for strong personal boundaries and individual freedom, and that part of us that is most in need of connection with others. The huge rock-concert industry provides a context for thousands of people to experience the connection and common purpose that can come from sharing the aspirations expressed in a musical rendition, and to do so in ways that seem to break loose from the rhythms and constraints of daily life as shaped by the market. The surge of energy typically experienced at these events expresses a common longing for a deeper connection that is unfulfilled in daily life. The sense of being in it together, of sharing common fates and common hopes, of recognizing in one another a community of people who remain attuned to the life energy that has not yet been extinguished—all of these emotions feel self-validating to the participants and can never be fully explained to those who have not been there, or who have not allowed themselves to be fully there even when physically present.

Like sports and sex, music and dance can express the isolated individualism of our contemporary world. They can function like religion or nationalism, as the locus for pseudo-communities that provide temporary feelings of connection and relieve pressure that might otherwise be directed in acts of self-destruction or against economic and political institutions that thwart meaning. Yet, from a more positive perspective, all of these areas that surge with energy and evoke our suppressed hunger for communities of meaning testify to that which has been lost in our daily lives and which people crave. They are constant reminders that this hunger may be redirected but cannot successfully be repressed.

TELEVISION AND HATE RADIO

I have listened to Rush Limbaugh denounce the politics of meaning, and me personally, often enough to know that this man is a political enemy. In fact, he has personally attacked me so often that I eventually called his show to ask for a few minutes of airtime in which to respond to his ridiculous, false characterizations of me and my ideas. My request was denied—Limbaugh does not want to have on his show any other kind of live energy that might counter his voice.

Even if one dislikes Rush Limbaugh, however, one cannot deny the basis of his appeal. Like so many other talk-show hosts, Limbaugh embodies a kind of passionate life energy. It naturally attracts people as an alternative to the boring and deadly policy discourses offered by high-minded public radio or television commentators, whose fascination with technocratic details is rarely matched by their psychological sensitivity or spiritual vision.

If public television and even some of the commercial television news networks are unable to generate large constituencies, it is not, as they tell themselves, because they cater to a sophisticated audience rather than pander to popular tastes. It is, rather, that they misguidedly attempt to portray themselves as morally, spiritually, and politically neutral—in the process, emptying their reportage of all that could connect with our moral sensibilities and deepest hopes. Compared to this seemingly neutered and energy-depleted reality, hate radio feels alive and much less phony. People turn away from neutral and technocratic communications, and lose interest in a public realm that is devoid of emotional intensity or moral relevance. They withdraw instead into television that seems more connected to human reality (hence, the popularity of magazine-style human-interest programs), or media that are more connected to the passionate vision of social reality presented by right-wing hosts.

These talk-show hosts encourage a discourse of resentment against society's official shapers of consciousness: the media, Hollywood, the educated academic elite. Yet this resentment is not artificially created by the Right. It strikes a resonant chord precisely because people justifiably feel that many of the institutions in their lives, particularly the intellectual establishment and the media, have failed to give them an intellectual or moral framework through which they could understand the alienation and frustration in their lives. The hate radio of the Right validates this anger, directs it (often against the demeaned others in our society who are least capable of defending themselves), and celebrates it.

There is no reason, however, why life energy should have to be channeled in these fascistic directions. It could equally be directed against the ethos of selfishness and materialism, and toward a new affirmation of the right of people to be fully recognized, and validated in their desire to be more fully alive. I have achieved this with audiences of people who normally respond to right-wingers, so I know that it is possible and that our life energy need not find expression only in hurtful or hateful ways.

Meanwhile, mainstream television often functions as an energy deadener. Most of us can resist the specific political content of a program that has an overt political message. It is much harder to resist the numbing effect of presentations of reality that portray people with a one-dimensional lifelessness that masquerades as the way ordinary people really are. Our own moments of life and energy seem, by comparison, problematic or even pathological—reasons to start taking Prozac or some mood-changing prescription drug, or to go to therapy, or to start drinking, or to try to hide oneself more successfully. Our hunger for life that is more connected, more real, and more oriented toward higher meaning seems unconventional and bizarre.

News shows, of course, are the most obvious meaning deadeners—reducing the passion of politics to predigested sound bites. The predictable, scripted "spontaneity" of local newscasters pretending to joke or tease one another, or the unbearable deadliness of shows like *Firing Line* and the Sunday morning news-analysis shows, deaden our hopefulness that anyone alive exists beyond our small circle of friends. Not surprisingly, these latter serious shows draw smaller audiences, which permits the Hollywood moguls to conclude that "people just aren't interested in ideas"!

When tens of millions of Americans respond positively to the idealism and hopefulness of a movie like Steven Spielberg's *Schindler's List* or to a compelling television miniseries like *Roots,* they discredit the Hollywood excuse that the American public will only watch shows and movies that do not require us to use our heads or grapple with ideas.

Many of those engaged in shaping today's mass culture are disillusioned liberals and former idealists who, as part of the process of reconciling themselves to a life aimed at maximizing their own individual well-being, have come to believe that their own youthful commitment to social change was silly or potentially destructive. So they have become willing participants in the media assassination of any life energy that cannot be reduced to simplistic formulas that teach us to contain our desires for loving connection. Having bought into Hollywood wisdom about what the audience "really" wants, they use their often considerable creative talents to find innovative ways to present television shows and movies that, in the final analysis, repeat the standard cynicism and despair of the age.

The media works with other cultural forces as an idealism-quasher, particularly when it redefines in reductionist terms those moments in which a community has experienced transcendence and optimism. A classic case is the media's systematic lies and distortions about the meaning of the 1960s in general and the movement to end the Vietnam War in particular.

The repression of collective memory of the Vietnam War, the continuing refusal to acknowledge the millions of deaths caused by American intervention, and the inability to seriously confront the idealism of those millions of young people who protested at the time, have helped shape our current period and its despair. This enforced historical amnesia has made it impossible for anyone who lived through that period to integrate his or her own life with some larger sense of its historical meaning. Instead, the image-shapers have attempted to sidestep their own youthful idealism by allowing both sides (those who protested and those who perpetrated crimes) to come together in the empty image of "generational" solidarity and Woodstock nostalgia.

The media has developed a "master narrative" that focuses on momentary youthful enthusiasm and idealism, mixed with a distorting dose of sex, drugs, and rock and roll. Retrospectives define a generation's memories of itself, and how that generation quickly "grew up," recognized that it was on the wrong path, and except for a few dropouts and many drug-scarred casualties, went on to become a yuppified success story. Whenever a story is told about someone from the 1960s, that person is assimilated into the master narrative, and the parts that do not fit are ignored or denied. Measured against this media version, anyone who has remained committed to social change (and there are literally millions of baby boomers who are) must see herself or himself as an oddball who has no likely set of allies should she or he move from memory and fantasy to contemporary political action.

Most often, however, it is not the specific political slant of any particular television show or movie, so much as the quashing of our sense of hopefulness and possibility, that makes the media a crucial meaning-deadener.

The one place in the media where life energy is allowed to break through is in advertising. There, our sexual energies are taunted and awakened, our hunger for connection to others is explicitly acknowledged, even our fantasy lives are given credence—but only so that all this energy might be directed toward the consumption of consumer goods. The excited and agitated air of many commercials stands in stark contrast to the restrained and deadening, naively sweet, or cynically evil portrayals of reality that are otherwise so prevalent over the airwaves.

The Enduring Spiritual Crisis

Every aspect of our personal and public lives is decisively shaped by the deprivation of meaning. Alienation at work and the absence of opportunities to serve the common good, an economy that rewards selfishness and materialism while encouraging us to think of others as objects for manipulation and control, and a society that preaches looking out for number one, all contribute to the dissolution of relationships and ethical values in civil society and in private life. The triumph of mechanistic thinking and the de-spiritualization of daily life further intensify our hunger for meaning and our vulnerability to substitute forms of gratification. Because many progressive intellectuals and cultural critics fail to understand this elemental hunger for meaning and purpose, and the powerful attraction of anything that seems to offer us the life energy that has been drained from so much of our economic and political and social life, these thinkers conclude that they are surrounded by people who are irrational at best. The American majority, well aware of how contemptuously it is being treated, returns the favor by despising these intellectual and cultural elites.

3

The Failure of the Liberals

Many members of my family were murdered by the Nazis. As a child, I was surrounded by the grieving for those who had been killed, and by a family and community determined to ensure that this kind of thing could never happen again. Yet much of the energy expended by my parents and the Jewish community seemed to be based on the assumption that it was inevitable that vicious anti-Semitic haters would regain power in various countries of the world. So the critical task, in the view of my community, was to make sure that Jews would be in a stronger position to defend themselves the next time something like this happened.

By the time I was twelve, I had begun to question this assumption. Many of the non-Jewish kids I met in school were perfectly wonderful people, and I saw no reason to believe that hidden somewhere deep within their psyches or gene pools was a determination to hate Jews. If hatred won out at a particular moment, perhaps it was not the result of some inherent human evil, but something that had been produced in people by particular circumstances. I began to ask about the Nazis, "What made their ascension to power possible?"

I could not understand why the European Left had been unable to stem the popularity of the fascists. The Left had offered its typical program of individual rights, economic entitlements, and inclusion, but this had not seemed to speak to people's needs. The Left had warned, "They are fascists. They will not give you individual liberties and they will not protect you from the worst economic consequences of the free market." Yet people had shrugged and said, "So?"

What the Left had missed was that people were in deep pain in their lives, and that the racist, anti-Semitic, and xenophobic responses were part of a larger framework of meaning and purpose that provided some relief from this pain. The parades, the communal celebrations, and the music were not superficial add-ons that merely obscured the inner truth of hatred (of Jews, gays, non-Germans, non-Aryans, or whomever). On the contrary, the communal celebrations bespoke a hunger for solidarity, mutual connection, and shared values—and for many people, it was this hunger for community that attracted them to fascism. Their hatred of others was based on the degree to which they had come to believe (usually mistakenly) that the demeaned Others had actually caused the breakdown of their communities of shared meaning and purpose.

When liberals and leftists sought to explain German anger during the 1920s in terms of the harsh economic conditions imposed by the Versailles Treaty after World War I, this explanation simply struck me as insufficient. After all, other peoples have faced harsh economic conditions without turning to fascism. And the communists, too, had proposed solutions to the economic crisis, so people could have turned to the Left if economics had been the primary determinant of their political proclivity.

Wilhelm Reich's *The Mass Psychology of Fascism*, and later, Zygmunt Bauman's brilliant account of fascism in his classic, *The Holocaust and Modernity*, helped me understand how Germany's desperate economic conditions had been intensified by the larger breakdown of community in the world. In certain absolute terms, economic life had been far harder one or two hundred years before the 1920s. But prior to the triumph of the ethos of selfishness embedded in the competitive market, people had lived in traditional or feudal communities which shared an ethos of caring for one another. The church, the local community, and extended families living in close proximity provided a mutual support system on which people normally could count in the face of unexpected dangers. Moral and spiritual bonds helped sustain a sense of community that often felt overwhelming and intrusive, but simultaneously provided people with the feeling of rootedness and knowing where they belonged in the world. To many people facing rapid modernization, the loss of these communities and of their accompanying moral bonds may have seemed relatively unimportant, given the benefits of modernity: freedom to make one's own choices, absence of coercion, decrease in patriarchal authority, and economic and social mobility.

The promise of freedom and mobility seemed rather empty, however, when German society faced economic impoverishment after World War I. At that point, modernity began to lose its appeal to many people whose fortunes had so quickly turned. Nostalgic conceptions of a lost past wildly exaggerated the security and mutual caring that once had been available, and obscured the real oppression that many people had felt while living under the authoritarian, patriarchal yoke of feudal rulers and a self-serving church. Yet the appeal to the lost communities of the past, and the anger at those who were blamed for having destroyed them (most centrally, Jews, along with various other modernizing forces) can only be understood in light of people's quite legitimate hunger to be part of a morally and spiritually rooted community.

When we experience the loneliness, isolation, and emptiness of societies that value wealth and power above all, and devalue ethical and spiritual reality, we often feel desperate, angry, and ready to embrace any alternative. Economic collapse becomes so terrifying precisely because, without a community of meaning and purpose, each one of us must face the possibility that there will be absolutely no one to help us get basic food or shelter should we lose our job and savings.

Social democratic movements have proposed a solution: why not simply pass legislation that will provide a generous economic support system for the poor? This seemed like a good idea, and it has been tried for the past half century. But the problem with the social democratic solution is that when it is embedded in the framework of the competitive market, and functions as a restraint rather than as the embodiment of a whole new way of living, the individualistic values of the market will eventually predominate over the caring values implied by social democracy. Selfishness, materialism, and cynicism increasingly triumph, reducing society's commitment to sustaining its social support system. In this context, new leaders come to power (as they already have in the United States and several Western European countries) who advocate dismantling many aspects of that support system.

In short, there is no quick policy fix or economic shortcut that can, by itself, provide safety. It is only when a society shares caring values that its people can feel secure.

From the standpoint of many on the Right, the only way in which caring values can be inculcated is to return to variants of traditional, patriarchal, or even church-dominated societies. From the standpoint of a progressive politics of meaning, however, caring values need not be associated with repressive communities, but the major focus of politics must be on creating a society committed to loving and caring.

Unfortunately, this crucial focus on values and on creating a community that could address our deepest spiritual needs has seemed irrelevant to many liberals in the Democratic Party here at home, in the Labour Party of the United Kingdom, and in the various social democratic parties of Europe. They have imagined that the appeal of fascism was a momentary worldwide upsurge in irrationality that was cured by the Allied triumph in World War II. They never have sought to understand the real human needs addressed by xenophobic nationalism and racism, however distorted the means. So the liberals and social democrats have believed that the whole problem of fascism is behind them, and that their primary task has been to ensure that the capitalist system never faces the kind of economic depression that led to the last surge of right-wing irrationality.

Instead, liberals and social democrats have concentrated on manipulating their way through the electoral system in order to get the power to pass specific pieces of legislation that would provide the poor with economic benefits. In the 1980s, when my colleagues and I first approached the liberal and social democratic forces and the labor movement to tell them that their own constituencies were feeling the impact of the crisis of meaning, we were told by their prominent leaders that they had nothing to fear from the Right, because the economic programs of the Right would self-destruct on their own. Dealing with the meaning issues, we were told, would be too impractical and divisive.

Yet, it is really the liberal position that has proved to be the impractical one. Without having forged a politics of meaning that could combat the growing individualism and cynicism embedded in the competitive market, one country after another has begun to dismantle the elaborate social support systems that liberal legislators had constructed. While these politicians were busily focused on maintaining power within the established political system, their constituencies were losing faith in the values that underlie the social democratic enterprise. Many former supporters have now turned to the Right to find the sense of community and meaning that liberals, social democrats, and the Left always thought was irrelevant or necessarily reactionary. At the end of the twentieth century, we suddenly find ourselves confronting fascistic possibilities that many thought had faded out with the defeat of the Nazis half a century ago.

I do not mean to suggest that the crisis of meaning will necessarily take the form of fascism or xenophobic nationalism. Under some circumstances it may, while under other circumstances it may merely manifest itself as an apathy about politics, a withdrawal into personal life, a decline in social solidarity, and an upsurge in various forms of individual or social pathology.

Nevertheless, what does seem clear is that the established categories of liberal thought were inadequate to understand the rise of fascism in the 1920s and 1930s, and they remain inadequate for understanding the rise of right-wing movements throughout the advanced industrial world in the late 1990s. Though I remain committed to liberalism's insistence on the importance of individual rights, I shall try to show in this chapter why many of the fundamental categories through which liberalism interprets the world are inadequate and must either be modified or replaced in light of the insights that derive from a politics of meaning.

Although the Left—particularly the twentieth-century communist and socialist Left—has often spent a lot of energy counterposing itself to liberalism and exposing its inadequacies, in many important respects it has bought into many of the conceptions being criticized in this chapter. Though very little remains of a coherent Left in advanced industrial societies at the end of the twentieth century, what does remain (and finds expression in academic radicalism and in many leftist journals) is often willfully ignorant of human needs for meaning, and shares with liberalism an inability to speak to the ethical and spiritual crisis of our contemporary world. Although at moments of its greatest popularity the Left often has attended to the meaning-dimension in its political activity, it never has incorporated into its theory an understanding of the legitimacy of the need for recognition or caring, much less of the hunger for ethical and spiritual meaning. If the Left were as different from liberalism as it imagines itself to be, the decline of liberalism might have led to an upsurge of interest in a leftist alternative. For several decades, the Left has criticized liberals for failing to mobilize the American people around a program to extend democracy into the economy, to protect the environment, and to limit corporate power. But because most people understand the Left to share with liberalism a fundamental misunderstanding of their needs, liberalism and leftism have shared a common fate.

The Illusion of the Autonomous Individual

I shall begin my reflections on liberalism by focusing on the important and praiseworthy commitment that liberals have made to individual freedom and to a neutral state that protects individual rights.

A just society, according to liberalism, does not seek to promote any substantive aims of its own, but rather enables its citizens to pursue their own ends. Rather than having any goals that it wants to implement, the liberal state refuses to choose in advance among the competing purposes that exist in the society. The highest value for the liberal state is to promote the individual's right to pursue his or her own wants and desires, unimpeded by others. These rights ought not to be sacrificed for the sake of the general good.

This central philosophical tenet of liberalism emerged out of the struggle with feudalism. Feudal societies subordinated individual freedom to what they described as "the common good." All too often, the common good actually was nothing more than what was good for the most powerful elements within the feudal communities. To counter the fallacy of the common good, people developed liberalism as a philosophy that insisted on the primacy of the individual and of the right to pursue individual interests without interference from the church or the larger community. All of humanity owes a debt to philosophical liberalism for the way that it helped undermine the static and oppressive realities of traditional, patriarchal, feudal societies.

Nevertheless, while I honor and support the struggle for individual liberties that has been fought against repressive communities—and which still is being fought in parts of the world where the liberal vision has not yet been achieved (including China; many parts of Asia, Africa, and Latin America; many Islamic countries; and some communities in the United States)—I cannot help but notice that by fetishizing the freedom to choose as our highest goal in life, liberalism has sometimes joined the capitalist market in fostering a conception of human beings that reinforces selfishness, materialism, loneliness, and alienation.

By giving highest priority to individual choice while avoiding questions about the content of that choice, liberals have seemed to suggest that there could be no possible basis for an objective ethical standard from which that choice could flow. Moreover, liberals have seemed to suggest that the welfare of the individual must always take precedence when making judgments or facing difficult choices.

The highest goal of some forms of liberalism is to maximize the choices available to the autonomous individual who has learned to stand by herself or himself without dependency or need for others. If individuals by chance should meet and enter into a voluntary contract, wonderful; however, these liberals believe that what we most value should not be the connection among people but the ability of each individual to exist autonomously. Granted, I may not be describing the *reader's* variant of liberalism, but I am describing a liberalism that has increasingly come to dominate the public sphere. It is this version of liberalism that has become its public face and has been the source of its diminishing prestige.

A politics-of-meaning perspective, on the contrary, asserts a very different foundational theory: that human beings are fundamentally *in relationship*. There is no such thing as a "self-made man." Nobody has ever taken care of himself or herself in the first year of life and survived. No inventor or innovator or entrepreneur has ever developed a plan or an idea without depending on the language, technology, labor, agriculture, and intellectual life that preceded over the course of one hundred centuries and through the efforts of millions of people before us.

Far from being autonomous, human beings need one another, as well as a relationship with the spiritual reality of the universe. The healthy human being gives genuine recognition to others, and acknowledges them as embodying the same preciousness and sanctity from which her or his own rights derive. Such a person acknowledges vulnerability, interdependency, and our fundamental need for others and for connection to a higher spiritual purpose that exists outside as well as inside of oneself.

Whereas liberalism builds a worldview from the standpoint of the autonomous individual, the worldview of a politics of meaning begins with the relational human being who is in deep need of recognition and connection to others and to the spiritual, transcendent dimension of the universe. Moreover, a politics of meaning identifies an objective and universally binding ethical foundation: that human beings are infinitely precious; deserving of love and respect; and entitled to actualize their ethical, loving, spiritual, aesthetic, intellectual, and joyful capacities.

The difference between these worldviews has immediate political consequences. To the liberal, the issue of building loving relationships may seem to have nothing to do with politics. Building a relationship is just one of the many possible things that one might do with one's individual freedom, according to liberal thinking. On the other hand, from the standpoint of a politics of meaning, the sharp decline in long-term, loving relationships represents a broader dysfunction that cannot be ignored. Human beings are essentially beings in relationship, so if we have a society in which people are unable to sustain relationships, we do not have merely a different set of choices, but a social pathology. Similarly, a society that promotes selfishness and restricts our capacity for ethical and spiritual sensitivity is not merely an alternative lifestyle; it is distorted and ought to be changed.

Of course, we must be careful not to revert to communal norms that disrespect unmarried people or that suggest that people remain in oppressive marriages. Nor do I support any approach that dictates some particular form of spiritual life or religious practice. People must have maximum freedom of choice to determine the best means to achieve our goal of loving relationships and spiritual authenticity.

Liberalism, however, cannot commit to this ethical goal, since its formal commitment to choice precludes the favoring of any particular kind of choice. Yet, leaving things up to individual choice often amounts to leaving things up to the strongest pressures in the society. Surrounded by people who are fanatically focused on their own success and are willing to manipulate others for the sake of their own interests, most people feel that they must participate in those same dynamics and "do unto others before they do to me" as a necessary form of self-protection. A society dominated by this kind of "freedom" feels profoundly unfree, because the option of being with others in a more caring and mutually supportive way has been subverted from the start under the guise of maximizing our individual choices.

In effect, liberal freedom becomes the freedom to function as a lone individual within a heavily competitive market society. As a market consciousness increasingly dominates each individual, and people become increasingly used to distrusting and self-defensively manipulating one another, it becomes harder for people to find a world of loving relationships and friendships. Is it any surprise that many people thus conclude that the kinds of freedom they are getting from liberalism are inadequate; that something terribly important is missing from life; and that the liberals seem unable to understand or articulate what is missing, or how to restore it?

Moreover, liberals also seem not to understand that some things have become harder to obtain in the world that they have created. What if we do not want more choices in cars, computers, and electronic wonders, but more options in communal living, or more opportunities to be together with people who genuinely care for us and will take care of us when times are rough? What if you want to live in a world whose environment has not been severely damaged by turning it into an object of consumption? Liberals have a difficult time understanding why some people believe that these kinds of spiritual needs are harder to fulfill in the modern world. Yet, many other people feel that our increased number of material choices has only come at the expense of losing some of the most important aspects of life that are no longer available to us—a choice that we did not make but that the competitive market made for us.

More Rights, Less Power

Liberalism encourages people to continually assert the existence of rights not previously recognized and then to seek governmental backing of those rights.

To some extent, this is a good thing. Rights are a narrow, legalistic way to ensure that people get treated with the recognition and caring that they deserve. Still, they reflect a fundamental affirmation of the dignity of human beings and their entitlement to decent treatment. In a world where systems of domination continue to impart the message that people do not deserve anything more than the demeaning treatment that they often receive, an insistence on individual rights is a step toward self-respect that is inconsistent with oppression. The many courageous lawyers and liberal legislators who have fought for these rights have often done so with an implicitly meaning-oriented worldview, growing out of an ethical and spiritual vision that could not be fully expressed in liberal ideology. Their efforts deserve support and honor.

However, there are some negative aspects to the "rights orientation" of contemporary liberalism. The central focus on rights tends to encourage us to see ourselves primarily as individuals seeking protection against the larger society. Rather than focusing on the ways in which we might join with others in a struggle to change the larger society, the rights focus pushes us back into the position of the individual who, together with his or her champions in the

Supreme Court, can chart a solitary path without the support of others. So we win our "rights," but in the process create a society filled with individuals who feel unsure that they can count on anyone, even their own family members. They return from work or school each night to families whose members are more sensitive to their own rights than to their love for one another. Pained by the absence of shared spiritual and ethical vision and of deep mutual recognition, many people seek solace in the malls or in television. Imagining that their freedom now consists in not having next-door neighbors tell them how to think or dress or live, they meanwhile have their wants shaped by a constant flow of media images as they soak in a steady diet of indoctrination from their televisions.

These newly "freed" human beings increasingly derive their sense of freedom from the consumer choices that they are encouraged to make in the market. Corporate interests, recognizing this growing estrangement, sell products by offering the image of connection with others through the purchase of various commodities and lifestyles. In short, the freedom obtained through this process increasingly feels empty, and people in fact are trapped and dominated by a subtler but equally coercive power, now operating by shaping their consent rather than by opposing it.

Economic Entitlements

Liberalism could not have lasted long if it had relied only on its principle of extending rights. As people began to exercise those rights within the context of the new free market, they soon discovered that the capitalist system, building on the inequalities of inherited wealth from the feudal era, tended to concentrate power and riches in a small group of individuals and corporations. These victors in the free market seemed unwilling to take much responsibility for the well-being of everyone else. Ironically, while people were accumulating liberal rights, they were feeling more powerless.

As a result, liberals had to broaden their approach. They moved from philosophical liberalism to a political liberalism that *did* endorse at least two substantive goals: first, that society should ensure that working people were not impoverished (as they had been by depressions, recessions, and unrestrained corporate rights to prevent labor from organizing, becoming too powerful, or making too many demands); and second, that people who had been excluded from the system's economic benefits should now be included.

In this modified version of liberalism, genuine freedom required certain social and economic prerequisites. If people were not going to reject the entire liberal system, their economic needs would have to be addressed. Many liberals would have favored significant use of governmental power to rectify economic inequalities. However, their elected representatives had to raise large sums of money in order to run campaigns. And in order to do so, these representatives had to appeal to corporate liberals—leaders of major corporations who wished to use government to stabilize, but not transform, the economic system. These corporate liberals did not want to tamper with the economic marketplace or challenge its concentration of wealth and power in the hands of the few. So they came up with another solution: continue to allow people to pursue their own ends in the marketplace, and let the resulting inequalities persist, but use government to rectify the worst consequences of this market by providing certain goods that would compensate for the way the market operated. For much of the twentieth century, liberals followed this strategy by fighting to create a system of economic and social supports that brought employment, housing, health care, education, welfare, and social security to millions of people in the advanced industrial societies of the West. If everyone had individual freedom plus a minimum level of economic security, liberals argued, people would be empowered to create fulfilling lives for themselves in any ways that they might choose.

Corporate liberals used big government not only to offset potential radicalization that might have been engendered by economic hardship, but also to provide a wide variety of services for the corporate world, including basic research and development, transportation, and communication services that might otherwise have been extremely costly for businesses. At times, the rest of the liberal movement questioned this corporate welfare drain on the public coffers, but liberals mostly accepted the following "reality": that their elected representatives would have to make significant compromises with their corporate funders in order to stand a serious chance of being elected to office. This was the nature of politics in a society where the cost of electoral campaigns was extraordinary, and the cost of being presented as "a responsible and serious candidate" by the media was usually to show fundamental agreement with the existing distribution of wealth and power.

For the rest of the liberal movement, the cost of this compromise often seemed reasonable. After all, together with their elected representatives and the corporate liberals who funded them, the liberal movement could take credit for some important and valuable accomplishments in building the social infrastructure that the competitive market had been unable to generate. Labor unions, liberal intellectuals, members of ethnic minorities with a progressive bent, and other key elements of the liberal alliance, in tandem with the corporate funders of liberal legislators, deserve much credit for providing leadership in the many struggles of the past half century to build schools, clinics, hospitals, roads, urban transportation systems, and other institutions neglected by the market. In this sense, liberalism used big government as the primary mechanism for showing our caring for one another.

Unfortunately, the modern liberal state has not been a meaning-sensitive instrument for delivering caring, nor for providing us with opportunities to experience ourselves as acting in caring ways toward others. It has provided instrumental caring without expressive caring—that is, it has sometimes taken care of us, but in ways that have not made us feel taken care of. In fact, because corporate liberals share with their conservative corporate colleagues the same fear that people may become *too* enthusiastic about using government to serve the common good at the expense of corporate profits, they have resisted as "too ideological" or "too soft" any suggestions that could have encouraged governmental programs to focus on the subjective experience of giving or receiving governmental assistance. Nor were corporate liberals challenged on this point by labor movement activists or hard-nosed liberal theorists, since they too shared the notion that what *really counts* is the economic "bottom line," so if government is delivering the economic services, the consciousness of support for government will automatically follow. Imagine the liberals' surprise when many who had benefited from these services became a major constituency for a renewed right wing that explicitly argued for dismantling of these services! Having largely ignored the experiential and subjective level of reality, liberals were unaware that many of those middle-income people who had benefited from governmental programs (like low-cost education, veterans' benefits, health-care research, mortgage subsidies, and low-cost transportation fees) did not view themselves as having received anything, and in good faith were buying into accounts of the world that allowed them to construe themselves as having been "self-made" or having pulled themselves up by "their own" bootstraps. The current popularity of conservative philosophies results in part from the fact that liberals never worried much about whether the recipients and donors of government services really understood themselves to be involved in communal acts of caring for one another.

Can We Show Caring for Others by Paying Our Taxes?

Suppose, as in the case of many entitlement programs, that the benefit received *does not come close* to providing a dignified minimal level of economic survival? What if it provides unemployment insurance for less than a year, but there simply are not enough new jobs available compared to the number of people who wish to work? What if it provides a level of welfare at which no one can possibly feed a family without causing eventual malnutrition? What if it provides public housing that is so shoddily and tastelessly constructed that people feel better provided for in prisons? What if the quality of public expenditures seems to improve dramatically depending on the wealth of the recipients, so that public services for the upper middle class and the wealthy, as well as for the poor, seem far superior to those that serve the lower middle class?

Skepticism about how much the government expresses real caring is reinforced when government simultaneously seems wildly excessive in its spending for programs that primarily benefit large corporations but not the public as a whole. What if one of every three dollars in the federal budget is used to fund a huge military-industrial complex, even at a time when there is no country in the world actually or potentially threatening our country?

The short answer to these questions is that the recipients of this instrumental government caring do not get the idea that their economic entitlements represent an act of caring by society as a whole. Consequently, they do not feel particularly grateful. Rather, they hear themselves being discussed as a social problem that must be managed and controlled, and the benefits they are receiving appear to be part of a scheme whereby others (who have more wealth than they do) will exercise social control. To the recipients, these acts of instrumental caring actually feel more like patronizing and paternalistic gestures, not like genuine attempts to treat them as equally cared-for members of a concerned community. Some recipients feel guilty and ashamed; others feel angry and full of rage; few feel gratitude. The rage intensifies when their inability to find jobs at a living wage is blamed on them, and they are characterized as having created a pathological culture of poverty that keeps them from enjoying the opportunities that would otherwise be theirs.

Nor does the way in which services and benefits are delivered express an ethos of caring. Governmental officials who originally entered public service precisely because they desired to care for others soon discover that they are not rewarded for the degree of caring they show to the public. On the contrary, such concerned behavior is seen as soft and foolishly idealistic. The task of government workers is to administer people and things, to provide benefits or services that are often underfunded—and hence, incapable of achieving the goals for which they were created. Overextended in demand and greeted with suspicion or outright hostility by some recipients of the services that they provide, government officials soon develop a protective emotional shell that makes it difficult for them to act in a way that conveys genuine caring to the public. At best, what the public receives is objective caring (namely, some service or economic benefit is really being given to them) in a way that does not feel subjectively, genuinely caring.

As a result, even though we continually benefit from government services that may objectively represent our mutual generosity and willingness to care for others, it is very rare for us to feel that we directly experience that generosity and caring. Even services that are provided efficiently and at relatively low cost, such as the U.S. Mail, rarely feel like a manifestation of collective caring. Our actual benevolence is rendered invisible, and hence fails to create in us the sense that we belong to a world that benefits from mutual goodness and generosity of spirit, as manifested through the mechanisms of government.

Tax Revolts

The taxpaying public as a whole does not think of itself as engaged in acts of collective caring when it pays taxes. Perhaps, one might think, people will never be happy about having to make sacrifices for the collective good if that means giving up something of their own, with which they could have taken care of their own personal needs. So of course people are going to be unhappy about paying taxes.

Yet, as Robert Heilbroner has convincingly argued in *The Worldly Philosophers,* the notion that people are motivated solely by material self-interest is a relatively recent one, and does not correspond to the experience of earlier societies, the records of seventeenth- and eighteenth-century "explorers," or the data of modern anthropologists. People's reluctance to pay taxes is far stronger in class-dominated societies that began to emerge some 3,500 years ago. In those societies, taxpayers began to suspect that the wealth appropriated from them was not being used for the common good, but for the benefit of a particular class or group. When people feel that their food, land, possessions, or money are being taken to serve the selfish interests of others, resentments grow. In such cases, sacrifices required by the community begin to feel oppressive.

For a different model, one need only look in the Bible. It does not fail to describe the moments in which the people of Israel were rebellious or disobedient to various portions of Moses' laws, but it rarely mentions resistance to the paying of sacrifices, or tithing. For the first many hundreds of years after the giving of the Torah, there was no central authority or police force or army to enforce the payment of taxes. Yet, three times a year, the people voluntarily appeared at the great festivals to bring sacrifices and to donate the produce of their land to the priests, first at Shiloh, later at the sanctuary in Jerusalem. Moreover, these great festivals were times of immense joy and celebration rather than mourning over having to yield the tithe. Giving to others—in this case, a priestly caste which had no ownership of land and had to depend on the generosity of the populace—was experienced as joy.

Throughout history there have been societies in which people voluntarily gave what they had to a common and collective storehouse (most recently, the kibbutz movement in Israel). When people believe that they can trust one another to use their collective wealth in ways that would benefit everyone, they are happy to share what they have.

Tax revolts and growing support for cuts in government services have spread through much of the Western world in the closing decades of the twentieth century. These are products of a popular conception that government is not working—that it has not been solving societal problems, has ignored the plight of middle-income people, and has become captive to "special interests."

The perception that "government isn't working" has resulted partially from a powerful conservative campaign to debunk all government spending in order to reduce the tax load on the rich and the corporations and to undermine the government's ability to implement environmental, health-and-safety, and other societally oriented regulations of the economy. To be successful, conservatives have had to focus people's attention away from popular programs like the G.I. Bill, Social Security, and other middle-class entitlements, and away from the important impact that Great Society programs have had in helping to create a black middle class. Instead, conservative critics have emphasized the persistence of poverty and crime, which government has failed to end.

The willingness of many Americans to accept this conservative redefinition of reality is connected to a deepening understanding by the electorate that liberal reforms have not eliminated social problems, but have only tried to soften their worst impact. After decades of funding "poverty" programs, poverty has persisted. Of course, the liberal programs have never actually been oriented toward a systematic restructuring of the economy in ways that would wipe out poverty (such as serious income redistribution, coupled with guaranteed full employment at respectable wages for every person who wishes to work). In fact, left-wing radicals have always criticized liberal programs precisely because these have been too timid. Liberals who have justified on pragmatic grounds their tinkering with the system, rather than adopting more far-reaching measures, must now face the reality that it might have been more pragmatic in the long run to fight for larger social transformations that might have produced more dramatic and popular outcomes.

People certainly have been correct to perceive that the programs they have funded have not eliminated the problems. Looking ahead to decades of paying for programs that do not seem to make a dent in the basic problems of the poor and that ignore the crises of meaning in their own lives, many people conclude that they would rather keep their money in their own pockets rather than pay higher taxes.

Full Employment

Liberals have not pressed for full employment in any serious way. Instead, particularly during the past several decades, they have put far more energy into competing with Republicans to see who could create the best business conditions for American capital to succeed in the global market. New Democrats, in particular, have argued that the problem with the Republicans is not that they have been barking up the wrong tree (in trying to strengthen the economic success of American capitalists), but that they have been less efficient and imaginative in doing so than the Democrats might be. Democrats have proposed government-subsidized job retraining, investment in the social and economic infrastructure, expansion of research and development, and creation of an electronic superhighway as ways to use government creatively to help make American industry more competitive internationally. Others have suggested ways to impose trade restrictions that would strengthen America's economic advantage vis-à-vis other countries that have been using trade barriers to effectively privilege their own populations, to the disadvantage of American workers.

These may be useful moves, given the current context of politics, but they certainly do not make American working people feel particularly secure. The impact of full employment would be to dramatically empower working people. This would be precisely the kind of economic benefit that would flow from the caring advocated by a politics of meaning. If all workers knew that they could leave one job and find another, as a matter of right, they would feel much freer to press demands to make their own workplaces healthier, less stressful, and more fulfilling. Employers would have to do much more to satisfy their workers' needs.

Working people no longer feel that there is a political party that considers their economic security as the bottom line and insists that full employment (or full coverage, in case jobs are not available) must be the departure point for all other policies, which must coordinate with that goal. On the contrary, working people are being told by *both* parties that the market is the ultimate arbiter, that there is only a limited amount that government can do to influence corporate decisions, and that each party can only compete politically within the framework of determining who will be better for the capitalist class. Given this frame of reference, working people logically no longer feel that the Democrats or liberals are the ace in the hole that will provide them with the economic security that they need.

From the perspective of a politics of meaning, the demand for full employment only makes sense if it is done as part of a larger, meaning-oriented, social transformation. Like so many earlier liberal reforms, full employment could end up having negative repercussions if it is enacted as a new economic entitlement within the existing framework of a liberal society. Introduced into a society whose dominant ethos is self-interest, full employment could quickly lead to a decline in productivity as working people simply become lazier and less subject to management discipline, because they know that they can always get another job. Labor unions have at times moved in a similar direction, making contract demands that have undermined the ability of firms to operate effectively or to discipline workers who were actually obstructing the entire production process and irritating fellow workers. These occasional moments of narrow self-interest by unions have given ammunition to union-busting corporate firms that seek to undermine all unions, eventually leaving workers with no protection beyond the good will of their bosses.

This observation leads to a larger point: if workers' rights are enhanced without challenging the basic framework of a selfishness-oriented society—in other words, if reforms are implemented within a liberal rather than a politics-of-meaning framework—the social consequences are likely to be both salutary and destructive. Salutary, because anything that gives workers more power is inherently valuable; destructive, because power to get for oneself, when not modified by a concern for the consequences to others, can further societal disintegration and despair. Workers may begin to take advantage of their guaranteed employment by working less, because they no longer have the fear that drove them in previous capitalist societies, nor the incentive of caring for others that a politics of meaning might validate. This is one example of why it is difficult to present separate planks for a politics-of-meaning program—because as long as each change is being introduced into a society whose bottom line remains committed to selfishness and materialism, it is easy to envision how each change by itself could fail.

As communist societies in Eastern Europe showed, the worst of all possible configurations is to have a society that speaks of the common good but actually is organized in the interest of a ruling elite. People quickly see through the rhetoric and realize that they are being asked to make special efforts or work harder to benefit a small group that holds all the real power. Without the "whip" of a competitive market and the fear of unemployment and economic deprivation, people in *that kind of a society* will not work. The free market will be much more productive under such conditions—but these circumstances presume the logic of selfishness. Extension of workers' power and rights would make sense in a different context—one dominated by a politics-of-meaning framework.

As with any other particular demand or policy element, the key question is to understand the larger context within which the demand or policy is being made. Clearly, the meaning of full employment, and its actual day-to-day operation, would be very different if society's assumptions remained attached to the selfishness paradigm, or if the assumptions were those based on a politics of meaning.

One reason why workers do not fight for more power for the working class, or join movements calling for "worker's control," is that most people suspect that their fellow workers might take advantage of increased benefits to become lazier or more selfish. Working people usually are willing to leave things in the hands of management, in part because they accept management's argument that some element of coercion is necessary in order to get workers to work. By this reasoning, if production were left in the hands of workers themselves, they would quickly fall victim to the desire to make life so easy that society's entire productivity would fall dramatically. Deep down, many working people suspect that this argument is true, and that "worker's control" would become another scheme whereby people take advantage for themselves without worrying about the impact on others. And these worries are quite legitimate, given the context of our liberal society, in which everyone has learned that the only rational activity is the pursuit of his or her own narrow interests. Only a very different kind of society, based on more communitarian assumptions, could make possible an extension of workers' power in ways that actually served rather than undermined the common good. And only a labor movement that showed that it understood this need to move beyond an "entitlement consciousness," and began to show a sense of social responsibility (*not* to the corporations, whose definition of responsibility is often limited to maximizing corporate profits, but to the larger society and its legitimate concerns), could get its own members to really believe that they had the right to more social power.

This last point reveals a major problem with all economic demands made by the liberals. To the extent that these demands are made within the dominant framework of contemporary politics, they tend to be seen as extending benefits to some particular group at the expense of everyone else, and thus merely serve as a triumph for that group's selfishness. "If government is about providing economic benefits for someone," many people may ask, "then why not for me?" Rather than creating a sense of common caring, liberal economic entitlements have led to a mass psychology of resentment toward those who have received government support, and a distrust of government itself.

Racism

So far in this chapter, I have concentrated on showing that popular estrangement from liberalism is based partly on the failures of liberalism to speak to people's fundamental needs. But liberals sometimes respond to this argument by suggesting that the real problem they have faced is not the inadequacy of their programs or worldview, but simply and solely that the American people are bad in some way that policy-makers had not fully anticipated. The most frequent example of such a pathology is racism. "It is racism," the liberals say, "that undercuts our popularity—and there is little that we can do about that."

But there *is* something to be done, if one has adopted a meaning-oriented analysis of racism.

The essence of racism is nonrecognition. It is the inability to see the members of another race as fundamentally human: having the same needs and desires as ourselves, having the same pain from misrecognition, and having the same sanctity and right to be fully realized as a being created in the image of God.

I can imagine many different scenarios that might explain how this nonrecognition all got started. Imagine, for example, a tribe that lives in the hills, depending on the hunt and often frustrated because its food supply is unreliable and its people are starving. Another tribe, down in the valley, has developed agriculture and seems to be quite successful in maintaining a stable food supply. At first, the hill tribe might approach the valley tribe and ask them to share their harvest. However, the farmers may believe that if they share their food with the hunters, there will not be enough to go around for themselves, and they too will suffer starvation. So the farmers refuse to share.

Over time, this inequality will breed anger and struggle. Some people will conquer others, and create social arrangements that justify unequal distribution of whatever is available.

If people felt comfortable about taking from or not sharing with others, or turning their backs on the neediness of others, they would do so with full heart and no need for an inner story to justify this behavior. But it is precisely because we have a natural inclination to see other human beings as precious and worthy and reflecting inherent sanctity, that we must find a way to misrecognize, to keep ourselves from seeing other people for who they really are. And this is where racism starts—in the need to imagine the dominated other as really, utterly Other, not as a fellow human being who is just like us. That is why it has always been easier to sustain a system of domination if the dominated people could be portrayed as fundamentally Other. If the dominated look different, for example, it becomes much easier to believe that they *are* different.

All systems of inequality and oppression require some type of justificatory belief system, precisely because they contradict our more fundamental recognition of others as having the same legitimate claim to be valued as we do ourselves.

Racism, sexism, and the like are forms of selfishness that have been institutionalized in a system that gives us alleged reasons why we should have more of the world's goods than others do (be those goods material or spiritual). No wonder, then, that our current system—which has universalized the principle of selfishness—has produced a world abounding in racism and its brother, xenophobic nationalism. These behaviors are no more than the principle of selfishness acting itself out in national, ethnic, or racial terms.

Racism, of course, is not just an attitude; it is also a form of social organization. American racism is not confined to stigmatizing African-Americans as inferior (an accusation recently boosted by the pseudo-scientific claims of Charles Murray and Richard Herrnstein's *The Bell Curve*), lazy, or prone to violence. It is equally manifest in economic practices that concentrate unemployment in African-American communities, ensuring that African-Americans with equal skills and training are less likely to be hired, and less likely to earn equally, than similarly skilled and trained whites.

Racism also springs out of a hunger for community, although this hunger is satisfied in a distorted, harmful manner, because the communities involved define themselves in opposition to others. Trying to satisfy this hunger in a healthy way must become an immediate project for liberal and progressive forces. Unless people can find communities of meaning that do *not* require racism, sexism, homophobia, and so on, many will gravitate to communities that *do* exhibit these distortions. They prefer distorted communities to the alienation and loneliness that lies just below the surface of the liberal world of individualism and unlimited free choices.

Racism also is a way of externalizing anger that has been internalized previously. This is a legitimate need, even if it often is illegitimately fulfilled. The task of anyone involved in trying to combat racism is to provide people with a legitimate focus for externalizing their anger, to replace the illegitimate target of the scapegoated Other. The legitimate focus is on all those social forces and realities that have caused us to experience underrecognition or misrecognition throughout our lives. A progressive politics of meaning aims to refocus people's attention in this very way, and hence to undermine one of the direct sources of racism.

Conversely, part of the task of any antiracist movement is to provide positive ways to achieve genuine recognition, community, and economic security. Because they don't fully address two out of the three, the Left has failed to undermine racism. They cannot help people understand that the recognition and community Americans really want cannot be achieved through racism, since many liberals believe that racism is precisely what many Americans really want. No wonder then, also, that so many Americans feel misrecognized and demeaned by these liberals! When liberals and elitist intellectuals adopt a politics-of-meaning framework, however, they can develop a better understanding of what leads Americans to racist politics without writing these people off as inherently racist.

Racism Works Against Our Interests as Human Beings

It is ironic that so much of the way in which liberals frame their analysis of racism is in terms that show how white people benefit from racism. In fact, only if one has a very narrow conception of self-interest (namely, the one that is dominant in this society and that is incorporated into far too much of liberal thought) can one even begin to argue that racism works for white people's self-interest.

Let me consider the strongest version of the racism-as-white-people's-self-interest theory. It argues that, in the short run, it is in the rational self-interest of people to set up society in such a way that somebody has to get hurt, because of necessary shortages of goods. In that case, does it not make sense for people to ensure that some racial or religious minority has to take a disproportionate share of the resulting hardships? And is that not precisely what happens in America, whose racist system now ensures that unemployment falls disproportionately on blacks, thus giving whites a far better chance of avoiding it than they would if unemployment were spread evenly through the population in a race-blind manner?

There are two answers to these questions. First, the short-term result of such a system is not only that unemployment falls disproportionately on blacks, but also that the rest of society is depoliticized (because it is "only blacks" who are suffering). The resulting general apathy permits the depression of wages and reduction of services that affect the quality of life of most whites as well. In narrow material terms, American workers would be doing far better if they had developed the kind of solidarity that racism undermines, because with that solidarity they would have been able to build a more successful labor movement, which could have won material benefits (such as health care, child care, and better retirement plans) that are available to workers in many other advanced industrial societies.

Second, the selfishness-benefits of a racist system are far outweighed by the social costs of creating human beings who can shut their ears to the cries of others and who focus only on themselves. It is precisely this kind of human being who will be central to the triumph of selfishness and the corresponding erosion of loving relationships, families, and friendships, as well as the crippling of moral and spiritual discourse in our society. The price to be paid for racist discourse, in short, is far too high because the underlying selfishness that it requires has consequences far more destructive to the self-interest of white people than any purported material benefit could possibly repay.

To put this idea in other terms that may summarize some of my discussion so far of the ethos of self-interest, it is not in anyone's self-interest to live in a society in which people are narrowly, materially self-interested.

Critics may object that people will not accept this kind of argument, but when exactly was the argument made to the general public? Which American president carefully and repeatedly has taken people through these kinds of arguments to show why racism is not in our self-interest? When has the struggle against racism ever been framed in terms that reach beyond compassionate concern for the victims to a portrayal of how racism hurts the rest of us?

The major attempts to speak to Americans about racism have been framed through the language of individual rights, justice, and fairness to the oppressed. Never have they been posed in a political discourse that validates the pain of the white majority. Liberals have never understood the crisis of meaning and how it operates to undermine the well-being of whites as well as blacks. They have never been able to effectively link the struggle against the ethos of selfishness, in the form of antiracism, with the necessary struggles against the subtler forms of selfishness that undermine families and friendships, and generate the insecurity and alienation that most people face in daily life.

I am *not* suggesting that racism would go away the moment that a meaning-oriented progressive movement came forward with these arguments. Many Americans perceive themselves as more powerless than they actually would be were they to join with others in a struggle to change their world. As a result, they cannot imagine that anything fundamental, such as economic inequality, could be different. But if little could be different in the fundamental distribution of wealth and power in our society, then it is not hard to understand why many people choose to remain in a situation of relative advantage in comparison with African-Americans. If the actual outcome of a struggle for economic equality would only be a sharing of poverty more equitably with the poor, many people will opt to stay where they are and close their ears to the cries of pain of others. It is their surplus powerlessness—the degree to which they imagine themselves as more powerless than they actually need to be—that is foundational to their racism.

Moreover, racism serves another function that cannot be eliminated merely by talking about the way it undermines our real interests. As I have argued throughout this book, people who do not get the respect, recognition, and loving that they deserve, and who live in a society that systematically frustrates their meaning-needs, are often filled with rage. To the extent that the Right provides an outlet for that rage by urging people to direct it at some demeaned Other who is supposedly the source of our nonrecognition, people are able to reduce their own self-blame and externalize their anger. Racism, sexism, homophobia, and anti-Semitism all function to legitimize this externalization of rage. Given this dynamic, the only plausible strategy for defeating racism is as follows: in the short run, to redirect people's anger toward the real source of their frustration, namely, those institutions and social practices which prevent them from getting the respect, recognition, and caring that they deserve; and, in the long run, to create a meaning-nourishing society that *does* provide the respect, recognition, and love that people desire and deserve.

Affirmative Action

Many of these issues come into clearer focus around the current attempts to dismantle affirmative action programs. Liberals and the Left are unable to sustain popular support for these programs, despite the fact that they were originally instituted at a time when the majority of Americans recognized the historic injustices suffered by African-Americans and women, and wished to find some way to redress those injustices.

But affirmative action took this basically idealistic inclination and channeled it into the existing framework of liberal rights. Supporters drawn to the civil rights movement's vision of universal justice found that the political energy generated by it was being directed into a more rights-oriented legalistic strategy, which sought redress through the courts. The idealistic impetus to right a wrong and to heal a lasting injury was transformed by liberal legislators into an entitlement to compete in the capitalist market on better terms.

The original idealism embodied, albeit in partially inarticulate ways, a transformative vision for change. Martin Luther King Jr. and the civil rights movement gained support precisely by appealing to notions of justice that asserted the importance of mutual recognition of the worth and dignity of every person, and the right of every person to caring and love. As Peter Gabel puts it, within

King's idealistic vision "affirmative action was an expressive call to act together affirmatively to eradicate the antihuman humiliation of racism. And affirmative action does still retain an echo of this deep ethical meaning that spread through American culture as a result of the transcendent energy and spiritual presence of the civil rights movement itself."

When this ethical vision was implemented as an affirmative action program that struck many people as little more than giving someone else an entitlement to compete in the market, it assumed the market's selfishness-generating aspects. The transformative and spiritual dimension of the civil rights movement was lost amid a flurry of claims for the "right" to compete on better terms. Implicit in this transformation was the affirmation of the market ethos: that the real goal of life is to accumulate as much money or power as possible, and that blacks and women have been unfairly prevented from joining in this pursuit.

The implicit message, then, that affirmative action communicates goes something like this: "You white people and you men have already had your chance to make it in the society. If you haven't made it, you have no one to blame but yourself. We, on the other hand, are groups that never got a fair chance, so now we want ours."

Few Americans know exactly what is wrong with this message, but they feel angered by it. Although most people accept the view that we live in a meritocratic society, they also feel put down by this assumption because they know that, in their own lives, they have not "made it" or achieved "the good life." The more sophisticated may well suspect what Left-oriented economists have been arguing for decades—that there never has been a meritocracy, that there is in fact a class structure, and that where they have ended up in it does not solely depend on their own individual merit. But since America is so deeply founded on the notion that ours is a land of limitless opportunity, few people are ready to challenge the meritocratic underpinnings of the society. Instead, most people adopt the meritocratic ideal, and consequently feel bad about themselves and their lives. They feel deeply misunderstood when liberals seem to refer to them as a privileged group enjoying the pleasures denied to those who are "really oppressed." They feel that liberals are mocking them, by suggesting that for them (as opposed to the "truly oppressed") the playing field was fair. It seems that liberals are criticizing them for enjoying the few material pleasures they have worked so hard to accumulate, over the years, as compensation for lives that often are stressful and painful.

Changing the Criterion of Merit

The discourse of affirmative action provokes a powerful rage, which right-wing opportunists are able to manipulate. The right-wing message is that most Americans are being denied the recognition and caring they deserve, and it is all the fault of these liberals, who have been giving that caring to these others—African-Americans, women, gays—who deserve it far less than do average Americans. What liberal programs are really about, argues the Right, is using big government to redistribute the recognition and caring away from deserving ordinary Americans to undeserving Others.

A politics-of-meaning perspective points out that the pain being addressed by the Right is real—not just a clever way to mask racism or sexism. Most people in the advanced industrial world really *are* being denied something they very much need—the recognition and caring that should have been there for them throughout their lives, but has not been. The Right's analysis of why this happened and who took away the recognition and caring is wrong, but it correctly points out that something real and important is missing and that people have a right to be angry about this.

The best way to counter the Right is to help people understand that in a society governed by the ethos of selfishness and materialism, their own worth will always be judged by their usefulness to the powerful. Our fundamental worth as human beings—our sanctity as beings who embody the image of the divine and who can be partners with God in healing the world—is systematically denied in a world governed by market cynicism. Instead, we are continually being forced to prove our worth by passing the tests established by the powerful to show that we deserve to have the opportunity to work for them.

Liberals seem to be endorsing the essential fairness of the existing system when they endorse affirmative action. They are understood to imply that the normal operations of the market system are fair and reasonable, and are based on objective standards that make a great deal of sense. However, liberals argue, given the market's history of previous exclusion, we now need to make exceptions for African-Americans and for women.

Liberals thereby seem to be agreeing with conservatives that these beneficiaries of affirmative action do not "really deserve" it, because these people have not shown themselves to be worthy by some "objective standards." It is only by dint of belonging to a historically oppressed group that they deserve special treatment.

No wonder, then, that white men get angry. They have spent much of their lives jumping through hoops, often unsuccessfully, in order to secure the love and caring of their parents and teachers, or later, to prove to potential employers that they could perform according to whatever criteria were imposed on them. Now they are told by liberals that these hoops, although fair when applied to white men, are going to be dismantled in the case of these other people. These white men's hurt that they were not as successful as other white men is made worse because, it turns out, the tests and other criteria for success were not really necessary for judging who should make it and who should not. Naturally, the white men feel resentful. Liberals might be far more persuasive if they began to wonder about the legitimacy of the hoops as applied to anyone, rather than providing some group with a way not to have to jump through them.

From my standpoint, much of the affirmative action debate is deeply misguided. The "objective standards" rarely measure the most important qualities that our society needs in order to function in the way that a politics of meaning wishes it to function. If we take seriously the new bottom line proposed by a politics of meaning, it will not be long before we notice that the qualities measured by most objective tests are not necessarily the most important.

For example, we probably could start by abolishing the Scholastic Aptitude Test (SAT) and similar objective tests for entry into higher education (and subsequently, professional training). High scores on the SAT exams are unlikely to predict who among us can figure out how to appropriate the wisdom of Western civilization in a humane way. On the contrary, based on the actual experience we have had, there is at least a prima facie case to be made for the notion that those who do best on the SAT (and particularly in the intense preparations that many of our most competitive, achievement-oriented students make to sharpen the tested skills) are most likely to embody the competitive ethos that has helped lead our society to its current crisis of meaning.

Like so many of the hoops through which children and teen-agers have been required to jump during their education into alien-ation, the SAT does not measure how smart we are. Peter Gabel, who favors the abolition of the SAT, points out that it measures our capacity to think like a machine, and to detach our thought process from ethical and spiritual intuition. Like so much of our education, the SAT rewards meaningless thought—thought which assumes the separation of mind from body, of thought from feeling, and of analysis from intuition. There is no room for the empathic under-standing of human longing that is indispensable for living a morally centered life. As Gabel puts it, the test is "brutalizing to the soul of everyone who is subjected to it, because it requires that we alienate ourselves from everything that matters to us in order to be recog-nized by the prevailing criteria of merit as deserving, worthy, intelli-gent members of our community." Many of the people I see in therapy are survivors of the psychological conditioning process de-livered by our schools, and reinforced by the competitive market that the SAT and similar criteria of merit embody.

Certainly, I do not mean to suggest that reading and math and comprehension skills are unimportant or merely "subjective." I value these skills. But I know all too well that many of the people who dragged my family members to the concentration camps were quite suited to these objective tests, but poorly qualified to use the mechanisms of Western civilization in a moral way. So I do not want these to be the only skills we use in evaluating who should be getting an education or a job.

Instead, a politics-of-meaning approach will seek to shift the cri-teria of merit. While reading and math and comprehension should be one part of what is evaluated, we need also to weigh other criteria. These should include people's capacity to be empathic, cooperative, and aesthetically and spiritually sensitive; their ability to motivate others to participate in projects aimed at the common good, and to see through media obfuscations; their willingness to question authority, and to struggle for their goals against overwhelming odds; and their ability to see the morally relevant aspects of a given situation. We also should be looking at additional character traits, such as stability, honesty, sensitivity, and joyfulness.

These criteria are not arbitrary choices. They are, in my estimation, central characteristics that we as a society need in order to make our society more productive in the politics-of-meaning sense (namely, as a society that produces ethically, spiritually, and ecologically sensitive human beings capable of sustaining long-term, loving, and committed relationships).

Yet, if we do shift the criteria in this way, we are likely to find that African-Americans and other minorities would score just as well as other segments of our population on the rating systems we set up to measure these capacities. One result would be a dramatic rise in the number of African-Americans who were being judged as having merit.

By switching the criteria in this way, we would be avoiding the apparent unfairness of affirmative action. Race-blind criteria of this sort would likely yield racial equality, in a way that whites could accept, because it would be based on criteria of merit that made intuitive sense and which were universal.

The assault on affirmative action today cannot be fully separated from the more general assault on African-Americans, orchestrated by the Right and supported by many people who have succumbed to the ethos of selfishness. Nevertheless, this one aspect of the anger toward affirmative action ought not to be discounted. The task of a politics of meaning is to find another way to validate this anger without allowing it to find racist expression.

In the short run, many of us will oppose ongoing efforts to dismantle affirmative action, recognizing these as the current form of the assault on blacks. But we will simultaneously challenge the notion that established criteria of merit are fair and appropriate, and we will try to find new ways to shift our society to reward a broader set of skills and characteristics.

Peter Gabel, writing in *Tikkun* magazine in May 1995, suggested the following ballot initiative:

> Public employees in the State of California shall be hired not on the basis of race, gender or other external characteristics, nor on the basis of standardized tests, but on the basis of a history of service to their community and State as revealed by exemplary work with church groups, schools, the elderly, and other populations in need. In order to increasingly link public employment with an ideal of service emerging from all of California's communities, hiring policy should to the extent possible seek participation from every neighborhood within each locality and from each Assembly District within the State. The capacity to foster the development of racial harmony, as demonstrated by an applicant's history of service, may be one factor considered in determining qualification for public employment as defined in this initiative.

The point of this initiative is that it begins to highlight our commitment to empathy and caring for others, and redefines worthiness in terms of moral commitment to others. It makes the inclusion of all communities, rather than the favored treatment of any given community, the goal of our policy. Unfortunately, because this initiative requires a switch in the dominant liberal paradigm—away from rights and toward caring—it is unlikely to become a major element of the liberal program in the near future.

Instead, we are likely to witness a fruitless debate, in which right-wing racists will present themselves as concerned about universal values ("no special treatment, but everyone equal before the law") while liberals are portrayed as captives of "special interests" and insensitive to the problems that their programs have caused for the American majority.

It may take a few major defeats of affirmative action before liberals are prepared to really examine the problem through the politics-of-meaning framework I've proposed above. I will not welcome those defeats, because they will give succor to right-wing and racist energies that may have more lasting consequences. But political defeats are on the agenda for liberals until they can begin to address issues from a meaning-oriented perspective.

Multiculturalism

Most liberals and leftists have been unwilling to acknowledge the declining appeal of their worldview, preferring to blame this decline on external factors such as inadequate resources, poor spokespersons, or lack of sophistication with media and direct-mail technologies. Some people, however, have begun to question the narrow appeal of a politics based primarily on individual rights and economic entitlements. Members of the academic Left have sought another foundation for their critique of society, and many have chosen the route of lionizing the communities of the oppressed.

The problem with past left-wing politics, they assert, is that it has been based on the interests and concerns of the white male majority, while ignoring the interests of women, gays, and Third World communities. In this analysis, left-wing thought has focused on the universal needs of the oppressed, but in a way that has obliterated the historically specific needs of the communities being oppressed. Therefore, the task is to develop a new multicultural approach that gives adequate space to the specific needs of these various communities.

The politics of meaning seeks to create a society in which people can fulfill their desire to serve the common good. But the very notion of a common interest or common good has been challenged by some academic radicals who have replaced the spirit of the 1960s ("We are the people") with a multiculturalist focus that insists that there can be no unifying shared ethical vision, because there is no unified community.

Some multiculturalists believe that people of color, women, gays, and other oppressed communities should resist all efforts to move our society toward a common good, fearful that the distinctive values and insights of these particular cultural traditions will be obliterated by a dominant white male discourse. Using the powerful tools of literary deconstruction, the multiculturalists have made a compelling case for how the dominant discourse of Western civilization has been a discourse of white men, and how it has systematically excluded the experience and insights of ethnic minorities, women, and homosexuals.

Some multiculturalists have gone further, denying the possibility of any unifying culture or shared ethical themes. They claim that every attempt at such a unified culture or ethics could only be an attempt by some group to impose its intellectual and cultural hegemony on others. The most radical multiculturalists have insisted that there are communities that have incommensurable discourses. Accordingly, heterosexual white males have no business judging the culture of gay black females because there could be no language of common values.

This extreme version of multiculturalism should *not* be confused with the struggle for greater inclusion of the 1970s and 1980s. Women, gays, and minority groups quite legitimately argued for greater inclusion in institutions from which they had been systematically excluded. And, following some initial confrontations and struggles, many liberals have responded to these demands. Yet, as they have done so, a multicultural rhetoric has begun to emerge in these communities of the oppressed—a rhetoric that seems to suggest that the goal of inclusion was not to create a more harmonious community, but to give specific groups more power which they could use to pursue their own particular interests.

It is not very hard to see why many Americans would resent this kind of double-dealing. Here are people who have demanded inclusion on the basis of our shared value of equal respect for others, but who, once included, have then sought to deny that we really do have much in common or that there ever could be shared values.

When multiculturalism is allowed to extend to the denial of the common good or the possibility of objective ethics, it undermines the basis for building a more caring community. Under these circumstances, the Right has been able to offer itself as speaking for the general interest. While its specific programs actually lean toward the interests of the large and powerful corporations, its rhetoric evokes a shared community of caring that touches the hearts of many Americans. Even the Right's argument for the individual pursuit of people's own special interests in the marketplace (in order to produce the most wealth for the entire society), has appeared to show an interest in the well-being of others that these destructive forms of multiculturalism explicitly have derided.

Ironically, the Left's quite laudable commitment to inclusion has been derailed by a multicultural rhetorical commitment to a variety of separate communities, each contending for its own interests. Indeed, the rhetoric of multiculturalism mirrored the actual practice (though not the ideology) of the Reagan years. What could be more in tune with the spirit of the 1980s than for each group to be watching out for itself, certain that any larger community would take advantage, and exploit or oppress it?

Conversely, the moral relativism underlying the theory of incommensurable discourse has been a perfect counterpart to the glorification of selfishness generated by the competitive market. If there is no shared language, on what basis can the economically deprived or the politically oppressed appeal to those who are not similarly oppressed? Without any shared language or shared values, there really is no basis for critiquing the discourse of selfishness. At this point, the issue boils down to power, and upper-middle-class whites have been more successful and are likely to continue to be more successful than people of color in mobilizing power.

Some "tough-minded realists" on the Left may suggest that, at the heart of liberal society, the pretense of equality has hidden the realities of inequality and the selfish desire of the ruling elite to protect its own interests. Their use of deconstructive language does not create but only unveils the truth that the struggle for power underlies all the pleasant ideals and moral vocabulary of contemporary discourse.

From my standpoint, these deconstructing radicals fail to realize that part of the success of the civil rights movement, and even of the women's movement, derived from the support it received from people whose narrow material interests were *not* served when these movements advanced. Many people responded to the moral discourse that these movements articulated, even when those ideals arguably conflicted with their own narrowly defined interests. Yet so powerful is the logic of the marketplace that many social change activists cannot imagine that people would be motivated by a set of concerns that transcended narrow self-interest.

Aping a certain form of vulgar Marxism, some leftist social change activists feel that material interests must necessarily underlie all of human behavior. But those in the liberal and progressive ranks who share this assumption have trouble accounting for their own motivations. Against the moral relativists and economic reductionists, I would assert that many social change activists primarily have been motivated not by narrow self-interest but by some transcendent idealism connected with their view of the common good.

Conclusion

Liberals have important ideas to contribute to American politics. But without a politics-of-meaning framework, liberal ideas often foster a way of thinking that creates a society very different from what many liberals hope for.

Most liberals in America actually oppose the triumph of the market. Yet their political philosophy seems so congruent with the ethos of selfishness and individualism that it is easy for conservatives to blame all of societal dissolution on liberal political ideas. The Right is then able to turn people against what is good in liberalism, because most Americans are fed up with a world that seems to continually frustrate their desires for connection, caring, and idealism. The Right convinces people that it is the liberals' fault that there have been declines in ethical and spiritual sensitivity, in solidarity, and in mutual trust.

The great irony here is that the Right manages to resent the Left for fomenting the individualism and selfishness that is in fact generated by the economic system that the Right extols. Liberals take the rap for the capitalist market! Liberalism does not have an adequate response, because it cannot claim commitment to a particular vision of a good society without violating its prior commitment to have no commitments—except to a political procedure that guarantees individuals the right to go for whatever they want. This hands-off approach to a substantive vision of the good simply will not work anymore.

Some liberals believe that there is a danger in my argument. If liberalism adopts a specific vision in politics, they warn, they will be unable to ensure that the Right will not also introduce its vision, and maybe the latter will be the one that wins out. So, they conclude, liberals are better off trying to fight for a state that has no substantive commitments.

This concern is legitimate, but out of date. The Right's political vision *already* is prevailing—precisely because liberals offer nothing more than a promise of individual rights, economic entitlements, and inclusion that inadequately speaks to the fundamental needs of the American people. When liberals fight to keep values and spiritual visions out of the public arena, they only manage to succeed in keeping out *their own* values and visions. And this absence has left a clear path for the Right to put forward its vision and to win popular support.

Some liberal groups have protested the political role assumed by the Christian Coalition, the Moral Majority, or other religion-based political organizations. Religion, they argue, should be kept out of public life. Such liberals face a losing battle, both because the first amendment does not prohibit religious groups from advocating their political vision, and because most people actually *want* a meaning-based political framework.

The problem with the religious Right is *not* that it is advocating politics, but that the content of its politics is based on a perversion of religious values. Instead of building on the Bible's injunctions to love our neighbor, thus bringing glory to God by showing that a theological view of the universe would maximize our caring and compassion for others, these people build on isolated biblical passages that reflect fear and anger. In my book, *Jewish Renewal: A Path to Healing and Transformation,* I present in some detail a reading of the Bible that could form the basis of a full-bodied alternative to these right-wing distortions. But my point here for liberals is that they must combat the Right's vision with a better and more engaging one that goes far beyond their traditional principles of freedom, economic security, and inclusion.

As a final note, I should add that I have learned a lot from liberals and the Left. While I find little to admire in the corporate liberals who have shaped congressional policies to their own interests, I have a great deal of respect for the hundreds of thousands of liberal activists who gave their life energies to build the labor movement, the civil rights movement, the antiwar movement, the women's movement, the gay and lesbian movements, the environmental movement, and the movements for civil liberties and human rights.

Through generations of struggle, these people have held high a vision of hope and possibility against seemingly overwhelming odds. Their accomplishments are impressive, including the winning of basic protections and rights for working people, eliminating segregation, decreasing discrimination against women and minorities, weakening the hold of patriarchal assumptions throughout the society, protecting us from repressive interventions of the state, and providing a modicum of dignity for the aging and the disabled. It would be a terrible mistake to ignore this record of accomplishments.

And yet, liberalism is on the decline.

To the extent that liberals are trapped within a worldview that excludes human spiritual and ethical needs, they misunderstand what it is to be a human being, and hence are unable to acknowledge the ways in which our society frustrates the natural hunger for recognition and meaning. Consequently, they develop political strategies which are one-dimensional and increasingly unpopular. Revamping the "old-time religion" with a better spokesperson or a new party will not change this situation. Liberalism needs to be transcended—and the way to do so without losing the important insights and contributions of liberalism is to create a progressive movement for a politics of meaning. Otherwise, liberals will continue to feel the pressure of public disaffection and continue to misinterpret their decline in popularity as a mandate to buy into conservative assumptions. Thus, if by chance public revulsion at the extremism of the Gingrich Congress produces a Democratic victory in 1996 and the reelection of President Clinton, these Democrats will be unlikely to return to a visionary liberalism that extends and renews the most progressive aspects of liberal philosophy. Rather, having positioned themselves increasingly as people who share conservative assumptions about the budget, the immediate need to eliminate the deficit, and the need to dramatically limit the power of government in many spheres, we can expect that the Democrats will present our country with politics that in many ways resembles the liberal wing of Republican President George Bush's administration.

Yet, public disaffection with liberalism does not mean that people want a more centrist politics or some elusive mush that the press refers to as "the moderate center." The failures of liberalism call not for a move to the Right, nor for a move to the Left (that is, a militant revival of the old one-dimensional assumptions of an economistic and rights-oriented liberalism), but rather for a move to transcend the old ways of thinking and begin to acknowledge the meaning-needs that liberalism cannot fully grasp within the limits of its existing categories. Because liberals do not understand this, they find themselves trapped in a fruitless debate between those who imagine that they will be more popular by moving to the Right and those who advocate a return to a pure version of the old-time liberal or Left politics. Both views are mistaken for reasons I've explained in this chapter.

4

The Failure of the Conservatives

J ust as liberals deserve credit for their commitment to individual
freedom, economic security, and a politics of inclusion, conservatives also deserve credit for what they bring to the table. Their
valuable insights include an insistence on the value of tradition, an
acknowledgment that much of the good we seek cannot be achieved
through government or politics, a healthy suspicion of utopianism
and social engineering, and an understanding of the importance of
small communities.

Yet conservative politics is deeply flawed. In practice, it is committed to maintaining existing systems of power without subjecting
them to moral critique. Conservative ideals are often used as a prop
to maintain the current unequal distribution of wealth and power,
the primacy of the competitive market, and the sanctity of the large
corporations.

Conservatives rightly insist on the importance of communities and bemoan their erosion. But they fail to acknowledge the community-destroying impact of capitalism and the competitive market. Conservatives remain silent, for example, about the dislocating effects of the high mobility required of Americans who must move to find new employment opportunities. They downplay the destructive impact on a community when a corporation that has operated there for decades pulls out and moves to another area, where it can pay workers less and hence maximize its profits. In general, conservatives fail to see the negative social and spiritual consequences of a market that must continually create the need to consume new products while encouraging the devaluation and disposal of old ones. The very economic system that conservatives support erodes the values that they claim to champion.

Moreover, conservatives in power almost always resort to the demeaning of women, domestic minorities, or perhaps another nation that is defined as an enemy. Their dilemma is structural. The Right comes to power because it identifies and appeals to the electorate's anger about the disintegration of communities, the collapse of traditional relationships, the instability of contemporary life, and the erosion of moral values. But once in power, conservative leaders are unable to stem these problems, which are deeply rooted in the psychodynamic consequences of the materialism and selfishness that are central to the competitive market.

Because the Right is unwilling to look at the community- and tradition-destroying impact of the economic system it champions, it has to place the blame elsewhere—on scapegoats. It is not mere coincidence that the primary anti-Semitic forces in the world historically have found their homes in conservative and right-wing politics. Nor is it any surprise to me that Louis Farrakhan's anti-Semitism is espoused in precisely that part of the black community that is most explicitly pro-capitalist, subordinates women, and believes that blacks can pull themselves up by their own bootstraps without relying on others.

It is no accident that other contemporary forms of racism, sexism, and homophobia have more easily found expression on the Right than on the Left. "Although we are in power, and haven't eradicated your pain," right-wingers implicitly tell their supporters, "we could have created a wonderful society, except that there are forces in our community (or outside), which are responsible for polluting and undermining what would otherwise be a fulfilling, caring, and sensitive social order. If we can root out the vermin—isolate or destroy the influence of these others—then we will have the community we promised you."

This externalization of anger on others is a central tactic whereby the Right has won support during the twentieth century.

A Meaning-Oriented Political Realignment?

The Right has been extremely articulate in condemning the ethical and spiritual crisis of the modern world. Many people on the Right understand the distortions of materialism and selfishness. Many understand the hunger for meaning. Right-wing Christian evangelists often provide compelling analyses of people's personal problems because they uncover the meaning-dimensions that are frequently ignored by those who rely on a narrower or more technocratic account of reality.

So it should be no surprise that in the first stages of fighting for a politics of meaning, progressives and some right-wingers may make common cause in critiquing the dominant technocratic way of understanding reality. In the course of struggling for a progressive politics of meaning, we may find ourselves allied with right-wingers who similarly bemoan the ethical and spiritual bankruptcy of the current order, and who challenge the individualism and me-firstism that is built into the prevailing version of contemporary liberalism. Similarly, aspects of the Right's critique of the self-indulgent ethos of the 1960s counterculture are essentially on target, even though that critique is often formulated in a distorted way to obscure the fact that the vast majority of hard-core New Leftists rejected countercultural fatuousness, and were driven by idealism and moral seriousness.

Those on the Right who embrace a politics of meaning often find themselves at odds with the more centrist and establishment conservatives who share the technocratic framework supported by establishment liberals. Centrists of the Left and the Right often embrace the materialist, empiricist, and one-dimensional, scientific worldview that dominates public discourse in the West. Establishment conservatives often end up trying to distance themselves from the meaning-oriented right wing of their own movement, and may find it easier to deal with the more compatible establishment liberals.

Conversely, I sometimes feel that certain aspects of reality are better understood by the most reactionary elements of the Christian Coalition than by some of my most sophisticated allies in the liberal or progressive worlds. It makes life messy when one's political enemies are speaking important truths, but for those of us who are more committed to truth-telling than power-accumulating, it is occasionally necessary to acknowledge that people who are deeply wrong on many issues are also sometimes more insightful on other issues than are one's best friends.

I have often heard people on the Left say about some aspect of the politics of meaning, "But that position is held by people on the Right"—as though this fact in itself were enough to discredit the position. But it is not, and so, particularly during the first stage in the struggle for a politics of meaning, we need to be prepared to see some people on the Right as partial allies on some issues.

The Right is unlikely to provide *consistent* allies, however, because of its unwillingness to acknowledge the inherent contradiction between lamenting the impact of selfishness and materialism in private life, on the one hand, and championing those same values in our economic, political, and social institutions, on the other. Rail as it might against the ways in which civil society and private life have been infected by the ethos of materialism and selfishness, the Right is an inherently untrustworthy ally in the struggle for a new societal ethos, because of its blind allegiance to the competitive market.

Conservative columnists, radio talk-show hosts, political leaders, and policy experts are often deeply cynical people who use the language of conservatism to justify their own unbridled self-interest, self-promotion, and lust for power. In contrast, many rank-and-file conservatives are basically decent, sensitive human beings who share the same concerns for an ethical and spiritual world that lead progressives to a politics of meaning. Many of these people who currently are drawn to the Right will eventually be drawn to a progressive politics of meaning, when they understand more fully how the existing economic system undermines ethical and spiritual values. Precisely because many conservatives are *not* hypocrites, they ultimately will realize that they cannot be cheerleaders for selfishness and materialism in the economy, and then act surprised when these same values show up in the few hours each day when people are not involved in economic activity.*

Yet that realignment is far away. Few people in the United States have ever heard anyone with liberal or progressive instincts articulate a politics of meaning, so they have not been forced to consider the progressive critique of right-wing versions of a politics of meaning. Although the Republicans have been masters at charging that poor people are bad at taking responsibility for their own lives, they have had a very poor record themselves of taking responsibility for the impact of policies that they have adopted. Nor have they seriously asked themselves why, in other countries where conservatives such as Margaret Thatcher have held power, the ethos of the larger society becomes ever more dominated by selfishness and materialism. This oversight demonstrates the unconscious splitting between two kinds of selfishness, a contradiction which characterizes conservative politics: on the one hand, conservatives laud market-generated selfishness; on the other hand, they attack civil society and private selfishness. Yet they have never faced seriously the politics-of-meaning critique: that the "bad" selfishness of civil society and private life is intrinsically connected to what the conservatives think of as the "good" selfishness that operates in the economic market. Because they avoid this issue, conservatives often misunderstand two of the most serious problems facing advanced industrial societies: the ecological crisis and the growing rate of violence. To understand these problems, we need to apply a progressive politics of meaning.

*I am *not* claiming that most conservatives are selfish or materialistic. In fact, in my own experience, I have often met conservatives who show considerable caring for others and willingness to share. Linguist George Lakoff misinterprets the politics of meaning when he hears it denying the kindness or generosity of many individual conservatives. What I do assert is a kind of intellectual/psychological splitting in conservatives that allows them to lionize the pursuit of unrestricted self-interest in our economic lives (where most people spend most of their waking hours) while deploring this same ethos when it shows up in our families and personal lives.

The Ecological Crisis

The Industrial Age triumphs of a materialist worldview and a mechanistic science led people to view the earth as a "resource" which could be used for any purposes that we chose. The biblical injunction that human beings should be stewards of the earth was abandoned in the modern era, and in its place we began to think of the earth as something that we could manipulate and exploit for our own private purposes.

Given the dynamics of the competitive market and the concentration of wealth and power that it produced, it would hardly be fair to say that it is "we" who have exploited the world's resources. It would be more accurate to note that a wide variety of corporations have found that they can make profits by depleting the earth's resources; by producing products that people did not previously know they wanted, but which they could be induced to want through sufficient advertising and social conditioning; and by abusing the environment with toxic waste.

Corporations traditionally have justified their actions by saying they only try to satisfy the desires of the people. They argue that markets are supremely democratic and efficiently communicate what people want. Corporations claim that they only respond to these desires, or they would go out of business. So, their argument goes, if one wants to change corporate behavior, one first has to change people's desires.

The argument is misleading in three ways. First, it is misleading because people do not vote in the market on the basis of "one person, one vote," but on the basis of "one dollar, one vote." And since dollars are not equally distributed (and are even less equally distributed once one subtracts money that must be spent on food, clothing, and shelter), the market reflects the wishes of people unequally, depending on how much disposable cash they have available. By this calculation, the rich will do far better than most other people, since a much higher proportion of their money is available for nonessential consumption.

Second, the corporate argument is misleading because it does not factor in the complex ways in which corporations can use their economic power directly and indirectly to foster needs for their products. When General Motors bought up the existing rail line in Los Angeles in the 1940s, proceeded to dismantle it, and thus ended the possibility of mass transit; or when other auto companies use their political power (exercised through direct and indirect contributions to candidates) to prevent the construction of adequate mass transit, or to postpone laws requiring tougher auto emission standards—they are creating certain needs, not responding to them. Similarly, when tobacco companies spend millions to promote among teens and preteens a set of images that cigarette smoking is cool or sexy behavior, they are not responding to but helping to create a certain need.

Third, the corporate argument is false because the market has no mechanism for registering desires by a majority that a certain kind of product or process *not* be produced, as long as there is a small minority that wishes to purchase it. For example, people may want to stop producing a product that pours carcinogens into the air, or another product that requires killing all the seals in the world, or that leads to the destruction of the ozone layer. But even if people *know* about these harmful consequences (which often are difficult to learn about, as long as corporations have the *right* to produce without studying the long-term effects of their production on the environment), they do not have a market mechanism for stopping this production. They *must* resort to politics. Economists call such issues as environmental consequences "externalities," and recognize that the market has no mechanism for dealing with them. Given this arrangement, it is nonsense to say that the market represents our democratic choices.

Luckily, we have learned to use democratic mechanisms of government to curb some of the worst environmental excesses of the unrestricted operations of the capitalist market. Ever since a group of people decided to make environmental destruction a major focus for political activism, starting with Earth Day in 1970, there have been local and national organizations doing their best to mobilize government to act on a variety of ecological issues.

Of course, most corporations do not set out to destroy the environment. Their goal is profit, and environmental consequences often are simply irrelevant within their hierarchy of values. But if the research, development, production, marketing, or consumption of goods has negative environmental consequences, too many corporate decision-makers regard these as unfortunate by-products of the market, to be ignored if possible. Some of the worst offenders, like oil companies responsible for major oil spills and air pollution that have done incalculable damage to the environment, have in recent years launched advertising campaigns touting their new ecological consciousness—usually, to rehabilitate their corporate image after public exposure of some environmental disaster for which they are responsible.

Though environmental awareness has grown, so too has the sophistication with which corporate offenders spread disinformation, downplay environmental hazards, support candidates for office who can be counted on to oppose serious limitations on corporate operations, and block legislation that might more effectively protect the environment. Both President Clinton and Vice President Gore came into office with an environmentally conscious agenda, yet they found themselves relatively powerless in the face of corporate interests, which have assembled a congressional coalition that was ready to block serious change, and, when conservatives came to power, sought to rescind environmental advances of the past thirty years.

One important way in which corporate interests have managed to block environmental reform has been by popularizing the notion that government itself is incapable of solving any problem, and that therefore all problems should be left to the market. No matter that it is the market itself that has wreaked havoc upon the environment. This conservative canard immediately resonates with the many Americans who want lower taxes (given their disillusionment with government, often for legitimate reasons). So, by funding think tanks and television shows and ads and candidates for public office—all of which spread the gospel that government can do nothing, and hence should be reduced in size—the corporations create a climate that is hostile to environmental action in particular, and to all government initiative in general. (That this position derives from selfishness and *not* from genuine conviction is clear from the failure of these same conservatives to support dramatic budget cuts for defense and law enforcement, though these huge governmental bureaucracies are at least as inefficient as any other.)

If the conservatives in Congress are successful in dismantling environmental protection, the danger to the life-support systems of our planet will soon be greater, not less, than when the environmental movement first emerged into public consciousness in the 1970s. While ideologues have spent the past few years celebrating the triumph of the free market over the communist system, future generations may look back on the end of the twentieth century as a period of unprecedented social and individual irresponsibility. Ours will be remembered as a period in which the facts were available about the destruction of our environment, and yet only the most piecemeal measures were taken to address a crisis that would yield permanent damage for the people of the world.

The frustration of efforts to save the environment, and the failure of corporations to take serious actions to prevent or undo the damage, or to create mechanisms through which these issues could be reasonably decided, directly results from the ethos of selfishness that permeates the contemporary world.

It is a favorite theme of contemporary conservatives to talk about teaching "responsibility." But it is impossible to teach responsibility to the rest of society when the largest and most powerful forces in the economy continually act irresponsibly, elevating their own self-interest over the common good of the human race. People growing up in this society learn that all this talk about spiritual sensitivity and ethical awareness stops at the boundary of economic life. For the sake of making a buck, it becomes permissible to ignore the well-being of others and to close one's eyes to the impact on future generations. What better way to teach an ethos of selfishness? If the very survival of the planet seems less important than the "right" of individuals to make a profit, how in the world do conservatives expect to teach an ethos of caring and spiritual sensitivity? They cannot, and hence they do not. The words of caring and spirituality begin to sound empty the moment we take serious account of what the Right is willing to do to this planet in order to protect the "right" of some individuals to amass wealth and power.

Moreover, once people become accustomed to separating the realm where an ethos of spiritual sensitivity and ethical awareness is appropriate (civil society and personal life) from a realm where it has no application (the economy), this bifurcation of consciousness (what psychologists call "splitting") takes on a much greater role in shaping public behavior. First, Americans learned to push ethical and spiritual concerns outside of the economy so that these would only arise in civil society. Today, many make that psychological split in their treatment of whites versus African-Americans, or of the middle class versus the poor. Tomorrow, that same disjunction may divide young and old, or inner-city and suburb, or North and South, or create some other invidious division. Once the bifurcation of moral consciousness becomes sanctioned, people cannot be certain that next time *they* will not end up as part of the group for whose spiritual and ethical welfare the rest of society no longer cares one iota. Unconsciously, many people suspect that they could be part of the next group left out in the cold, and this fear accounts for the tenacity with which they try to reassure themselves (through frenetic participation in some particular ethnic or racial or religious community) that they are still in fact part of the group that is "saved."

For those of us who recognize the environmental crisis as one of the most fundamental threats to the survival of the human race into the twenty-first century, the struggle for a progressive politics of meaning takes on greater urgency. On the one hand, through this lens one can see more clearly why conservative politics is so destructive. On the other hand, it is only by organizing around meaning-needs, and by helping to address the paralyzing pain that faces so many Americans, that an environmental movement could ever be in a position to mobilize an American majority for the kinds of dramatic changes necessary to save our planet.

Crime and Violence in a Rip-off Society

Conservatives have dominated the crime debate for the past three decades with their endless appeals for law and order. In recent years, liberals and conservatives have vied for the mantle of being "toughest on crime." Conservatives often fault liberals for championing the civil liberties of the accused, citing this tendency as proof that liberals are not really serious about fighting crime. On the other hand, when Presidents Nixon, Reagan, and Bush were accused of various crimes while in office (such as violating laws that prohibited arms sales to the Nicaraguan contras), conservatives were quick to avail themselves of these same safeguards, and have shown no interest in eliminating them when applied either to corporate or white-collar crime.

Liberals and progressives have recently come to understand the popularity of the anticrime position, and many have sought to jump aboard this bandwagon. Bill Clinton positioned himself as a "New Democrat" and ran as a tough-on-crime candidate, then helped enact a crime bill that called for the death penalty for dozens of crimes. Billions of dollars will be spent on building more prisons and putting more police onto the streets. The underlying assumption of these policies is that criminal behavior can be repressed through strict punishments.

Yet the general strategy, endorsed by both conservatives and New Democrats, has been tried and failed. No amount of repression seems sufficient to stem the rising tide of violence. On the contrary, the more that we incarcerate young felons, the more quickly they learn the most sophisticated techniques of killing, robbery, rape, and assault.

In his book, *Why Americans Hate Politics,* E. J. Dionne has described the lack of substance in the crime debate, demonstrating that it is not *about* anything except who can position him or herself better to get elected. Playing to the legitimate fears that Americans have about the astounding level of violence in our society, both parties have attempted to show that they have no sympathy for criminals but do care sincerely for victims of crime. Republicans have sometimes used this issue to play to overt racist sentiments. George Bush's infamous Willie Horton campaign ad used code words and images to send the message that criminals are likely to be African-American men, and reminded the public that Democrats have been overly sympathetic to the plight of such men. But even when racism is not involved, neither conservatives nor liberals who follow the same logic are willing to question why their measures have failed so miserably to reduce crime or violence. Nor are liberals particularly willing to ask themselves why their minimal social-support policies, sometimes touted as the more compassionate response to crime, have been equally ineffective.

Commenting on the 1994 Omnibus Crime Bill debate, U.S. Senator Bill Bradley suggested that although Americans believed that government intervention could solve the problem through more federal legislation, the problem in fact was closer to home—in the boardrooms of America.

In the 1990s, a growing number of Americans are willing to see through the charade and recognize that there is a spiritual crisis in America that may be at the root of much crime and violence. In many instances, crime and violence may be part of a cry for help by young people who feel homeless in the spiritual wasteland that they encounter in daily life. Shorn of any sense of living in a community of meaning and shared purpose, and seeing no positive communal values that are taken seriously, these youngsters grow up imbibing the dominant value of our society: "Take care of yourself without regard to anyone else."

Indeed, when they look around at the rest of society, most young people see a world in which many ordinary people, in every walk of life, are prepared to rip off as much as they can of the available collective goods and services, as long as they can get away with doing so. As our impulses toward caring for others are systematically degraded and ridiculed in this society, we learn that we are being foolish if we do not join in the general pursuit of selfishness.

Though our caring impulses are never fully suppressed, they take an increasingly subordinate role to our more "rational" assessment of self-interest. As a result, many Americans put morality on the back burner. We confine morality to issues within our personal lives, while imagining that moral sensibilities simply are out of place in the public arena and that we would be naive to try to introduce them there on a policy level. (Nevertheless, we happily flagellate leaders for their alleged personal immorality.)

Some corporations are masterful manipulators of the society's rip-off mentality. In an instructive study of the decline of public morality, sociologist Charles Derber points out in his book, *Money, Murder, and the American Dream,* that many corporations are as given to "wilding" as any inner-city youth. When tobacco companies, for example, target teenagers for special promotion of a product that is known to cause cancer, or when pharmaceutical companies raise the costs of medicines to levels that are prohibitive for the poor, they are doing physical harm on a larger scale than any group of irresponsible inner-city teenagers could do. The media, however, leave us with indelible impressions about the latter while rarely highlighting the damage done by the corporate world.

There are, to be sure, a number of corporations that distinguish themselves through their attention to the social or environmental consequences of their activities. Sensitivity to these issues moves some corporate leaders to understand the need for new investment policies, for an entirely new approach to social responsibility by society as a whole, and even for a politics of meaning. Organized in groupings such as the Social Ventures Network and Businessmen for Social Responsibility, these corporate leaders give the lie to any blanket assertion that all businesspeople are inevitably corrupted by the dominant ethos of the marketplace. But while these leaders should be praised and encouraged, it would be foolish to overstate how many such people have been able to flourish, and how far even the best of them could go should their responsible practices seriously cut into corporate profits.

Those who own and control corporations end up owning wealth that is vastly disproportionate to everyone else's. The top one percent of the population owns forty percent of all the wealth in America. The people in this tiny minority make certain that this inequity remains legal, through their ability to donate vastly larger amounts to political candidates and through their ownership of the media, which in turn define those political positions that are and are not deemed responsible and serious.

Will those Americans who have a lot share with those who do not? Unlikely, given the ethos of selfishness. Rich people do donate—though many of them do so only on the premise that their contributions can be deducted from income taxes and hence save them some money. Moreover, a very large portion of charitable donations go to projects that the rich develop for themselves, but which then are shared with others: supporting the symphonies, the operas, the art museums, the hospitals, the universities, and other institutions that will be of eventual use to themselves or their children. Furthermore, as any fund-raiser knows, these projects typically are financed through elaborate fund-raising events that are rituals of self-congratulation. The rich give one another honors for giving one another their money, and various cultural and political figures come to sing the praises of the givers, who in turn feel important and recognized for sharing a small portion of what they have. It is much more difficult to persuade the rich to give money to help the poor, and almost impossible to persuade them to support programs aimed at systemic change that might negatively affect their own economic interests.

Nor is this me-firstism a problem of the rich alone. Many who aspire to accumulate money have come to believe that they will not succeed if they spend "too much" energy worrying about the welfare of others. Many middle-income people feel ashamed to admit that they have not taken every possible opportunity to advance their own interests, and imagine that the reason why they have not been still more successful is because they have focused too little on looking out for number one.

Though there is a part of each of us that wants to be more caring and giving, it is not unusual for middle-class Americans to believe that they are being foolish and sentimental when they have those feelings, and to castigate themselves for not being more realistic about how the world really is. Despite the desire to be more moral, people yield all too often to a competing desire to be more selfish, particularly in regard to public causes. Cheating on income taxes is so common that it is widely acknowledged and winked at by many people. Whenever they feel that they can underreport income or exaggerate expenses and charitable donations, millions of Americans do so, unless constrained by the fear of being caught. Giving more money to society than the income-tax laws require, by contrast, is simply unheard of.

Moreover, our society is replete with tales of manipulative business practices. Many people will pursue an advantageous though morally ambiguous angle if they can find one. I do not mean that most people regularly break the law, though some do. What I do mean is that the bottom line of selfishness does not apply only to the rich and the corporate elite, but extends into every corner of society.

People repeatedly tell themselves that they do not really want to be this way, but that everyone else is, and that they would be foolish to put themselves at a disadvantage for principles that no one else is willing to take seriously.

I think that these people are telling the truth: they really would prefer to live a more moral life, but they have come to believe that doing so is impossible. Thus, many readers will respond to the thesis of this book by saying, "It's not realistic, because everyone is motivated by self-interest." While I maintain that they are wrong about our possibilities, they are right about the behavior that they most typically see manifested (without denying the reality that there are also millions of genuinely caring acts that happen every day in this society).

It is in this moral climate that a small percentage of the poor become involved in selling drugs or other criminal acts. The poor live in the same society in which everyone is constantly telling everyone else that the bottom line is to take care of number one. They live in the same society that honors and rewards corporate leaders who meanwhile are directly involved in plundering the planet's resources. They live in the same society in which corporate gangsters are commended for their large contributions to the arts, education, or public broadcasting. They live in the same society in which the politics of meaning is ridiculed for imagining that we could make the promotion of ethical sensitivity our new bottom line. Yet the rest of society imagines that the poor ought to live by a *higher* morality than everyone else. *That* is unrealistic.

We would be more realistic if we realized that all of life is a seamless whole, and that the way people learn to think and act in one part will have consequences for the other parts of the whole. If our society structures life in such a way as to reward selfishness, we cannot be surprised if that selfishness and insensitivity to the needs of others, that willingness to exploit others and to ignore the common good, permeates every part of society.

Violence and Misrecognition

More shocking than crime per se is the degree to which violence pervades our communities. Violence offends us in particular because it violates our understanding that every human being is precious and holy and of ultimate value. Violence is a denial of that holiness; it is a willingness to treat human beings as though they were mere objects to be manipulated at someone's whim.

But seen through a politics-of-meaning perspective, violence clearly is concomitant with the decline of spirituality and the triumph of contemporary forms of materialism and selfishness. There are very few institutions or social practices in the modern world that actually reflect in their daily operations the fundamental holiness or sanctity of human beings. Whether growing up in our inner cities or in affluent suburbs, young people are unlikely to come into contact with many institutions or adults who embody this sensitivity toward the sanctity of other people. They may hear these ideas in religious settings or in speeches by public officials, but they are unlikely to see these ideas actually instituted. They do know that police frequently use unnecessary violence, particularly against groups that are relatively powerless (such as the homeless).

Yes, young people know that certain kinds of violence are illegal. But they also know that other kinds of violence, including violence against children by parents and violence to achieve the ends of the state (such as the U.S. intervention in Kuwait or the use of the death penalty) are sanctioned and even honored. So, they may conclude, the issue is not violence itself, but violence by whom and for whose purposes?

Once young people get to this point, they might become a bit cynical. They have learned that the powerful are the ones who define how society's resources and institutions operate, and for whose purposes. Accordingly, young people may find the popular injunction against violence to be yet another hypocritical proclamation by a society that does not live up to its own moralizing. "Why should I?" young people ask.

Violence is a spiritual issue. It is a manifestation of the failure of a society to take seriously the spiritual nature of human beings. And when we are not recognized as beings who are infinitely precious, creative, and intelligent, we feel misrecognized and undervalued. Yet we often feel that we have no choice but to accept the misrecognition we get, for fear that the glimmers of love that still filter through would be lost to us if we were to demand full recognition, and because we learn early in childhood that our hunger for recognition is dangerous and unjustified. For many, then, childhood becomes a complex amalgam of subordination and dutiful submission (to the picture of who we are, presented to us by parents and teachers and supervisors) and a simultaneous rage at being misrecognized.

The rage at misrecognition can be channeled in socially acceptable ways (such as the vicarious gratification of watching a football game or a boxing match); or in militarism, xenophobic nationalism, or religious fundamentalism—each of which presents us with an enemy upon whom to vent our frustration. Alternatively, this rage may express itself in violence that is not useful to some larger group, and hence is defined as "crime."

It is futile to imagine that people will suddenly embrace the concept of human beings as ultimately precious, in a society that rewards those who treat human beings as means to an end. This is simple fantasy.

The rage of misrecognition can only be cured by providing real recognition—which is not only a psychological task, but a task of reordering society at large in ways that attest to the sanctity of every person within it. To give real care to our individual souls, we need to create a social reality that is consistent with the sanctity of each human being. Otherwise, most human interactions will continue to be based on the false self that each of us develops in order to accommodate our earlier misrecognition, and we will continue to not see others or be seen ourselves as the sacred and valuable beings that all of us are.

Is misrecognition just a momentary distortion which, once noticed, can quickly be fixed? Not at all! Misrecognition is the necessary concomitant of a society that treats people as objects. The deeper the objectification, the deeper the need for misrecognition. The more we wish to have people prepared to close their eyes to the destructive consequences of living in such a society, the more we must foster people who are out of touch with the ways in which they, too, have been forced to repress their deepest desires for recognition. Moral and spiritual insensitivity run counter to our fundamental being. They can only become prevalent to the extent that we have learned to be out of touch with our deepest selves. Learning to be out of touch in this way is a product both of our own personal psychological development and of the constant conditioning given to us by our broader society.

Much of our societal training is directed toward moral and spiritual insensitivity. Take, for example, two amazing realities of contemporary life: our treatment of the homeless and our attitude toward unemployment. In virtually every previous historical period up to the sixteenth century, the homeless and the unemployed were seen as victims of a world that did not provide adequate shelter or jobs. In the past four hundred years, however, and primarily in market societies, the homeless and the unemployed have been blamed for their own situations, and society has felt it appropriate to punish them for their misfortunes. Colonial America became one of the first societies to regard the poor as a pestilence; by the mid-nineteenth century, the poor and the homeless were widely viewed as a subspecies, genetically inferior to others and a blight on society at large. Hence, they were effectively quarantined into penitentiaries and almshouses.

These same dynamics can be seen in the actions of contemporary urban mayors who attempt to sweep homeless people off the streets, in order not to offend the sensibilities of middle-income people who do not wish to be confronted with the reality of poverty in their midst. Just as working people have punished themselves by internalizing the meritocratic ideology of the marketplace, so they have increasingly turned on the poor and seen them as enemies. This behavior would be all the more bizarre if working people could see how the technocratic revolutions of the present may lead to their own unemployment in the early decades of the twenty-first century. But most people do not see this possibility, in part because Western societies have successfully concentrated the victims of unemployment and homelessness disproportionately in minority groups. By viewing the poor as Other, it becomes easier to avert our eyes, to let them sleep in the cold, or to imagine that their unemployment is deserved or chosen.

Yet the cumulative impact of closing our eyes to the fate of others, and learning not to notice their pain, is a society-wide decrease in the level of moral and spiritual sensitivity—and this becomes the necessary and, at times, sufficient condition for crime and violence. Nevertheless, since thinking in these systemic terms is seen either as unrealistic ("because the system can't be changed") or soft ("because the only things criminals understand is tough behavior"), public discussion instead focuses on the "hard" choices about what forms of incarceration and punishment will work best. All the while, society hides from itself the obvious truth that none of these alleged deterrents has worked in the slightest, and that the crime and violence problems of the United States are far greater proportionally than those of many other societies, and are directly related to our spiritual crisis.

The debate surrounding the 1994 Omnibus Crime Bill is an example of how both liberals and conservatives participate in this process of denial. Conservatives attacked the bill for being full of "pork," as they referred to a variety of crime-prevention programs that included monies for community centers and midnight basketball. Liberals relabeled some minimal attempts to provide the infrastructure for community self-help as "crime prevention," since in the conservative political climate, this stratagem seemed the only plausible way to get needed programs funded. It apparently never occurred to the liberals that until the climate of selfishness and individualism is publicly confronted and defeated, attempts to sneak acts of public caring into legislation are likely to be caught and repudiated. And that was exactly what happened. The good programs in the crime bill were dramatically reduced in order to appease the conservative forces, who then could rightly point out that these weak programs were unlikely to have any dramatic impact on preventing crime. Liberals were exposed as manipulators, which is exactly what they were (although for a good cause).

More importantly, though valuable in themselves and on other grounds, these social programs would not prevent crime and violence. Perhaps they might become components of a successful prevention program, but only if they were seen as part of changing the dominant ethos of the society, were presented as such, and were created as such. Separated from the larger context of a transformation of the dominant ethos, they become "pork," that is, a further elaboration of the take-care-of-yourself mentality which is at the root of crime. So we see that liberal reformers and conservative hard-liners *both* misjudge the nature of crime, and their attempts to prevent it tend to intensify rather than alleviate the problem.

Crime will be reduced when people feel a social bond toward one another. That bond cannot be imposed by government or social programs or education. It is the cumulative product of a society that validates the spiritual and ethical dimensions of human reality, that embodies in all its actions a respect for every human being, and that encourages and rewards mutual recognition and caring among all members of the society.

When children feel deeply recognized and cared for, and when they can see how the society for which they are being prepared is based on enhancing everyone's ability to be recognized, cherished, and cared for, it is unlikely that they will be attracted to acts of disrespect, violence, or abuse toward others or others' property.

We, however, live in a society which dehumanizes people. Caring and cherishing others, outside of one's immediate family and friendship circle, becomes the rare exception rather than the norm. Crime and violence follow.

Conservatives tend to dismiss all such talk as "soft" or "coddling the criminals" or "misguided compassion for the poor," but it is none of these. Rather, it is a hardheaded refusal to obscure the connections between what happens in public life from what happens in private life. Instead of providing simplistic solutions for crime and violence, the progressive politics of meaning recognizes that these problems are intrinsically linked to the dynamics of a society based on selfishness and materialism. It does not pretend, as the Right and Left both do, that we can deter crime and violence without healing our souls. To accomplish this requires healing a society which, through its embodiment of the ethos of selfishness and materialism, and its consequent need to misrecognize, does so much damage to our souls.

The real miracle is how little violence there is, given our society's spiritual deprivation, the systematic frustration of our meaning-needs, the ways that we have individually experienced lack of recognition throughout most of our lives, the absence of social change organizations that address and help us understand these issues, and the paucity of outlets through which we can express our justified anger.

What prevents violent expression of this anger in many people is the tremendous spiritual power of the God-energy manifested in every human being, which is so overwhelming that it breaks through all of these angry feelings. It does not dissipate them, but reminds us that they ought not to be expressed through violence toward other beings, similarly created in the image of the divine and similarly hungering for recognition and spiritual connection. The God-energy in the universe continually allows us to break through the mis-recognition we feel, and thus subverts what might otherwise be a much higher level of violence.

How to Be Tough on Crime

Democrats and Republicans vying for the title of "toughest on crime" or "leading the campaign against violence" deeply misunderstand what is really happening. But they necessarily misunderstand, for to think otherwise would raise fundamental questions about the nature of a materialistic and narcissistic society that neither party wants to think about seriously.

Raising such questions is precisely what a politics of meaning *does* want to do. Such an approach, however, does not try to *excuse* criminals or violent people. The poor person who steals or who attacks another individual is no less morally corrupt than the corporate executive who recklessly produces goods for profit that use up our planet's resources without regard to the needs of future generations. The person who grows up being battered and then becomes a batterer is no less morally corrupt than the rich person who uses his or her wealth to elect officials who will vote against public funding for family support groups, parental education, and psychological services aimed at stopping the cycle of family violence. Corruption is pervasive throughout our society, and it is wrong in every class and in every racial, ethnic, or religious group. It should not be winked at or defined away as "understandable."

I am as much outraged as any American at those who perpetrate violence. I want them punished and isolated. I want to be protected from them. But I also know that I *cannot* get the protection I want without addressing the spiritual needs of others in our society. No matter how many people we lock up, the spiritual repression and frustration of our meaning-needs will create more human beings ready to act out in irrational and hurtful ways. This will continue until we can sustain genuine recognition of the God-energy within each of us, and can build social institutions that are predicated on that.

Both liberals and conservatives misunderstand the problem of violent crime. Conservatives, who usually bemoan the ineffectiveness of big government and its inefficient interventions in society, suddenly advocate an expansionist and interventionist government on this issue. Their repressive measures only legitimize totalitarian thinking, however, without having any lasting impact on decreasing crime and violence. Liberals are equally misguided, because their talk about "prevention" in fact is limited to jobs programs or distractions for people who might otherwise be attracted to crime. Neither of these approaches begins to reach the moral and spiritual crisis that underlies crime and violence; hence, neither one is likely to make any substantial difference.

The wish for an answer has led some in our society to search for magical solutions, or for ingenious techniques that nobody has thought of before. Perhaps people hope for a way to identify violence-producing genes or chemical imbalances or the like, and then treat these. Biologically and chemically oriented psychiatrists who depend on drugs to replace psychotherapy are gaining popularity. But this is just another avenue for society to avoid the deeper ethical and spiritual crisis. Eventually, people will realize that the way to greatly reduce levels of crime and violence is to create a society based on love, caring, and spiritual sensitivity. To be tough on crime is to be willing to have the courage to take on the spiritual crisis.

At this point, the skeptical reader may ask what I mean when I write of creating a society based on love, caring, and spiritual sensitivity. Is there any meaning to these high-sounding words?

In fact these words *do* have meaning, though it cannot be easily explained within the prevailing American worldview.

Creating a society based on love, caring, and spiritual sensitivity requires dramatic changes in how we organize our economy and civil society. But it is not merely a matter of social policy, though that is part of the solution. It is also a matter of us making deep changes in our personal lives and in the way we think about the world in order to create communities of meaning and purpose sufficient to the task of dramatically reducing violence. When we take part in communities that embody moral and spiritual sensitivity in the daily functioning of our social and economic and political institutions, and when we feel recognized as fundamentally valuable beings who are deserving of honor and respect and love, we will be far more sensitive to others and far less likely to think that it is acceptable to disregard one another's pain. We all will tend to worry about the common good, to have that concern play a significant role in many of our choices, and to be cautious about doing anything that might cause unnecessary pain to anyone else. This is the only campaign against crime and violence that has any chance of succeeding. Anyone who avoids this dimension of the problem is truly being soft on crime.

Why Conservatives Are Soft on Crime

Conservatives adopt the stance of being tough on crime to mask their fear of looking squarely at the problem. They are afraid to look at what makes people violent, and to devise systemic approaches to quell it, because they themselves often feel violent impulses that they fear might get out of control. Their deep fears about themselves are projected onto others.

This analysis may sound like a psychological dismissal, but it need not be. I do not engage in this analysis in order to adopt the tactic of the contemporary media, which seek to unveil the dirty secrets of our leaders in order to discredit any inclination toward idealism. If conservatives' fears of crime are based on a defensive move to protect themselves against their own inner violence, the appropriate conclusion is not to dismiss conservatives for having those fears, but to take those inner fears seriously and rethink what they are about.

My point, of course, is *not only* that we all have this deep inner violence, but that the tendency toward violence in all of us results from the frustration of our deep hunger for meaning and recognition. However, in order to see the world this way, we would have to be prepared to challenge everything—starting with our parents and

how they (themselves victims of a world of misrecognition) participated in the process of misrecognizing us and thus, in some important ways, betrayed us. It was hard for us as children to see the
world this way, or to allow ourselves to feel anger, partly because
we knew ourselves to be deeply dependent on these adults, and
partly because we experienced their anger toward us whenever we
showed our anger toward them.

Equally important in keeping us from expressing our anger as
children was that we saw adults' vulnerability and neediness. Many
of us intuitively understood that our parents' desperate need to impose their definitions of reality upon their children—and even their
acts of actual or threatened violence—bespoke powerlessness, not
power, and deep unhappiness. The best way we had to protect our
parents was to not challenge their way of thinking. Instead, we
adopted our parents' perspective: imagining that our own needs
and our own perceptions were irrational, suppressing our own desires for deeper recognition, and defining our own needs and our
own rage as irrational and dirty.

For many people, it was only a short step to imagine that whatever we discovered as being irrational and dirty about ourselves
(once we had taken our parents' perspective) was also really irrational and dirty about *everyone,* because this was what it *meant* to
be a human being. No wonder, then, that theories of innate evil,
and psychologies of pessimism and despair, have had a large and
expanding market—precisely because they provide us with relief
from the self-blame that we would otherwise engage in as part of
our deeply held suspicion that we are really not very wonderful.

Yet, no matter how hard the child tries to accommodate to the
perspective of the parent, to internalize the critical parent judging
oneself as errant child, there is an inevitable anger that accompanies
this process. Though it can be internalized and repressed, the anger
can never be fully eliminated, and often it manifests itself in surprising and irrational ways.

Precisely because these parent-child dynamics are so threatening
to acknowledge, conservatives and liberals unite in dismissing any
serious discussion of psychodynamics. They label it all as psychobabble or worse, never permitting it to reach the political arena in
a serious manner. Some practitioners of psychotherapy serve as

enforcers of this implicit ban, arguing that the only legitimate use of psychodynamic insights is to promote changes within the inner lives of their clients, not to help create changes in the larger society.

Feminists made inroads against this limited way of thinking when they insisted that memories of childhood abuse must be addressed not only interpsychically, but also socially, through recognizing the extent to which women have been subjected to actual abuse in the real world. The Swiss psychoanalyst Alice Miller has been one of a handful of contemporary analysts who have deepened our knowledge of childhood abuse and called for social change.

Unfortunately, the misrecognition and denial of our desire for deeper recognition are widespread and routine. Dealing with these hurts would require a fundamental rethinking of how we organize our society. This challenge explains the otherwise incredible fact that people in politics systematically refuse to publicly discuss the widespread pain that permeates our society and its direct link to violence, depression, drug and alcohol abuse, and many other problems that conservatives (and now, even centrist Democrats) mistakenly think can be solved through greater repression. The fear of dealing with these issues in any way, other than to dismiss them with innuendo or ridicule, crosses political boundaries and reflects their explosive potential.

Conclusion

It would be psychological oversimplification to assume that people drawn to conservative politics are moved in that direction simply because they wish to reassure themselves that the authority figures in their lives really were right, and that their own internalized self-blame is appropriate. Among conservatives, just as among liberals and progressives, there is a wide variety of personality styles and psychological histories. Those critics who wish to reduce conservative politics to an authoritarian personality style, or to a reaction to fathers who were unable to provide empathy and nurturance, seem unaware of the many liberals whose liberalism derives from rebellion against such parents. My own experience as a psychotherapist leads me to believe that rigidity and the ferocious need to repress our desire for connection to others is shared across political boundaries. Indeed, it showed up frequently among liberals and leftists that I encountered over the years. These are not personal problems but societal realities, and they are just as useful in analyzing the inner life and political proclivities of Bill Clinton or Jesse Jackson as of Jesse Helms or Newt Gingrich.

In this chapter, however, I have tried to explore a particular aspect of conservative pathology: the tendency to engage in psychological splitting in order to avoid acknowledging the connections between the specific societal problems they rightly decry and the larger organization of our economic and social life, which is based on nonrecognition and the resulting primacy of selfishness as compensation. Consequently, conservatives are prevented from even beginning to understand the rage that the denial of our meaning-needs engenders. Instead, they see human beings as irrationally angry, which then validates conservative instruments of repression.

Conservatives' psychological splitting makes it impossible for them to address crime and violence in the terms that have been proposed here. It guarantees that conservatives will push for policies that avoid the real problems and focus instead on vindictive punishment, rather than for a world in which the pathologies and destructiveness of the contemporary world would be reduced. Conservatives, I believe, *do* have some important perspectives that need to be understood by liberals and progressives, and I have some sympathy for aspects of the critique of the contemporary world offered by supporters of a right-wing politics of meaning. But in the final analysis, a progressive politics of meaning is very different from the worldview of the Right. Although the Right should be commended for asking many of the important questions, its answers are so misguided and, when engaged in blaming others, so destructive, that ultimately conservatism must be put on the shelf with liberalism as a philosophy that no longer can contend with the realities of the contemporary world.

5

—ɷ—

Giving White Men (and Other Supposed Oppressors) a Break:

A Repudiation of "Political Correctness"

....

One reason why liberals and progressives have lost so much political support in the past thirty years is that they seem insensitive or even hostile to the desires and needs of most Americans. Under the guise of a political correctness that valorizes the economically or politically oppressed, whole groups of people have been made to feel that they are the enemy, that they have been benefiting from a system of oppression, and that the goal of liberals and progressives is not only to take away what they have but to demean them for being who they are.

The most frequent target of liberals and progressives is white men. I have known several men who participated in the social change movements of the past thirty years and have told me privately that they wished they were female or gay or black, or part of some other group that was considered oppressed, so they would be spared the experience of being labeled as oppressive by such groups. (It just is not politically correct to have been born a man.) Other white men have told me about leaving social change movements because they felt that their ideas or leadership were discounted because of their race and sex. Of course, most white men do not react this way to the assumption that their very being is oppressive. Rather, they respond by closing their ears to the liberal or progressive agenda and turning to the Right.

These same dynamics apply to many other Americans. The way that liberals and progressives conceptualize politics pushes the vast majority of people into some category in which they are forced to think of themselves as the oppressors. There is always somebody, somewhere, who is worse off than we are—and if we regard anyone who is doing better than the worst off as "benefiting" from the system of oppression, we can easily make all people feel bad about themselves as participants in an oppressive world.

But encouraging people to think this way is not smart and it is not accurate.

It is not smart because when people are told frequently enough that they are oppressors, they start to identify with that position. They feel that perhaps they have the most to gain by identifying with the interests of other oppressors, and *not* with the oppressed. One way that Americans are kept in line is by our dominant culture reminding us that America is doing better than everyone else in the world, and that we should feel pleased that we are doing so well. Instead of asking how we are doing compared to the elites of wealth and power in the United States, we are told to compare ourselves to those less fortunate in the rest of the world. Far from leading most people to identify with those more oppressed, this logic leads them to identify with American elites and to feel that they have a stake in defending the status quo. So when liberals and progressives tend to emphasize the ways in which we all are oppressors, they strengthen the hands of the oppressors.

The dichotomy itself is false. The world is not divided into oppressors and oppressed; such a typology does not capture the complexity of social reality. Most so-called oppressors are also victims of the very same social system from which they derive certain economic or political benefits and privileges. It makes more sense to look at the shared victimhood as well as the shared privilege.

There has been a supposition that men are so deeply entrenched in power that they would never give it up unless it were forcibly taken from them. This "us/them" mentality assumes that the oppressors all are evil and the oppressed all are good, and that in some fundamental way the evil ones must be wiped out. I want to systematically challenge this us/them worldview, and propose instead a compassionate attitude toward all human beings, even those who seem to be benefiting from the oppression of others and who resist the changes I support. In this chapter, I have chosen to focus on compassion for men as one example of how to apply this principle, but it applies to others as well.

People are born into a social world that is already constituted in ways that degrade ethical and spiritual values, and deny *everyone* the possibility of full recognition as ultimately valuable or embodying God's image. Though the details vary with each family and are shaped by issues connected to class, race, and gender, every child goes through the shock of misrecognition: first by family, then by teachers and friends, and finally by supervisors or colleagues in adult life. Depending on one's position in the class structure, varying degrees of compensation are available for the pain of misrecognition. But there is no one who is not *also* a victim, no one who has not been spiritually and emotionally negated as a child. There are only degrees of victimhood, and degrees of material compensation. (It may be easier to live with the pain of misrecognition if one is born into a family of multimillionaires, though the few such people I know make me doubt that money ultimately is much of a compensation.)

I do not deny that the forms of victimhood differ, and that the suffering of Jews sent to concentration camps is not identical to that of upper-middle-class white American males, who have plenty of material compensation for their oppression. Of course we do not all suffer in the *same* way. However, it is a political error to imagine that we can quantify or create hierarchies of suffering. After acknowledging the real pain of those whom liberals have correctly identified as oppressed, we would be wiser to focus on how the supposed beneficiaries of this system of oppression actually are among its victims. To understand how this is true, we need to acknowledge and take seriously the ways in which all children in our society are victims of the pervasive misrecognition I have discussed earlier.

Many of the distortions of daily life are rooted in our responses to misrecognition and the denial of our desire for meaning, and in our accommodation to a society based on selfishness and materialism. If one could look at all other people, and oneself, as having lives that are in part shaped by this dynamic, one could then take a much more compassionate attitude toward people drawn to xenophobic nationalism, racism, anti-Semitism, sexism, homophobia, or religious fundamentalism.

I do not propose here to take a tolerant attitude toward the manifestations of any of these hateful behaviors. To be compassionate toward the people involved does not mean accepting their behavior. A central element in a meaning-oriented strategy for societal healing is compassion. If one can learn to see oneself, one's parents, and eventually all people as having been denied the opportunity to actualize their most fundamental ethical and spiritual needs, one can develop this compassionate attitude. Such an attitude is not based on condescension, nor is it manifested in love without boundaries. Rather, it is communicated in a trust that each of us has the capacity to transcend who we have become. The ancient Jewish notions of atonement and repentance are important to a politics of meaning. Human beings do evil deeds, but they can always return to their deepest inner truth and allow themselves to be motivated by their highest vision of the good. We have missed the mark, but we can always return to God through acts of loving-kindness. This atonement, however, is not simply a change in one's inner state. To be real, it must manifest itself in new behavior and an end to acts that are hurtful to others.

The kind of compassion that I am advocating does not preclude anger at oppression, but we must distinguish anger at a person from anger at that person's actions. Our goal must be to learn to convey to others a deep and profound respect for their beings, even as we struggle against their oppressive actions.

Having this kind of compassion for others and learning to see the ways in which they were victimized does *not*, as some conservatives suggest, further demean people or disrespectfully dismiss them as "nothing but victims." I am not arguing for absolving individual responsibility for oppressive behavior, and I am not arguing for tolerating violence when it comes from oppressed people. I *am* calling for real compassion for the people involved—in this case, for the right-wingers and others who act in oppressive ways. This means conveying to these people that we are willing to accept *them* even though we are not willing to accept certain forms of their racist, anti-Semitic, sexist, or homophobic behavior.

Such compassion is a tall order, and I do not expect that many liberals or progressives will find it particularly easy to achieve. It takes a lot of self-knowledge, and compassion for oneself. We must first be able to look at ourselves and recognize our own cruelty and hurtfulness toward others, and to see this behavior as resulting from the process by which we, as children, had to cope with a family and a world that systematically denied us recognition. Only then will we have enough compassion for ourselves to be able to give real compassion to others. And this kind of compassion is a far deeper process than merely giving poor people some economic benefits: it involves a whole different way of understanding.

I am fully aware that those who have never gone through such a process of self-acceptance will find much of what I say seemingly empty. There is a lot of psychobabble out there in our contemporary culture, and it often substitutes for serious thought. So it is important to stress that the process of self-acceptance and recognizing pain in others is not meant to be the sum and substance of a politics of meaning, but only one important dimension of it. Its primary importance lies in challenging the way of thinking about politics that reduces the process to "the issues." In fact, most people do not have a strong sense of what the issues are in any given election or political movement, but are moved by other levels of need—including, crucially, the need for recognition and for spiritual affirmation.

Give Men a Chance:
Understanding Homophobia and the Desperate Struggle to Prove One's Manliness

Up to this point, I have talked about the psychodynamics of childhood as though they were gender neutral. But they are not.

One of the many useful contributions of the feminist movement has been our wider understanding of how the contemporary organization of gender distorts the development of women. The ways in which a patriarchal order oppresses women is well known and its psychological and spiritual consequences have been well documented.

But men, too, are victims of the current gender system. They, too, are in a great deal of pain, and one of the primary causes has been the injunction that real men are not supposed to be in pain.

One way to understand the distinctive nature of the pain that many men face is to look at the area where they most frantically insist on their manhood, and most imagine that their manhood is about to be violated: namely, in relationship to the fear of homosexuality.

An instructive example was President Clinton's need to retreat hastily on the issue of openly allowing gays in the military. In the ensuing debate, liberals spent their energies attempting to provide rational arguments to counter the claims that gays might undermine families or the ethos of commitment to long-term relationships, or that gays might rape or sexually oppress other men. But rational arguments missed the point: homosexuals reawaken deep fears that many men have about their own nurturing side, which they have been doing their best to repress.

Many men feel desperate to prove themselves to be "real men," to show that they are not weak or overly idealistic. They try to embody the toughness and meanness and self-interest that manifests itself as cynicism or conservative "realism." This feeling is not based on some set of rational arguments; rather, it is a response to the pain that these men experienced while growing up in a patriarchal society.

The fear raised by the issue of gay rights strikes so deeply into the psyches of many people precisely because it touches on one of the greatest tragedies of patriarchal society: the asymmetrical way in which boys and girls develop a sense of identity.

In the nuclear families of patriarchal societies, the woman usually provides the early nurturing for children. She feeds them, caresses them, touches them, changes their diapers. The helpless infant would be unable to develop into a human being without this mothering, so it is no wonder that the mother takes on unimaginable importance for the baby. On the other hand, it is also the mother who frustrates the needs of the baby: taking the breast away, setting limits, toilet training, saying no. As the infant becomes a toddler, it develops resentment and profound ambivalence toward the mother. The child learns that its initial identification with the mother must be superseded by a knowledge that the mother is "not I," and it is the mother who must enforce this suppression of the child's identification with her.

As Nancy Chodorow points out in *The Reproduction of Mothering*, the identification stage is likely to be longer, and the separation-individuation stage murkier, for girls than for boys. The mother is likely to prolong the identification with her daughters longer than with her sons. The boy child, on the other hand, quickly learns from his mother and the surrounding society that he must differentiate himself from his mother more completely if he is to become a man. The boy child learns that he must suppress the "female" inside of him: the part of him that previously identified with his mother and her nurturing.

To achieve the required individuation from his mother, the boy will seek to establish a tie to his father. In a society where most men do not share child-rearing and are absent from the household much of the time, the identification that the boy seeks will often be tenuous. The boy will have to identify more with the position that his father holds in the world than with the actual experience of a specific human being. Given that distance, his father cannot begin to replace the emotional intensity of the boy's relationship with his mother, and the resulting ambivalent attitude will be reflected in the boy's treatment of girls and women. As Dorothy Dinnerstein puts it in *The Mermaid and the Minotaur*, "If woman is to remain for him the central human object of the passions most deeply rooted in life's beginnings, his relation to her must embrace . . . both the worshipful and the derogatory, the grateful and the greedy, the affectionate and the hostile feeling toward the early mother."

Boys will bond with one another to reinforce their ability to separate from their mothers, and in adult life they will continue or strengthen the male bonding to control and mask their emotional dependence on women. They will seek to be cool, distant, and unemotional in order to feel in control rather than desperate about their need to be close to women. Adult women will often restimulate (intentionally or unintentionally) the feelings of child-hood—the sense that women have overwhelming power from which the boy must escape, lest he reexperience both his vulnerabil-ity and his rejection. One way in which men escape from this threat is to infantilize women by removing them from political, technolog-ical, or religious areas in which they might appear powerful. And male bonding allows men to minimize their emotional dependence and reassure themselves that they are not so needy.

These dynamics face all men in a patriarchal society that is re-fracted through nuclear families in which men are rarely involved in child-rearing. But the exact way in which these dynamics are refracted through the specific cultural and psychological inheri-tance of *particular* families makes a great deal of difference. Not all fathers are equally absent; not all mothers are equally harsh in ma-nipulating or rejecting their son's affection and anger; not all cul-tures are equally committed to the ideal of an emotionally detached father. There is a continuum of responses on these and other issues that creates a set of variable responses among men to the basic asym-metry of their position. But in most patriarchal societies, achieving male identity requires repressing those parts of themselves that are most nurturing, caring, and maternal.

To some extent, the separation from mother is an ontological necessity, required in order for any child to achieve independence. But in societies with extended families and where men do a greater share of the child-rearing, the mothering roles are more shared—and cross gender boundaries. This arrangement buffers the degree to which the complicated feelings of desire and anger are focused exclusively on women. Similarly, though independence and separa-tion from mother is necessary in every society, the degree of inde-pendence and isolation required in advanced competitive market societies is considerably greater, and the degree of rejection of mother-ties hence is all the more intense.

Feminists have tended to place this asymmetry within the con-text of male power and to focus on the fact that men enjoy great compensation for the pain of separating from their mother: namely, the special privileges they receive in a patriarchal society. There certainly is no denying or minimizing that privilege. But if our goal is to help men come to understand that patriarchy is not really in their interest, it makes sense to return our focus to the pain that men have had to endure in this process, in order to remind them of what they have had to give up. To varying degrees, depending on the specific psychological and cultural framework through which patriarchal expectations were refracted, men have had to lose their soft, nurturing, and caring sides.

The more pain is involved in giving up mother, and the more difficult it is to establish a tie with father, the more desperate is the need to repress feelings of pain and loss that arose in this process, and the more exaggerated is the attempt by the boys or men in question to adopt stereotypical male qualities and to defend their macho identity against actual or imagined assault. Yet the repression of our soft, nurturing, and caring parts is a very difficult task. The more we are enmeshed in a macho life, the more we actually need the softness, nurturing, and caring that we are forced to repress.

Sometimes these needed qualities can be supplied by a woman. But as women have increasingly entered the job market and have found that these very qualities tend to be disadvantageous in the world of work, men have found it increasingly difficult to use women as their only source of nurturing. Women, too, have gained a sense of their own right to seek nurturing for themselves, and it makes them less willing to be involved in unequal relationships in which they do a vastly disproportionate amount of nurturing. As women resist lives totally dedicated to nurturing men, men's needs for nurturing increase, forcing them to reexperience the original need for their mother's nurturing, as well as their own desire to be nurturing—the very parts of their psyche that men had worked so hard to repress.

One attraction of conservative politics to some men is precisely that it promises rigid boundaries and assistance in repressing those parts of the male psyche that are traditionally seen as feminine, soft, caring, and giving. Conservative politics provides a variety of rationales for negating those qualities, and for seeing them as not functional for society. Such politics strengthens traditional sex roles that reinforce the macho energy needed to repress this desire for nurturing—in particular, those parts of the male psyche that might still be struggling with the desire to *be like* the nurturing mother.

Whenever we see a man rigidly insisting on the traditional macho style of being with others, we should allow ourselves to see underneath all this a child desperate for love, attention, and caring, who has been forced to deny and repress those needs. Similarly, the cynical journalists and intellectuals who belittle the meaning-needs, and who ridicule contemporary movements seeking spiritual renewal, may themselves be the most oppressed, because so many of them are victims of internal voices that require the denial of their own need for love, caring, and recognition.

These dynamics come to the fore most intensely in the male homophobe. The little boys on the school playground who continually test one another for softness are, in fact, trying to reassure themselves of their own control over their desire to be, like their mother was, soft and nurturing. These are qualities that they know will make them look "like a girl." Such identification has become painful for them, because first their mother herself, and then all of patriarchal society, has betrayed, abandoned, and repressed this part of them. The more unresolved the conflict, the more intense the need to assert our maleness, and the more we feel threatened by those who are not also doing so. The degree of macho behavior directly corresponds to the degree of unresolved pain.

Men who have made careers for themselves in the male-dominated, male-bonding, military establishment are often those who are most intensely in need of external supports to buttress their defenses against the allure of the caring and nurturing that they were forced to abandon when they were young. No wonder, then, that they feel particularly threatened by any homosexual presence in the military. It is *not* that they fear that they themselves are really gay and will be seduced by gay men (though this fear may certainly hold true for some people). When they talk about gay men, they talk about people who are weak and, like women, soft—unable to maintain the toughness and courage that it has taken for the rest of the military to be "real men."

In fact, the gay men who are attracted to the military often do not reflect these stereotypes. What straight men most fear is precisely what they most desire: the permission to be caring and weak, a permission which they will not allow themselves because doing so would run against their own self-conception of being a male.

Our attitude toward all of these "tough" men desperately shoring up their macho psyche ought to be one of compassion and caring. However much we reject the way that they have dealt with their pain, however much we must and should repudiate the homophobia and macho insensitivity that their attitudes lead to, we need to see these people as victims rather than as the embodiments of evil. And it is as victims that we have a first chance to talk with them, not just at them.

We want them to hear the psychological account of their pathology because we want them to know how it becomes possible for us to care about them and their pain, even when they treat us as demeaned Others. And we want them to know that *other ways to be a man* are now available. Men who embody other ways of being a man—ways that reflect a willingness to be caring and nurturing *without* giving up one's sense of being strong and independent—must be leaders in delivering this information.

There is a men's movement in the United States, composed of men who are attempting to embody this perspective. To the extent that they see themselves as consciously engaged in bringing this message to other men, they deserve our support. But we need not be part of a men's movement to understand that the legitimization of a soft, nurturing, emotionally generous capacity in men can be key to the strategy to undermine conservative politics and to weaken the homophobia which is so central to it.

Championing this type of male desire—the repressed hope for soft and nurturing relationships in a more caring world—will inevitably generate furious assault by the very men who are most in conflict about these unconscious desires. Yet if those who call for this kind of nurturing can stand firm in their analysis and commitment, they can reassure their opponents, who will not be abandoned to the scorn of neighborhood bullies or public humiliation should they allow themselves to recognize their own needs for love and caring.

All the worse, then, that President Clinton abandoned his promise to issue an executive order eliminating discrimination against gays in the military. That such an order might have been overturned by Congress made no difference; it would have allowed Clinton further opportunities to address the underlying issues.

A president with moral courage and political smarts would have talked about homophobia in the very terms that I have presented here. Having made that analysis, he would have gone on to say something like this:

> I know that it's going to take special courage for those in the military to deal with their fears about their manhood. Underlying their panic at having homosexuals in the same room is their own doubts about whether they can sustain their manhood, and whether they can keep under control their own desire to be more caring, more nurturing, more like a woman. It's not that they fear that they are *really* homosexuals—most who oppose this ban certainly are not—but they fear whether they can stand the anxiety of being with men who might remind them of the part of themselves that has caused them so much pain to repress. The courage that it will take for them is *not* the courage to retain their current conception of manhood, but rather the courage to imagine a different kind of manhood: a kind of manhood in which one can be strong and still soft, one can be masculine and still nurturing to others, one can show courage not just by taking risks in war but by taking risks in changing traditional definitions of courage. I believe that this is the task not just for men in the military, but for all men in our society, and that's why I'm going to stand strong for my insistence that homosexuals really are nothing to be afraid of. They won't destroy anything, and we as a society are strong enough to allow their different way of being sexual without feeling that we will be overtaken by it.

As it was, President Clinton's capitulation to the military and to conservatives in Congress sent exactly the opposite message—a message that has been reinforced over and over by his compromises and by his abandonment of people, principles, and campaign promises: namely, that the softness and humanity in Clinton's demeanor necessarily gets attached, in the public's mind, to the kind of weakness that prevents him from standing up for what he believes in. And this connection reinforces people's worst fears about softness:

that it will be inadequate for defending our country and our vital interests, so instead we really need the macho style that goes with homophobia. Indeed, one of the basic fears that many Americans have about liberals (which is how Clinton is perceived) is that they are too liberal about their own principles, in other words, that they are too soft to fight for their own ideals. This fear makes the public feel unsafe, because if someone will not fight for what he or she believes in, or gives up too quickly, then how can people put their fate in such a leader's hands and imagine that their interests will be defended?

Some political "realists" argue that a president cannot talk this way without risking a major political backlash. Actually, however, it may be more realistic for all of us to speak the deepest truths we know, even if at first they engender resistance. The continued reliance by liberals on the language of technocratic mush that fills the policy debates in Washington does not do much for the popularity of those who seek genuine change. Speaking honestly and deeply, but in a way that does not tell the majority of people that they are wrong, is more likely to produce results than allowing the "going wisdom" to define our political discourse.

Naturally, pushing people to new levels of psychological insight often engenders resistance at first, as psychotherapists are well aware. For this reason, it is important to be careful about how the interventions are made—and this is as true on a societal level as in individual therapy. Yet, there also are moments where a major breakthrough can occur precisely because people *have* heard the larger theory and are able to apply it to themselves. Feminism, for example, generated intense resistance and denial at first. Yet many of those who resisted most intensely have come to accept many feminist insights, because the power of the theory to explain so much about our lives, coupled with the insistence of many women that we try to listen to the theory in all its subtlety and complexity, eventually overpowered the initial resistance.

We live during a period in the development of American society when people need to hear a coherent psychologically- and spiritually-based account of the relationship between their own personal lives and larger social and economic forces. Until our political leadership is capable of doing this, we will be stuck in an endless replay of the dynamics that led to the 1994 election and the subsequent decline in power and integrity of Bill Clinton.

Meaning and Caring:
The Feminist Dimension

Extending our caring to others, including those with whom we disagree, is a central focus of this chapter. Some women may object that by explicitly calling for caring toward white men, I have gone too far. Yet the impulse for a politics-of-meaning approach, particularly its suggestion that emotional nurturing and caring are equally as important as economic well-being, has deep roots in feminist consciousness.

Though there were those with narrower agendas, much of the excitement of early second-wave feminism (in the late 1960s and early 1970s) stemmed from the willingness to venture that the problem with existing politics was not only that women were insufficiently included in it, but that it embodied a male paradigm of human needs that was far too narrow. Women, some feminists insisted, had a different set of needs that had to do with caring and sustaining relationships.

These ideas received their first full articulation in Carol Gilligan's *In a Different Voice,* and have since developed into a lively feminist debate about "the ethics of care." Some feminist theorists in the 1970s maintained that caring was a distinctively female way of being in the world.

Caring, these feminists observed, had been devalued as a human activity, and caregivers tended to be lower paid than workers who were more highly valued. (Caregivers included nurses, child-care workers, social workers, elementary-school teachers, and others in traditionally female occupations.) Because women were more in touch with their own needs to care and to be cared for, they were thought to be more aware of the caring-needs dimension of the human experience.

Later feminists refined these positions by questioning the implicit suggestion of earlier formulations that women were somehow biologically destined to be the caregivers. These feminists theorized that women's bias toward caring was not biologically determined, but a product of women's position as caregivers in patriarchal societies. Women had developed a way of thinking that emphasized connection over autonomy, because this kind of thinking had been necessary for the tasks they had been assigned.

Some feminists have gone on to argue that a female attachment to caring is merely an extension of the sexual division of labor. Instead of trying to infuse work or economics or politics with caring, these feminists have built a women's politics on narrow economic and equal-rights demands that seeks little more than to insert women into a male-oriented system of power and wealth. They have proven that women can be just as insensitive to the meaning-dimension of reality as any man, and can create a limited framework for feminist politics that is just as hard-nosed and "realistic" as the most distorted consciousness that runs the male-dominated world.

While I have subsequently come to believe that even within patriarchal societies, men have often been in touch with the caring-needs, the discourse begun by the women's movement brought me back to the texts and concepts of my own tradition that tend to value caring. Indeed, this valuation of caring within Jewish tradition may well have been one of the dimensions that had made it easy for some non-Jews to dismiss Jewish men as "feminized." I began to discover that it was the repression of men's need for caring that was central to the development of patriarchal psyches, on the one hand, and to a deep yearning for something that often took on mystical dimensions, on the other.

Looking at life from the standpoint of the denial of our desire to belong to a caring and loving world, and to comprehend its relation to our desire for meaning, purpose, and higher spiritual direction in this world, one could get a very different understanding of human history than by looking at it primarily from the standpoint of being motivated solely by our desire to fulfill material needs.

One way of thinking about the politics of meaning, therefore, is in terms of an attempt to extend the important insights developed by the women's movement so that they can be applied to concerns that affect both men and women.

Nevertheless, some feminists have objected to this broader approach, not only because they fear that a politics of meaning takes central ideas of feminism without properly crediting their origins, but also because they fear that if we begin to acknowledge men's pain and validate men's needs, women's ability to validate their own needs will be undermined. My point in this chapter about the need to validate men's real pain could be misheard by women as a new plea or implicit demand that women put their own needs aside and come back to the rescue of men.

Women have been so deeply socialized to believe that their task in life is to take care of others that it is often difficult to acknowledge someone else's distress as just that, even when no implicit or explicit demand is made for comfort or anything else.

In yet another context, I know this same kind of objection to the form of my argument as it emerges from the Jewish world: "We have had so much pain and suffering; it is not fair to ask us to acknowledge *others'* pain. In fact, our liberal tradition has pushed so much in that direction that we end up not acknowledging our own pain, and hence not being adequately protected from those who would continue to assault us."

These are valid concerns. However, nothing in this chapter is meant to suggest that the struggle against sexism, racism, anti-Semitism, homophobia, or other societal distortions should be abandoned in an orgy of caregiving to those who historically have contributed disproportionately to the ranks of the oppressors. Rather, I am arguing that the *most effective way* to continue those struggles against oppression is to begin to recognize the pain and fundamental humanity of those who have in various ways been complicit with systems of oppression.

Compassion for Wounded Healers

One reason why it has been so difficult for a liberal or progressive movement to show adequate compassion for others is that it typically is composed of people who have not adequately developed compassion for themselves. Victims of the same childhood and societal dynamics as everyone else, marred by the meritocratic fantasies and resulting self-blame that dominate contemporary society, those who wish to heal our planet are themselves in need of healing.

The appropriate response to this paradox is not to say, "Physician heal thyself"—as though that were possible apart from the larger society—but "Physician, let us heal one another as we heal the world." Anyone who plays the role of healer is going to be like the rest of the population: a human being who is psychically and ethically less than what she or he ought to be. Socialized in a world of oppression and raised by parents who themselves were psychically flawed and distorted, the healer necessarily shares the limitations and distortions of others, even though to some extent and in some specified ways the healer has taken steps toward transcending these dynamics. But this transcendence is going to be limited and imperfect, so we should have compassion for the healer.

Indeed, all of the healers in our world need to adopt this compassionate attitude about themselves. To the extent that they do not do so, they become engaged in frantic efforts to lie to themselves and to the rest of the world about who they really are. They feel that they must present themselves as total embodiments of psychological health and fully actualized spiritual beings if they are going to have the right to help anyone else. But perfection is self-delusional. Grandiose fantasies of being fully healthy and actualized then lead many of these healers to be insufficiently attentive to the ways in which their behaviors may be insensitive or hurtful to others. Far better to acknowledge the inevitability of flaws in our healers, and then to set up mechanisms through which these healers can acknowledge to one another and to themselves the areas in which they still need to grow, and in which they could use help and support from their peers.

The supposition that one could be fully healthy psychologically and fully actualized spiritually leads to a second great distortion: the need to present one's own work as totally successful. If complete psychological health is available to healers, it should be available to clients as well, and the successful healer then becomes the one who can totally heal. There follows a tremendous pressure to present one's work as totally successful and one's clients as totally healed—something that can only be done by lying to oneself or one's colleagues.

I have watched how some of these dynamics play out among psychotherapists. Lacking any serious understanding of the psychodynamic impact of the world of work and the ethos of selfishness and materialism, and oblivious to the ways in which the market mentality and the ideology of living in a meritocracy subvert much of their healing work, many psychotherapists imagine that they themselves should have been totally healed through their own psychotherapy and imagine that they ought to be doing the same for their clients. So when they find themselves dealing with parts of themselves that are not fully healed, they face the monumental task of hiding any signs of this "imperfection" from their clients and from their colleagues.

Likewise, when their clients themselves have trouble and do not fully sustain their psychological well-being, the therapists must hide this fact from themselves and from their colleagues, lest it reveal that they themselves have not been fully healed. The result is a series of coping mechanisms that are often quite destructive. On the one hand, some therapists may blame the client, usually by providing some label that suggests that the problem is so deep in the client's psyche that no one could possibly have dealt with it. On the other hand, some therapists may revert to a psychoanalytic stance that asserts that their work is not really about health, it is about "self-examination and introspection." This explains why the analysis has gone on for five or more years. These are just a few of the techniques that psychotherapists use to defend the narcissistic, self-aggrandizing picture of themselves as having failed if the client is still troubled in some way.

One reason why therapists rarely hold self-revealing case conferences with their colleagues, and why as a result so many therapists in private practice are immensely isolated from professionals with whom they could openly discuss their cases, is that they imagine that other therapists will see through them. They fear that they will be seen as less together than they are supposed to be, and hence not really on the same high healing plane as everyone else. By hiding themselves behind a veil of self-sufficiency, these therapists protect themselves from self-punishing judgments about their own imagined inadequacy.

Similar dynamics manifest themselves in other ways in social change movements. Precisely because the people within these movements often feel inadequate, they promote themselves with a bravado which, ironically, produces what they most feared: the alienation of the people whom they sought to recruit.

Still worse things happen when social change movements adopt a perfectionistic imagery of what they are supposed to be. Those of us working for social change in the 1960s imagined that we were supposed to be the fullest embodiment of our own highest ideals. This expectation quickly destroyed our movements. First, we turned with anger on all those not yet recruited into our movements, acting as though those people were enemies for not being on the same high moral plane as we were. Second, we turned on one another within our movements, furious about the ways in which each of us continued to embody sexism or racism or various inflated ego needs. Rather than recognizing our own inevitable limitations, and trying to compassionately support one another to exercise some of our spiritual capacities for transcendence, we treated one another as enemies, and created a climate of suspicion and mutual accusation so deep that few people wished to remain associated with our movements.

Meanwhile, others who had more peripheral contact with our movements reported that they had been involved but rapidly had become disillusioned because the people in the movement were no better than anybody else. These peripheral others were right. But why did they expect something different? If a movement is going to be democratic and successful, it will constantly be growing and incorporating within itself many, many people who have come to understand some of the movement's truths, but who are not thereby transformed into different human beings. When people decide that they want to be more whole and more sensitive to others, it is a necessary condition for transformation and healing, but it is not close to being a sufficient condition. Indeed, given the powerful and compelling pull of our long individual and social conditioning, the unconscious forces that operate within all of us, and the ongoing ways in which we adjust to a world of selfishness, it is highly likely that people who are trying to build a more caring world will themselves be, like everyone else, far from embodiments of those ideals.

We can be sure that in a movement for a progressive politics of meaning, we will find many people who are uncaring, selfish, spiritually insensitive (or at least underdeveloped), unable to be fully loving, and unable to give others the recognition they really deserve. Are we supposed to throw such people out or prohibit them from holding any position of responsibility? Who exactly would make *that* decision, and how would it be implemented? It is exactly this ethos—of group supervision of the morality of its members—that can be most dangerous and most totalitarian. It must be resisted. It is one thing to articulate an ideal and encourage people to pursue that ideal, providing a network of support groups and other activities so that people feel that they are not alone in trying to challenge the ethos of selfishness and materialism. But it is quite another to have a movement that expects its members to already fully embody those ideals. Where this is the case, we can expect group coercion, self-deception, and eventually a desperate flight from that community into the kind of individualism that the group originally set out to combat. It is in precisely such a climate that people begin to batter one another with charges of being politically incorrect.

A more compassionate understanding would acknowledge from the start that any successful social change movement will necessarily include millions of people who do *not yet* live up to the ideals of the movement. The key is to maintain the ideals and encourage people to strive for them, while simultaneously welcoming supporters with all their flaws and inadequacies, and showing them that those who have been in the movement longer *also* have many flaws that they have not yet transcended, and that these veterans also do not hold themselves up as full embodiments of the movement's ideals.

Compassion as a Guide to Spiritual and Political Transformation

Compassion as I have described it in this chapter is a central guiding principle of a politics of meaning.

First, we must help people develop compassion for themselves and their own lives. Part of this process involves understanding how the pain in their lives does not reflect their own personal inadequacies, but results from living in a society whose basic human relationships have been deformed by the market-driven ethos of selfishness and materialism.

I have never supported those who used this notion of compassion as an excuse to avoid personal responsibility where it is warranted. Indeed, I have found in my own psychotherapy practice that it is easiest to foster this sense of personal responsibility precisely when the client can be unhooked from exaggerated self-blame. Much of the analysis of the politics of meaning is a guide for helping us to distinguish better between aspects of our lives that we can change individually and aspects of our lives that ought to be changed, but which will probably require the involvement of many others collectively seeking social transformation.

The women's movement provides a striking example of this balance. When women analyzed sexism, their analysis did not lead them to remain passive victims, but to engage in powerful activism whereby they improved their collective situation, and provided a context within which many individual women acted more effectively and powerfully in the world. Once they assumed a compassionate attitude toward themselves—based in part on their understanding that many of the issues that had previously appeared "personal" (for example, problems getting respect from men at work or in relationships) actually were connected to the dynamics of patriarchy and male chauvinism—women were better able to take personal responsibility for changing their collective situation. Some of this personal responsibility was channeled into struggling against the patriarchal dynamic in place in our world. Those skeptics who believe that compassion necessarily leads to disempowerment and a victim mentality have never seriously considered the empowerment that women have gained over the past few decades.

Second, we must move beyond compassion only for those who are obvious victims of the system to include those who are in some respects beneficiaries of that system. This group includes people who benefit from sexism, people who act in oppressive ways, and people who are wounded healers. This expanded compassion does not imply turning the other cheek or tolerating the behavior of oppressors, nor does it imply any letting down of our vigilance against sexist, racist, or homophobic behavior.

I am well aware of the resistance that this analysis raises among groups that have fought so hard to establish their credentials as oppressed. "Wait a moment," many are likely to respond, "we've worked so hard to get people to understand *our* pain, and now, before we've even begun to win that battle, you want us to switch our focus and pay attention to the pain of the oppressors? To show compassion for these oppressors is ridiculous and probably reactionary."

Yet my point is not that we must surrender our understanding of the pain of the oppressed, but that we must make room for an understanding of everyone else's pain. We must do this because it more truly reflects reality. Progressive social change has no stronger weapon than its willingness to tell the truth, even when the truth is complex and will be misrepresented by our opponents in the media.

There also is a pragmatic reason to tell this truth. Unless we are willing to talk about the pain of middle-income Americans, even people who are not in any immediate financial difficulty, we will never be able to deliver anything for the poor or the most oppressed. There are limits to how long people will respond to the pain of others when no one seems to care about their own pain. Unless we can provide the American majority with a deep sense of being recognized, it will never respond to the pain of the most oppressed.

When we look at the world in this expanded way, we allow ourselves to notice the complexities in the lives of those who had previously seemed to be merely privileged. Follow the lives of many surburban-dwelling corporate types as they assemble early in the morning on trains and buses or on crowded freeways, making their way to work, from which they will return exhausted and depleted in the evening, often too late or with too little energy to give quality attention to their children or mates. Follow them as they spend each day learning how to treat others as objects, and internalizing the message of the market: that we must look at one another from the standpoint of what we can get from other people, not from the standpoint of their being embodiments of the spirit of God. We can begin to see that many of these people are really living in corporate labor camps, and that their "privilege" is only that they get higher compensation than the rest of us for a wasted, frustrating, and empty life. Watch them as they become migrant laborers, moving around the country at the behest of corporate sponsors or in search of a better job. Watch them as their marriages fall apart, their children rebel, their neighbors don't know them, and their coworkers seek ways to best them in the economic marketplace. Sure, many corporate workers have more options than do others in our society. But this life of privilege that they live is often empty and stressful to them, as it would be to us. So, instead of buying into the self-promotional line that Western societies put out about ourselves as the best embodiments of humanity's highest truths, we would do better to begin to recognize that even those who seem relatively privileged are often themselves in real pain, and that it behooves us to acknowledge this pain and develop compassion for those who may have little compassion for us.

Finally, and perhaps most importantly, there is a deep spiritual reason for putting compassion at the center of our agenda: human beings fundamentally deserve to be cared for and cherished. Whether we see our sanctity as part of the fundamental spiritual reality that pervades all being, or whether we see ourselves as created in the image of God, human beings reflect that which is most honored and respected in the universe. So when people are not fully embodying their potential to be loving, caring, and spiritually and ethically sensitive beings, the appropriate response is not "politically correct" put-downs, but compassion and healing.

Of course, compassion itself can become a sappy, mushy concept that does not honor but denigrates human beings. If compassion were seen as equivalent to forgiving all offenses or assuming that human beings can never be held morally accountable because they are victims of their circumstances, we would quickly lose respect for people. But this is not how I have used this concept. Rather, I have argued for a disciplined compassion: one that continues to hold people morally responsible, but that simultaneously acknowledges situational limitations and tries to push for transcendence while recognizing the psychological and social constraints. I favor punishing perpetrators of violence, not merely giving them counseling. But I also want to go beyond punishment to changing the social conditions that generate violence in the first place—and for this, we need a compassionate understanding of how people get to be who they are.

In this sense, a politics-of-meaning approach to compassion is "practical spirituality." I have watched spiritual movements call for compassion in a very uncompassionate way, precisely because those movements did not understand the constraints on people's lives. In 1995 I was interviewed on a PBS television special by Peggy Noonan, George Bush's White House speechwriter. I pointed out to her that many conservative Christians who oppose government intervention to help the poor also seem to fail to take the biblically mandated steps of personally caring for the poor (for example, by bringing the homeless to their own homes each night to feed and shelter them). Noonan responded that she agreed that this was what conservatives who reject government intervention ought to do, but that those who do not do so "just aren't good Christians." Her response, in my estimation, was far too easy. The task of the spiritually sensitive person is to find out *why* others are not living ethically sensitive lives, and then to figure out how to change that. This is where practical spirituality comes into the picture.

To be practical spiritually is to be engaged in strategizing about how to change our world, not just lamenting that it has not changed. Practical spirituality means developing concrete strategies to change economic, political, and social institutions and practices that reward selfishness and materialism. And this, of course, is precisely the goal of the politics of meaning.

What I have been asserting in this chapter is that the way to build social healing and transformation is to develop a way of thinking and acting that manifests compassion for those who are living lives that do not appear to share our values or sensibilities. We can vigorously critique their ideas and social practices. But, as I have attempted to show through the example of white men and their homophobia, we must seek to understand how to address the underlying pain and anger in ways that enable people to begin to hear our ideas and strategies for possibly healing this pain.

Hate radio has mobilized legitimate anger in illegitimate ways. But to counter hate radio, we need to understand more fully what is the legitimate basis of people's anger. There is no point in dismissing it with a "politically correct" insight that, in relationship to others, many Americans are privileged. It makes far more sense to understand the ways in which this privilege does not really provide ethical and spiritual satisfaction, and then to speak to this dimension of people's experience—validating their anger and redirecting it away from the traditionally demeaned targets of hate-radio attacks, and toward the ethos of selfishness and materialism that systematically frustrates our meaning-needs and our desire for genuine recognition and love.

6

A Progressive, Pro-Family
Perspective

....

A society that rewards people for their selfishness should not be
surprised that it faces a crisis in its families.

A society that rewards people in the world of work for their
ability to manipulate and control others should not be surprised
that it has fostered narcissistic personality types who are incapable
of sustaining long-term, committed, loving relationships.

A society that makes work unfulfilling and alienating, and promotes a meritocratic ideology that encourages people to blame
themselves for having this kind of work, will produce people who
feel too burned out, depressed, or angry to have much energy for
their families.

If the Right were serious about supporting families, it would
seek to change the world of work in order to make it less stressful,
less alienating, less inducing of self-blame, and more rewarding of
cooperative and caring behavior. I will discuss how to do this in

chapter 7. For the moment, I want to note the perversity of a political Right that presents itself as the pro-family force and puts forward a Contract with the American Family, while supporting the very economic institutions and values that undermine loving relationships.

At the same time, liberals and progressives have been unable to counteract the Right, because their economistic account of family problems has seemed relatively shallow. True, the democratic Left and the labor movement have pointed out that families are under greater stress when they lack sufficient economic support, child-care, or health-care benefits. The Left certainly has been correct to charge that a right-wing pro-family program that does not include these kinds of supports cannot really be serious. Yet we all know that family breakdown is just as likely to afflict people in affluent suburbs as people in the poverty-stricken inner cities and rural areas, so a liberal program focused on delivering economic supports may be necessary but it certainly is not sufficient.

Family is important because it is the only institution in contemporary society that is unabashedly committed to love and caring as its primary function. Families seek to provide a place in which individuals can feel that they receive love, economic and emotional support, and a commitment that their needs will be given high priority without family members first having to "do something" to prove themselves worthy of this caring. When functioning in a healthy way, families provide a safe environment in which people can leave the goal-directedness of daily life and engage in play, humor, and spirituality. A healthy family can provide safety for children, to the extent that parents are genuinely interested in providing them with the experience of honest recognition and emotional connectedness.

These are ambitious tasks, and many families do not do a great job. But there is no other societal institution that takes on all these tasks as its goal. The family is the one institution committed to valuing people because of who they intrinsically are; hence, it is the one institution already and implicitly on the side of the politics of meaning.

Because very few nuclear families successfully fulfill all these tasks, many people are growing disillusioned with the family. After decades of unveiling all the distortions that exist in many families, we need not pretend that most families are healthy or doing their job well. The solution, however, is not to discard the family structure, but to ask ourselves what can be done to strengthen its capacity to generate loving, spiritually and ethically alive human beings.

The religious Right uses the "pro-family" banner to legitimize everything from gun control to anti-abortion legislation. However, most Americans respond to a pro-family perspective not for these reasons, but because they recognize in family an ideal of love and caring that they rarely hear articulated in any other societal institution. Most Americans resent the cultural Left for deriding these ideals as fantasy or for ridiculing their hopes.

What Is a Family?

In the culture wars at the end of the twentieth century, one central focus has been the Right's attempt to sanctify the nuclear family as the only appropriate family unit. But the nuclear family is itself a relatively recent development, an accommodation to and resistance to the vicissitudes of the capitalist market. Through most of human history, people have lived in multigenerational family units that are embedded in tightly knit communities. One could just as well argue that the nuclear family is an "alternative" structure, and hence not *really* a family.

The contemporary nuclear family is an inherently unstable structure. It tries to provide "shelter from the storm," but in so doing, it takes upon itself the impossible task of making up for the breakdown of larger communities by becoming, for many people, the main focus of meaning and purpose. The love of our "significant other," or of our significant other plus children, is supposed to compensate for the alienation and selfishness that we face in the larger world. However, throughout history, nuclear families have never been designed to take on this burden alone; instead, they always have been embedded in larger frameworks of meaning and purpose. Yet today, they are expected to provide "the meaning of life"—and to do so for people shaped by the me-firstism of the competitive market and weighed down by the self-blame, depression, and anger generated by the world of work. Popular culture encourages us to imagine that even though we cannot change the larger world, we each can find the one magical personal relationship that will make everything okay, and will compensate us for all that we lack elsewhere in our lives. Judged against this tremendous expectation, every little issue in our romantic relationships is magnified a thousand fold.

Meanwhile, the market consciousness that permeates our lives teaches us to think of our partners not as beings who deserve to be treated as embodiments of the sacred, but as instruments for fulfilling our needs. And since there is a marketplace of relationships, we think that we can always go on to find another partner who might possibly give us a better deal than the one at hand. No wonder that the nuclear family has been in trouble.

As the divorce rate has surged, people have begun to find other ways to build a stable context for love in their lives. Single-parent families and homosexual couples have sought to build alternative family structures.

It is important to support these alternative family structures in the face of a cruel and unjustifiable attack by the Right that claims these are not real families. Both single-parent and homosexual families can provide a context for long-term, loving commitments and a healthy environment for raising children.

On the other hand, very few heterosexuals who are raising their children as single parents are doing so because, on reflection, they believe that this is a better family structure than a two-parent family. Most are aware of the research that shows that, all other things being equal, children do better in two-parent families.*

But for these single-parent families, all other things are *not* equal, because the real-world choice that many people face is between remaining in a relationship that has been stultifying or emotionally destructive, on the one hand, or being alone and raising one's children as a single parent, on the other. And given *that* "choice," they have opted for single-parenthood—not because it seems to be the most attractive lifestyle, but because they have been unable to find a partner who would be compatible, loving,

* That research is severely limited. It may actually show little more than that children do better when they live in families that provide a basic level of material well-being, since single-parent families, usually headed by women, often face economic uncertainty or deprivation.

non-chauvinistic, emotionally available, and able to help raise these particular children in a committed and loving way. Though television shows may highlight the lives of a few women who have chosen single-parenthood because they are too snobbish or narcissistic to involve themselves with the available men, most single parents of both sexes would be very grateful for an opportunity to share their lives and their families with a partner.

It makes no sense, however, to deny that what single parents actually do build with their children are real families. The love and attention that a single parent can offer may be just as intensely nurturing and esteem-generating, or (to avoid romanticization) just as emotionally devastating and neurosis-generating, as in any family.

Indeed, the nuclear family is not immune to damaging behavior within it. There is evidence that the isolation of nuclear families has sometimes allowed them to conceal the physical and emotional abuse of spouses and children. As parents have become increasingly isolated from traditional extended-family and community supports, the stress in family life has grown, while at the same time, it has become easier for parents to hide from others behavior that would have seemed unacceptable or sinful in previous generations. Although we cannot deny that some of the memories currently being "recovered" in psychotherapy may have been influenced by the suggestions of therapists, or by the overheated emphasis on abuse in some sectors of American culture, nevertheless I am deeply disturbed at the recent flood of stories about child abuse or incest in nuclear families. Right-wingers who have zealously attacked other family structures have been curiously unwilling to confront the pathologies that have been revealed in the nuclear family.

Similarly, the Right has condemned the gay lifestyle as inherently narcissistic and immoral, while ignoring the growth of gay and lesbian families. Increasing numbers of homosexuals are seeking to consecrate long-term, loving relationships through rituals of commitment, and have sought to have these relationships sanctioned as official marriages by our society. Ironically, the very people who condemn these relationships as inherently unstable simultaneously resist providing any societal sanction for marriage, or other external supports that will bolster their long-term character. Many homosexual couples are now interested in raising children, either by adoption or, in the case of lesbians, by actually bearing a child with donated sperm. It is simply false to claim that homosexuals as a group have no interest in sharing the burden of raising the next generation. Gays and lesbians who build long-term, loving, and monogamous relationships are sustaining family life, not undermining it.

There is, to be sure, a subculture of homosexuals who glorify the ecstasy of uncommitted sexual encounters and who, despite the risk of AIDS, continue to insist that any talk of long-term commitments is oppressive to their lifestyle. But we hear this same nonsense among heterosexuals. In the early 1980s, when I joined with Betty Friedan, Benjamin Spock, and others to form a progressive pro-family coalition called Friends of Families, I was denounced by some heterosexual feminists. They charged that even though we intended to support a progressive family structure, the family itself was so intrinsically linked to patriarchy and "heterosexism" that we would unintentionally strengthen the Right and undermine the ethos of pleasure-seeking without commitment—which they saw as fundamental to any campaign for liberation.

Fourteen years later, most homosexuals and feminists support the idea of a progressive pro-family politics. Many now recognize that there is real danger in confusing an enthusiasm for sexual pleasure with enthusiasm for sexuality that is divorced from loving and nurturing relationships.

The general assumption about parenting in American culture is that it is an individual decision, and thus should be an individual responsibility. But this notion ignores the fact that we all have a communal interest in raising emotionally and physically healthy children who can inherit and transmit the individual legacies and collective accomplishments of the human race. Since everyone benefits from this process, everyone has some responsibility to share in the relevant burdens.

Overcoming Patriarchy as Family Support:
A Response to Communitarianism

Patriarchal families in which the power and wisdom of the father dared not be questioned, and in which women were expected to consistently yield to the desires and will of their husbands, may have been efficient economic entities at one point in history, but they were not likely to produce anything like what we mean by love. Real love requires the kind of mutual recognition that can only take place between people who see each other as equally valuable and equally free. Patriarchy assumed a fundamental inequality that tended to undermine our ability to see one another as created in the image of God, or, in secular terms, as valuable for what we are rather than as a means to someone else's end. In a different age, patriarchy may have delivered social stability, but probably never delivered what we think of today as loving relationships.

One of liberalism's achievements was that it delivered a death-blow to authoritative forms of state coercion, so that there were few legally sanctioned constraints, for example, on women leaving oppressive families. Though fears of violence and economic inequalities still keep some women chained to oppressive families, society has moved toward increased acceptance of divorce and toward economic and physical protection for women seeking to separate from emotionally and physically destructive situations. Those men who have tried to hold on to patriarchal patterns often undermine their family lives. By encouraging women to leave oppressive relationships, feminism, to its credit, has created an incentive for those men who wish to remain in their marriages to become more sensitive to and respectful of women and their needs. This is a politics-of-meaning move: to reward loving and caring behavior.

In this regard, a progressive politics of meaning diverges sharply from the version of communitarianism proposed by Amitai Etzioni, despite many other areas in which we are in fundamental agreement. Etzioni correctly notes that intact two-parent families are preferable to divorce. He cites statistics indicating that children of divorce often lose contact with their fathers (in the period soon after divorce, one-sixth of all children see their fathers at least once a week; after ten years, nearly two-thirds have no contact at all). Additionally, the sometimes bewildering array of their parents' new partners may generate in children a decreasing sense of security and, when these relationships do not work, an increase in self-blame. Etzioni acknowledges that "rotten marriages can cause as much harm as (or even more harm) than divorce," yet the thrust of his discussion in *The Spirit of Community* seems to put greater emphasis on his observation that, "personally, I do not know of a single instance in which the children were not harmed by divorce."

Etzioni suggests a number of methods for strengthening families, such as increased couples counseling, the ritual of a family meal, and even a waiting period after divorce before remarrying. He quite reasonably suggests that the Social Security numbers of parents should be written on a child's birth certificate, so that a parent reneging on child support can be traced and child support withheld from paychecks by the employer.

But Etzioni goes on to conclude that "if we wish to communicate that we care more about sustaining families than we did in the heyday of permissiveness, alternative lifestyle experimentation, and anti-family ideology, we should make divorce less easy."

Etzioni acknowledges that changes in the heart, not the laws, will build stronger families. "People need to enter marriage more responsibly and be more committed to making it work," he insists. I agree, but he misses the central point: the usual reason why relationships fail is because there is too little love and mutual recognition, not because there is too little responsibility.

All too often, people have internalized the ethos of the marketplace, and view the other person primarily in terms of what one can get out of the exchange. In the ethos of the marketplace, every commitment is tentative, based on assessment of what is in one's own best short-term interest. If a better deal comes along, in this way of thinking, one naturally moves on.

To counter the marketplace consciousness, we need to foster a different way of being in the world, a way that emphasizes the primacy of love and mutual recognition, that encourages us to see other people as fundamentally deserving of respect and caring, and that repudiates instrumental ways of viewing the world and one another. Loving another person involves an ability to transcend ourselves and to see the other as a wonder, a miracle embodied, a manifestation of God's spirit, a being who moves us to care and who automatically evokes in us a concern for his or her well-being. This is a whole new way of seeing, often closely aligned to the insights of spiritual and religious traditions that validate joyful embracing of the other and invoke notions of loving our neighbor, as well as the stranger. It is a far cry from the repressive overtones of Etzioni's approach to communitarianism.

Etzioni's emphasis on responsibility can too quickly be assimilated into a new conservative discourse, which attempts to counter the destructive impact of the marketplace by placing all responsibility for society's problems on the individual. Worse, his emphasis misses the psychological dimension of human relationships. People remain committed to one another when they feel mutually recognized and cared for, and no amount of moralistic injunctions to act responsibly can substitute for this. Our task is to foster a society that makes love and caring more available, rather than try to build a society in which partners will stay together despite the fact that their fundamental needs for recognition and love are not met.

On the other hand, Etzioni is perfectly right to say that we need to create a climate of opinion in which there is a "tilt" toward people staying together rather than breaking up relationships when they encounter difficulties. Societal support for people leaving situations in which they feel oppressed is so strong that, at least in some upper-middle-class and therapeutic circles, it may now exceed support for staying together and working things through. But family stability will *not* be achieved through the use of legislation, nor through economic and political coercion.

What would make family stability more likely is to build a society that encourages us to see one another as beings created in the image of God and fundamentally deserving of love and caring. If we were no longer learning to see others primarily in terms of what we could get from them, if market consciousness no longer governed our approach to the world, we would be far less likely to want to bolt from a relationship when problems arose. A meaning-oriented society would not have the kinds of legal constraints supported by Etzioni, but it would promote an ethos of commitment that encouraged people to put energy into their relationships. If people were surrounded by others whose first instinct was to try to make relationships work, in a society that provided easily accessible family counseling and family support networks, divorce would decline— not out of coercion but out of choice.

The work of keeping couples together should be shared by the relevant community: the people who joined together to sanctify the marriage, and the friends and family members who have subsequently become involved with the couple. I do not mean that this community should make people feel bad for considering the possibility of leaving a relationship. But members of the concerned community can help problem-solve and share their own experiences from having faced similar problems. More concretely, they can provide child-care support for couples who have not had enough time by themselves, away from their children. Unfortunately, sometimes the people we wish would function as a supportive community do not. In those instances, we may need to create family support networks.

Family Support Networks

Every community should teach family communications and parenting skills and provide tangible support, such as exchanging child care or helping with an aging parent who demands constant attention. Other family support activities could include organizing weekly communal meals or picnics and sharing skills (I can repair your car, you can help me edit my novel, and we both can help Neighbor X teach his kids how to play baseball or how to master algebra).

These activities could be organized through an informal family support network, which might meet twice a month and provide a place for people to exchange information and techniques for dealing with problems they are facing in their families. Each meeting might devote some time to this kind of "sharing" and problem-solving, some time to teaching specific communications or parenting skills, and the rest of the time to organizing an exchange of skills and concrete family assistance, such as child care.

I have found that these family support networks work best when led by someone who has particular expertise in family support skills. But I do not want to see the government run these networks. There are good reasons to worry that a government-controlled program of this sort might become politicized, allowing one group or another to impose its own agenda. It may be better, then, to seek governmental support only for the training of local family support experts. Each community could then form its own consortium of family therapists, teachers, and religious leaders whose task it would be to develop and supervise these networks.

The Tyranny of Couples

Peter Gabel has argued that one of the dangers of current attempts to support the family is that they may inadvertently play into a destructive dynamic, which he labels "the tyranny of couples." Some couples are so worried about preserving the relationship that they do so by deadening themselves emotionally and playing to what they know their partner expects. Of course, there is nothing wrong with being in touch with another person's desires, and sometimes making sacrifices or subordinating our own will in order to please others. But when this becomes a way of life, the result is emotional zombies. By presenting themselves to each other as part of "the good couple," people sometimes undermine the vitality and honesty that are the prerequisites of loving connection.

In general, we should insist that being pro-family does not mean covering up the problems in family life. Most people have experienced extreme disappointment and frustration in family life. The pain of this disappointment is all the more pressing, precisely because families touch upon our highest hopes for genuine recognition and honest loving. These disappointments stick in people's minds, making them skeptical about loving relationships, and hence skeptical about the possibility of a society based on love and caring. All too frequently, families exercise emotional coercion, dishonesty, and manipulation in the name of love and caring. This sends the victims running in horror, away from any politics that seems to suggest that the world could be based on these ideals.

My goal is not to get people to pretend that their families really did feel good, nor to encourage people to appreciate all the good things that were really there and to play down what was missing. Rather, in supporting families, I start with a focus on what *was* missing, and why the promise of families has not been achieved. From this standpoint, it is possible to imagine what kinds of social transformations would be necessary in order for families to really function and fulfill their promise. The last thing we need is a renewed family phoniness encouraged by a seemingly pro-family support network.

Pain and Disappointment in Family Life:
A Major Source of Cynicism about Love

To be truly pro-family means to recognize the pain and frustration that so many people experience in family life, and to get those secrets out of the closet and into the public domain. People can then learn from one another's experience, stop blaming themselves inordinately for those problems, and begin to help one another work them through. Far from idealizing family life, with its inevitable consequence of increasing self-blame, this approach acknowledges that most people have had troubling and sometimes contradictory experiences in family life. Sometimes they have achieved a closeness and sense of caring that they have never found elsewhere; sometimes they have felt deeply frustrated, disappointed, misrecognized, or manipulated.

It is all too easy to transfer the ambivalence we feel about our own family experiences to an ambivalence about any future attempt to construct more caring relationships in our society as a whole. When our childhoods and family experiences have promised but failed to provide us with the caring we wanted, resistance to such a project is natural. Ironically, many of those who most loudly proclaim the ideal of family life in the public arena are people who did not get what they needed in their families. They feel such personal shame at having failed to evince the love and caring that they needed from their parents that they try to cover their shame by loudly proclaiming how wonderful the experience really was or is.

Overcoming this shame and self-blame is one goal of a meaning-oriented family support program. Many children blame themselves when they do not receive the recognition and support that they need from their parents. They imagine that their parents see "the deep truth" about them, namely that they are not really lovable human beings. For such people, the goal of creating a society based on loving and caring actually evokes tremendous anxiety, because it brings to mind this distorted self-image in which they see themselves as people who have been unable to elicit the deep loving they sought as children, and hence as people who are unlikely to benefit from a more loving society. True, they may have worked out some kind of adult relationship, built a family, and been told by others that they are loved or lovable. But it is not uncommon for people to hold on to this deeper sense of self as unworthy of love, and then to build a series of relationships around themselves based on this diminished sense of worth.

These dynamics may help explain why some people cling desperately to a relationship that provides them with the barest amount of love or recognition. They are convinced that they deserve nothing deeper. Therapists often encounter this particular arrangement when one partner in the relationship, wanting something deeper and more emotionally alive in the marriage, brings the other into couples counseling. Often the therapist faces massive resistance from the other partner precisely because that partner does not believe that she or he could possibly elicit a deeper love. Becoming more "real" or alive in the current relationship threatens to put this person back in touch with her or his own unresolved childhood pains, and may also "expose" this person to others as being unlovable.

No wonder, then, that such people are often profoundly committed to resisting any notion that the world could be fundamentally changed in a more hopeful and loving direction. They develop intense cynicism about any kind of healing and transformation, which manifests itself in a variety of ways. They may dismiss psychotherapy (although sometimes only those forms of therapy that bring one back in touch with childhood memories), or they may dismiss all spirituality (or anything that connects one to a memory of a higher self), because they had to repress the memory of their own highest self in order to fit into the family system that they encountered as a child. They may dismiss any possibility that our world could be shaped to embody greater loving and caring.

Among the short-term goals of a politics of meaning is to develop family support networks, which help people think through these issues, reunderstand themselves and their own worth, and reject negative pictures of themselves developed in childhood. If the network's organizers can accomplish this, they will be able to help the participants avoid passing on these same dynamics to the next generation.

In the past few decades, hundreds of family support networks have been created in communities across the United States. While many of these networks have been very successful, organizers also report that people display a great deal of resistance to joining such networks. Consciously focusing on family problems sometimes seems scary, particularly to people who retain deep self-blame about their own "failure" as children to elicit love from their own parents. Fearful that anything even vaguely psychological might force them to get back in touch with these painful feelings, many people stay away.

To attract more participants to family support networks, then, one must design them in ways that affirm people's strengths as well as open people to their pain. People have to know that they are not identifying themselves as "sick" or "in trouble" if they elect to participate in a family support network. Moreover, parents who join these networks need to feel that the real sacrifices they have made for others in their family are acknowledged and appreciated. But they also need to feel that it is appropriate to acknowledge what was not or is not working in their own family—without having thereby proclaimed to the world that they personally are failures.

I helped people gain these insights in one context during my work at the Institute for Labor and Mental Health. We sponsored an event called Family Day, a day for public celebration of the good and hard work that people already were doing to keep their families together, plus an analysis of the problems that "we all face in family life." We staged family sports, swimming, a rock concert, a Latino music concert, folksinging, and movies. But Family Day went beyond celebrating the wonderful, to pay much attention to family problems. We ran over twenty topical workshops, such as "Workplace Stress and Family Stress," "Problems Facing Single-Parent Families," "New Directions in Homosexual Families," "Dealing with Toddlers," "Parenting Skills," "The African-American Family," "Shiftwork and Family Life," and "Dealing with the Stress of Aging Parents." We also held a series of workshops for children on how to deal with the issues they faced in family life.

Knowing that this kind of event would be less groundbreaking if concentrated only among upper-middle-class professionals, we systematically avoided the yuppie world and advertised in working-class communities, aided in part by churches and the school system. Over four thousand people showed up, most of whom had never had an opportunity to discuss personal problems concerning their family in a safe, affirming environment.

In public-service announcements on television, on radio and on the backs of buses, we advertised that "everyone faces problems in family life." This statement made it possible for people to feel that they were not "sick" if they participated in a discussion of issues which heretofore had been the private, secret parts of their family life. Many of these people joined ongoing family support networks that we created—so many, in fact, that we quickly found ourselves overwhelmed with the numbers of middle-income parents who wanted the opportunity to problem-solve and learn family support techniques.

I am well aware of the tendency in some circles toward superficial self-disclosure as a defense against real involvement or real confrontation with one's problems. But the people who came to our Family Day events were very much from what used to be called "middle America": people who were not part of a therapeutic culture or an alternative consciousness. They were, in fact, the very people who, in the popular conception, would have been least open to participating in anything that had the vaguest connection to countercultural, psychological, or spiritual activity. Yet, over the course of several years, Family Days and other events that we created to address occupational stress revealed a widespread hunger for connection and for opportunities to share problem-solving.

Singles

There are many people in our society who are single and do not want to be. Yet in contemporary Western societies, acknowledging this need is often filled with shame. The meritocratic framework that predominates in the competitive market shapes how we think about our private lives as well. Accordingly, many reluctant singles believe that they must be inadequate in some way that has caused them not to attract the appropriate person. This, to be sure, often is nonsense, but in our current society it feels like common sense.

It often is nonsense because most people have only very limited opportunities to encounter others in daily life who might be appropriate partners. One consequence of the breakdown of communities is that many people today find themselves with few contexts in which they can meet people who share their values. Although this is true for couples as well, and is one reason why many people find themselves with fewer friends who share their values than they might have in earlier times, it is especially true for singles.

Throughout most of human history, single people were introduced to one another by a community that concerned itself with arranging marriages. It is only in about the past one hundred years that a marketplace in relationships has emerged in which each person must fend for himself or herself. Moreover, given society's meritocratic assumptions, single people often feel embarrassed to acknowledge that they are looking for someone. They feel that just being single already makes them less desirable, so they engage in various strategies to make it clear that they are not "too" interested or desperate. Furthermore, many acquaintances think it would be intrusive or embarrassing for the single person if someone were to attempt to connect him or her with an appropriate partner.

A caring society would dispense with all this pretense. It would challenge the notion that the healthy individual is the person who knows how to stand alone without needing others, and instead insist that healthy people know and can acknowledge their need to be in loving relationship with others. It would consciously seek to create safe spaces for singles who want to meet other singles in alternative environments to the meat markets that contemporary singles events so often become.

We *do not* want to return to the period of arranged marriages, with all its coercive elements. But a caring community could actively take responsibility for introducing singles to one another. The only way this would work, however, is if it were accompanied by a systematic and sustained assault on the stigmatization of being single and not wanting to be. Needless to say, we do not want government intruding in this or in most other areas of family life. It would be the community's responsibility to, for example, organize coed functions where singles could be introduced in an unpressured environment.

Though a politics of meaning is pro-family, it ought not push singles into relationships by making them feel inadequate if they are not currently in a long-term, committed, loving relationship. In a society based on love and caring, it is quite likely that some people will choose to remain single, and society should support that choice as well. Otherwise, unstable families will result, because people have entered them under societal pressure, rather than out of a genuine desire to build a long-term, committed relationship with a specific person. For this reason, it is also important to build societal institutions that make it safe and acceptable for people to remain single.

Our society already has begun to recognize the need to provide support for women who are escaping emotionally or physically abusive relationships, including homes that will support such women during the immediate transition out of these kinds of families. But a much fuller network of societal supports for singles is necessary.

Ultimately, the most important support that a society can give to both men and women is to change how people understand relationships. Loving relationships would be greatly strengthened when rooted in a joint commitment to serve some larger purpose besides immediate self-gratification. Couples that saw themselves as coming together because of a shared vision of the good—a shared commitment to healing and repairing the world—would find that their relationships had a resiliency that is often lacking in the modern world. The community should not dictate the range of options for that particular shared vision, nor how the couple would incorporate that vision into their daily life together. But the community should encourage people to find some such vision, and it should help couples understand that each specific relationship takes on an aspect of holiness to the degree that it connects to a higher ethical or spiritual purpose.

Respect for Children

It is not because they have "rights" that children ought to be respected. Children embody the spirit of God, and one major task for parents and teachers is to overcome the many obstacles that make it difficult for us to focus enough attention on our children to be able to clearly see and respond to that spirit within them.

One way to attend to that holiness in children is to use our imagination and creativity to help introduce them to the accumulated ethical, spiritual, and ecological wisdom of our community. The language of rights can become particularly inappropriate in this context if it is used to question whether parents ought to inculcate children with their own values, or sometimes override children's own choices.

It is fatuous to assume that children automatically know what is best for them, particularly in a world in which television and the mass media hold such sway in shaping children's desires. The notion that children are in a higher place and, if left to themselves, would automatically make healthy choices, may contain a grain of truth. But it has increasingly little application in the modern world, in which children have been bombarded by media, advertising, and subtle forms of indoctrination since the earliest years of their lives.

In recent years, a spate of movies and television shows have reversed our old "parents-know-best" fantasies and fostered the notion of a world in which children are always right. This is just the latest pandering by the mass media to the children's market, the fastest-growing sector of the commercial marketplace. Parents must guard against this targeting of children, who are the least able to defend themselves against manipulation with the lessons of experience.

The parents' job, then, is not merely to allow, but also to instruct and to shape. This is a very difficult task, given the commitment of powerful interests that use the most sophisticated media techniques to influence children's desires, in order to create the kind of consumers that the marketplace needs them to be. The absence of public funding for child care, and of adequate funding for noncommercial television, puts most families at the mercy of commercial television as the child-care technology of last (or often first) resort.

Parental responsibility brings with it the obligation to respect children, because they share the same sanctity and holiness that commits us to fundamental caring for every human being. There is also a prudent reason for respecting children: because love cannot be coerced, and children who grow up being treated respectfully are most likely to know how to treat others respectfully. Children also will usually respond to the love they received in their early years by projecting love toward others, including their aging parents. Conversely, children who have not been respected are most likely to be disrespectful to others as adults, and hence are most likely to make it difficult to create the community of loving connections and caring that each of us needs if our lives are to work. So each of us has a stake in ensuring that we and others treat children respectfully. The more we listen to our children, consider their ideas seriously, and show them that their feelings are important to us and that their anger at us is allowable and worthy of our attention and concern, the more our children will feel that they are getting some of the recognition and respect that they need. Often, respect means allowing children the freedom to make their own choices, even though these may be choices with which we disagree or which are inconvenient for us.

Respect does not mean avoiding all forms of discipline. Self-discipline and learning to take responsibility are important gifts that parents must give their children. But, too often, parents use these words as a cover for passing on to children the same arbitrariness, emotional cruelty, and even violence that they themselves experienced as children.

All children deserve protection from the unnecessary infliction of pain. How much pain is unnecessary? These judgments are always made relative to a given historical and psychological context. We certainly do not want the state to try to raise children. The state ought to provide us with courses in school, support for community-controlled family support networks, and free access to family therapy, but we should not let the state make family decisions for us. Yet this will guarantee that we parents will unconsciously inflict at least some of our neuroses on our children. Part of the goal of family support networks is to help provide mechanisms that offset the worst aspects of this dynamic by giving all of us a way to learn and improve our parental skills. Those parents who raise caring children merit our special commendation, and we can learn from them.

Because children are our future neighbors, how they are treated is everyone's business. If they are emotionally or physically brutalized, or if the world they are introduced to is devoid of ethical or spiritual sensitivity, we all are likely to suffer the consequences—whether in random acts of violence or in ethically insensitive voting behavior. So our vital task is to do what we can to foster loving environments for children, without interfering in family life in ways that threaten to become communally totalitarian.

Senior Citizens

Senior citizens deserve more than economic security and protection from physical abuse and mental pain. They deserve our respect and honor for their years of contributions to the rest of us.

At the same time, the younger population deserves the opportunity to learn from seniors, and to benefit from their life experience and wisdom.

The issue of aging, then, is not simply an issue of how to respect the rights of senior citizens, but also how to create a society that honors rather than discards them.

Senior citizens' advocacy groups have tended to focus on securing certain economic and health-care benefits. It is truly outrageous that those who have worked all their lives and helped build the collective wealth of society should, at the end of their lives, face economic insecurity—particularly with respect to adequate health care and housing. No one should face these problems, but to the extent that society needs to make judgments about where to begin rectifying inequalities, it should start by taking care of the aging.

Liberal programs attempt to address the material needs of the aging, but rarely focus on the deprivation of meaning. Those older Americans whose retirement frees them from daily involvement in the struggle for economic survival often become deeply depressed, because of the loss of social ties that were provided by the world of work. Moreover, without the distraction of work, it is harder for seniors to avoid the feelings of isolation, loneliness, and alienation that the rest of us face but do not have as much time to notice.

Yet, precisely because they do have to face questions about the meaning of their lives, seniors are well situated to play a leadership role in creating a movement for a politics of meaning. The same dynamics that today lead some elderly people into depression, or into frenetic attempts to repress awareness of their pain, could be channeled into activity aimed at rebuilding our world in a more loving, caring, and ethically sensitive way. One area ripe for change is the way our society deals with the aging.

The major obstacle is that the competitive market has a strong commitment to glamorizing the new and the young, because it must endlessly create new needs in us to buy new products. The old, on the other hand, are portrayed as used up, not likely to produce good things, and a waste of our energies. Given the market's powerful influence in shaping the common attitudes of society, our political and social institutions tend to reflect this invalidation of anything that smacks of being old.

A commitment to seniors must challenge this ethos of the marketplace that endlessly celebrates the new and requires us to discard the old. This attitude leads to behaviors that are ecologically destructive and morally illegitimate, and ultimately produces a society that devalues elders.

Even those societal institutions and service providers who are dedicated to serving seniors have unnecessarily restricted their vision. Older Americans are frequently portrayed as a disadvantaged group, rather than as human beings still engaged in growth and the accumulation of wisdom, capable of creating beauty and sharing love. Betty Friedan's *The Fountain of Age* details the many ways in which even the most sophisticated liberals tend to squeeze aging into the category of "misfortune." This definition often permeates the consciousness of seniors themselves, causing them to regard the aging process as a curse, and blinding them to the new strengths and opportunities that may be available. Therefore, part of a politics-of-meaning program begins by encouraging elders to reclaim those strengths and sources of inner dignity.

Zalman Schachter's *From Aging to Saging* is one of the most insightful of recent books that outline important steps that we can take as a community to draw on the wisdom and talents of our elders. Every family, community, state, and nation needs a council of elders. The elders could gather regularly to celebrate, pray, exercise, talk, care for one another, and deliberate about the problems facing the family, community, and larger entities. The entire community would be greatly enriched if the media covered the deliberations in local, regional and national councils of elders—these could provide a useful countervoice to the drivel that sometimes takes place in official legislative councils.

Our communities would benefit from a seniors corps that facilitated the involvement of elders in the central service institutions of society. As assistants and advisors to teachers, child-care providers, nonprofit agencies, government offices, health-care facilities, and in the private sector, elders often possess the wisdom, experience, and know-how that their juniors lack. Besides government facilities, a huge number of nonprofit organizations could greatly benefit from the participation of elders, and numerous elders would enjoy sharing their skills if they knew they were needed. What we do not have today is any agency seriously devoted to making these connections in a way that is sensitive to the needs of seniors.

Families and communities need to structure ways to learn from the experience of elders. Though this ought to be part of the daily experience of our lives, it might be facilitated by an annual week-long celebration, nationally focused on learning from elders.

There are programs for elders in nursing homes, churches, and community centers, but all too often these only respond to a narrow set of needs, such as food, exercise, and entertainment. They fail to recognize that seniors have so much to contribute, both in transmitting the wisdom of the past and in leading the struggle for a more meaningful future. Teams of well-intentioned social workers and volunteers try to develop programming to "get the seniors involved," and are likely to dismiss the more expansive visions offered here as unrealistic because they know how hard it can be even to get seniors to come to the local senior center.

Here we note the same circular thinking that so cripples liberal do-goodism throughout our society. Instead of tapping people's most visionary spirits, it assumes that they are very reluctant to be involved in social change and so limits it scope to the most minimal baby steps. But many people are certain that those baby steps will lead nowhere, and since they see no one involved in anything more significant, they despair and sink more deeply into depression.

In discussing seniors, it is a mistake to underplay the impact that deteriorating bodily functions may have on people's self-esteem or capacity to be involved in larger communities. The danger of the "positive thinking" approach espoused by Betty Friedan is that it may unwittingly contribute to self-blame when some seniors find themselves physically unable to do all that the expanded conception of seniors says they can do. A self-fulfillment model of aging can be misused by conservatives to justify the dismantling of economic benefits and protective measures that seniors have fought for over the course of many decades.

Seniors do get sick and do die. But the way that this is experienced could be greatly changed if we lived in a society based on caring and not primarily on selfishness. The bitterness that many elderly people experience is often rooted in the feeling of being abandoned by everyone else—a perception that often is right. This abandonment is the final step in a process that has been going on all through their lives, lived in a society that has systematically undermined community ties. Without a framework for understanding their possible alternatives, the elderly despair.

Yet no politics of meaning can deny the reality of sickness, pain, and infirmity. It angers me to hear some New Agers talk as though Alzheimer's or other degenerative diseases could be overcome by people who had lived right or had the right attitude. A meaning-oriented society can help create a world in which we will have more love and caring, but it cannot eliminate the reality of pain, suffering, and death. Fortunately, how that pain and death is faced can be altered by a politics of meaning. In the first thirty years of the twenty-first century we will see a new crop of seniors, the baby boomers and veterans of the 1960s, who could bring a more hopeful and less cynical attitude toward aging.

Retirement centers, senior centers, and even nursing homes could be reshaped, or new ones could be built that would reflect our own highest values, and would seek to promote the kind of mutual recognition and solidarity that have so often been missing throughout the rest of our lives. They could also embody a spiritual sensitivity and honesty about death that would reject the technocratic focus on aging that usually results in a systematic denial of death, even in institutions where death and the fear of death are a constant presence (such as hospitals and nursing homes). It certainly is not too early for baby boomers to begin to plan the kind of meaning-oriented retirement centers that they wish to have. Otherwise, they will be forced to choose among options that culturally and politically express the worst of American consumerism.

Those struggles should not wait for a next generation of seniors. Useful legislation has already been through Congress, giving nursing-home residents a right to privacy, a right to participate in the planning of their own care, a right to know what medications they are being given and to refuse to take them, and a right not to be put into physical restraints solely for the convenience of the nursing-home staff. Some of these rights are now being challenged by Republicans who are set on dismantling government regulations, so the fight may have to be fought again.

We should also ensure that senior centers and nursing homes are democratically run by an elected council of elders. Some nursing homes have already implemented programs that encourage the elders to sing together; write poetry, plays, and letters to newspapers and local elected officials; and act in ways that restore the dignity that sickness or infirmity may have begun to erode. Another dignity-restoring mechanism would be to encourage residents of nursing homes to hold memorial services for residents who have passed away. By acknowledging death, and the fact that all residents are facing it, it will become easier to sanctify life.

The Christian Coalition's Contract with the American Family

In May 1995, Ralph Reed, the executive director of Pat Robertson's Christian Coalition, unveiled its Contract with the American Family, a surprisingly visionless document that failed to articulate any coherent theory of why American families are in trouble. The family crisis is too important to be used merely as a Trojan horse to

push through Congress a potpourri of unrelated conservative political programs, yet that seems to be the immoral game now being
played by elements of the religious Right.

Still, the Right sometimes makes important points about the
family crisis in America when it identifies the roots of this crisis
in an excess of selfishness. As I have already acknowledged in this
book, liberals sometimes give excessive focus to individual rights in
ways that sometimes (not always) accustom them to putting their
own individual needs above the needs of any community or any
family to which they belong. This inability to commit to a "we,"
argue some right-wing theorists, forms the rotten core of liberal culture, contributing to the weakening of relationships in general, and
to families in particular.

I think the Right has a point here. American culture does suffer
from an excessive individualism, a narcissistic focus on one's own
needs and desires without regard to the needs and desires of others.
But it is ridiculous to blame this selfishness on liberalism, which is
itself only a reflection, rather than a cause, of the dominant ethos of
the capitalist market which the Right so vociferously champions.

If we want to strengthen families, the way to do so is to
strengthen our commitment to the values of love and caring, and to
give these values priority over individualism and selfishness. That,
of course, is precisely what a politics of meaning does, and what the
Christian Coalition's Contract with the American Family fails to
do. In fact, the Christian Coalition's Contract has almost nothing to
do with challenging the ethos of selfishness and materialism. It is a
classic instance of my general claim that the Right merely invokes
the issue of family rather than actually worrying about how to
strengthen our capacity to nourish and sustain loving and caring
relationships.

Let's look at the Contract with the American Family in some detail to understand what I mean.

THE RIGHT'S CONTRACT

If we look at the details of the Christian Coalition's Contract, its
failure to live up to the Right's own best ideals becomes clear.

1. *A constitutional amendment to allow people to celebrate their religion in public spaces.*

This proposal is irrelevant to challenging the ethos of selfishness and materialism and will do little to strengthen families. Moreover, the kind of religion that would likely result from moves such as a moment of silence in schools, the reintroduction of Christmas, and other religious behavior into public space—like the kind of religiosity that flourished there before Supreme Court decisions barred it—would be a curiously lifeless form of public religion whose consequences would be to further the secularization process within religious forms. The fiery intensity of religious experience, and the compassionate connection among human beings that is one of the best aspects of many religious communities, would almost certainly be lost in most of these public-square religious observances. Far from making our society more religious, these observances are a disservice to God and undermine authentic spiritual life, replacing it with cheapened public showmanship.

2. *Transfer of funding of the federal Department of Education to families and local school boards.*

The Christian Coalition endorses a U.S. Department of Education report that parental involvement in children's education results in higher student performance. But it then blames the lack of involvement on bureaucracies and administrative costs and federal restrictions. This claim is ludicrous on its face. Underlying the Right's concern is their recognition that federal standards have encouraged the development of curricula that include the experience of women, blacks, and other minorities, as well as the placing of the U.S. experience in the context of world history. Yet understanding that America has been racist or sexist does little to undermine families.

3. *Legislation to enhance parents' choice of schools.*

There is much to be said for some form of school choice, if and only if it were class-weighted in ways that gave working people and the poor the same economic power to get high-quality schools that is now available to upper-middle-income people. If, for example, there was a sliding scale based on disposable income after the basic food, shelter, and clothing needs had been met, so that poor people might be given vouchers ten or fifteen times that of upper-middle-income people, we might have a fair system. But none of this would help alleviate the ethos of selfishness. The introduction of a marketplace in educational opportunities, while desirable for other reasons, would probably further erode the kinds of social solidarity that contribute to family support.

4. *Enactment of a Parental Rights Act and defeat of the U.N. Convention on the Rights of the Child.*

This is the Right's attempt to protect the sanctity of individual family life from those who would scrutinize it with "external" standards, such as concern about physical or sexual abuse. Our society has only recently begun to consider how widespread this abuse is. Rather than challenge the distortions in daily life that create a society with so many physical or sexual abusers, the Right effectively protects the abusers behind the screen of family privacy. From my standpoint, this particular proposal represents the real threat to the needs of families and allies it with the sickest and morally most obnoxious realities of American society.

5. *Family-Friendly Tax Relief.*

Under this rubric, the Christian Coalition calls for a series of measures that pro-family progressives also support: tax relief for families with children, eliminating the marriage penalty, and allowing homemakers to contribute up to $2,000 annually toward an IRA, thereby providing equitable treatment of spouses who work at home.

6. *Freeing states to limit funds for abortions.*

While I support abortion rights, I understand some of the legitimate concerns raised by the Catholic Church and other anti-abortion activists (though I am also aware of the hypocrisy of many who care about life only until the fetus is born, then manage to lose concern as the child moves into poverty induced by current class-oriented economic and social arrangements).

The Right makes an important point when it questions the way liberals have defended abortion by placing the decision entirely in the realm of "individual choice," as though individual choices had no consequences for the rest of the society and as though we were accountable to no one but ourselves and our own desires. While I oppose the Right's attempt to legislate these issues, I do believe that liberals have too quickly reverted to a highly individualistic framework in defending abortion rights.

Seeing ourselves as isolated monads who possess rights and enter into relationships with others through voluntary contracts— the exact model suggested by the theorists of capitalism—has contributed to the breakdown of loving relationships. So while I oppose the Right's paradoxical attempt to bring the state into personal life, and believe that reproductive choice needs to be protected (particularly from those who would coerce or bomb abortion clinics out of existence, or penalize doctors who perform abortions), I also think that the liberal world should be crusading for voluntary restraints on abortion, creating an ethos which goes beyond "It's nobody's business but the woman involved," and which sees abortion as a kind of tragedy that may be appropriate in some circumstances but should be dealt with as a tragedy rather than as business as usual. While rejecting the Right's attempt to impose state control, we also ought to seek to create an ethos in our society that mourns the too-frequent need for abortion, and see this as a reason to speed societal changes that would make voluntary abortions less necessary.

Most women are already deeply conflicted and in much psychic pain when they undergo voluntary abortions. The appropriate attitude is not to make them feel guiltier. However, it would be appropriate for the rest of us to mourn each time such an abortion is performed, and to see it as a further impetus to work for changing a society that has made this painful choice seem the most plausible one to the woman involved. This attitude of collective penance is very different from the judgmental and recriminatory attitude of the religious Right, but also from the laissez-faire attitude of many liberals.

7. Enactment of legislation to enhance contributions to private charities as a first step toward transforming the bureaucratic welfare state into a system of private and faith-based compassion.

This is a valuable direction. Every citizen should be allowed to donate $200 of his or her federal tax obligation to any nonprofit organization with a total income of less than $20 million. (This prevents these donations from being totally manipulated by the wealthiest institutions, which can buy television time to convince people to donate to them while making smaller, community-based institutions invisible.) But while this is a good idea, it will do little to undermine the larger ethos of selfishness or to support family life.

8. *Restricting pornography.*

A good idea, though it should not be accomplished by big-government legislation, but rather by market pressures. Nevertheless, even if we had no pornography, family life would still be in deep trouble.

9. *Privatizing the arts, the National Endowment for the Humanities, the Corporation for Public Broadcasting, and the Legal Services Corporation.*

This proposal has absolutely nothing to do with families, and is opportunistically tacked on to the Contract.

10. *Crime Victim Restitution.*

Funds given to states to build prisons should encourage work, study, and drug-testing requirements for prisoners in state correctional facilities, as well as requiring restitution to victims subsequent to release. Again, this proposal has nothing to do with the problems facing families, though I support some of these notions.

In short, those elements of the Christian Coalition's program that *do* make sense do little to help families or to combat the ethos of selfishness.

A Meaning-Oriented Contract with American Families

Now let's consider a meaning-oriented approach. Government would not be the means for implementing the contract, for reasons

I discuss in the following chapter. Instead, a politics of meaning aims to institutionalize these changes in a more direct way through democratic mechanisms that we will establish throughout our society. With this arrangement in mind, here is a meaning-oriented Contract with American Families:

1. We will reduce the total selfishness and materialism in society by popularizing a new bottom line that evaluates the productivity of institutions by the degree to which they develop human beings who are capable of sustaining loving and caring relationships, and capable of ethical, spiritual, and ecological awareness and action.

2. Harnessing the technological advances of the Computer Age, we will reduce the work week to thirty hours, redistributing work so that everyone is employed, and thus allow working people to have more time and energy for family life.

3. We will increase employee participation in fundamental decisions that shape the world of work, thus decreasing the stress that results from powerlessness at work. As workers have less stress to bring home, some of the stress on family life will be reduced.

4. We will build family support networks in every community to provide voluntary frameworks of assistance for families dealing with the inevitable tensions of family life.

5. We will create a corps of family support volunteers in each neighborhood who are available to provide in-home supplemental care for children or the elderly. We will create councils of elders in each community and we will motivate every societal institution to learn from the accumulated wisdom of our elders.

6. We will fight for one year of paid "family leave" to ensure that parents are given enough time off from work to be with their children in the first year of life. We will also fight for flexible work schedules so that parents can be home when their children return from school.

7. We will support the creation of television programs and networks aimed at providing children's entertainment that avoids excessive violence and rejects the manipulative use of sexuality that commonly appears on contemporary television. In addition, we will challenge the ethos of selfishness and cynicism conveyed in the media, and focus on developing media programming that strengthens ethical, spiritual, and ecological sensitivity.

8. We will create an educational system that teaches and rewards awe and wonder at the grandeur of the universe, empathy, caring, the ability to discern the ethically relevant aspects of any situation, individual responsibility, discipline, and respect for the experience of others, plus appreciation for the spiritual traditions developed through human history.

9. We will fight for a society that provides full employment, housing, health care, and child care, but that does so in ways that empower the individual family and do not impose bureaucratic constraints or a particular lifestyle.

10. We will support the creation of public events where families meet to celebrate and honor as a community the hard work and energy that so many people put into building families. These events will provide a public space (through workshops, small group discussions, educational forums, and so on) in which to explore the many remaining problems in family life. We will build ongoing public campaigns to improve the quality of family life by honoring and rewarding those who are best at expressing love and caring in an ethical, spiritually centered way, and by challenging all those societal practices that undermine our ability to see and treat one another as fundamentally deserving of love and caring.

I believe that family life, loving relationships, and friendships would be dramatically strengthened if these ten points were implemented in a serious way.

Conclusion

Creating a society that is safe for love and intimacy is not simply a matter of passing some legislation. It involves a reshaping of priorities and a rejection of the societally dominant forces of selfishness, materialism, and cynicism.

To be pro-family, then, must start with a process that challenges the way we have come to internalize the market consciousness, that is, seeing other people in terms of what we can get from them. Similarly, loving relationships will grow stronger when we reject the cynical attitudes that teach us to distrust one another and to doubt the possibility that most human interactions really could be based on loving and caring.

It may take generations to create a society that is broadly based on mutual recognition and that fulfills our meaning-needs, but it need not take more than several years for us to create family support networks that operate not just for some oppressed Other, but for ourselves as well. Nor need we wait for societal approval before creating support networks for singles. Similarly, there are parts of our Contract with American Families that we should seek to implement within the next few years, even as we continue to challenge the Right and dispute its claim to be the only serious pro-family force.

7

Policy Implications:

The Economy, Education, and Health Care

························

Transgressing the Reality Police

In this chapter, I imagine what it would be like to violate the "reality police" who tell us that it is impossible to have a world based on loving and caring. Reality, they tell us, is the world of pain and oppression, a world in which all people are out for themselves. Thinking about a world based on a different principle violates everything that we have been taught is "realistic."

What I discuss in this chapter is *not* a set of ideas to be implemented inside our current society, but a vision of what a different society might look like. It is an answer to the question, "What would a society based on a politics of meaning be like?" rather than the question, "What should be the transitional program that we fight for next week?"

This distinction is important. Some of the following policy ideas, when placed in the context of our existing society with its ethos of selfishness, become easy to dismiss as impractical or even foolish, because they are unlikely to work given the current ways that people treat one another in a competitive market society. Nevertheless, the ideas I propose will put flesh on the philosophical framework I have described, and give some vision of what a society with a caring ethos might look like. I also hope to deflect the likely criticism from the Right that a politics of meaning is a cover for traditional liberal or left-wing politics, and the likely criticism from the Left that it is a meaningless slogan that can only mislead people into right-wing ideas.

For this reason, I have decided to put forward some representative thinking on economics, education, and health care, even though a full policy articulated for a politics of meaning would have much more to say about each of these issues than I try to address here. In addition, a full policy would address areas like foreign policy, criminal justice, and welfare, among others.

I am strongly committed to a society where social arrangements are evaluated on the basis of whether they support and nurture human beings who are able to provide one another with genuine recognition; who are able to sustain loving and caring relationships; and who are ethically, spiritually, and ecologically sensitive. But I feel no attachment to any of the specific plans outlined below. They are *not* the defining elements of a politics of meaning, but only our best guess at this moment about some of the constituent elements of that future society. In chapter 8, I will discuss briefly the first steps necessary to build a movement that might take us to the world I describe.

Replacing Big Government with Civil Society

I risk a certain danger in writing what follows: the ease with which each idea could be taken out of context and *misinterpreted* to be calling for a major expansion of government and its intervention in our lives. In fact, my program calls for the opposite. Many of its details would best be implemented by downsizing government and expanding civil society—the institutions that exist between our government and our private family lives.

What I propose is a much more serious downsizing of government than is being advanced by current conservative policies to return power to the states. The states are not a solution, because state government is just as flawed as the federal government. State government is just as accessible to manipulation and control by the most powerful economic forces in civil society, just as toxic to the average citizen's spirit and will as any federal bureaucracy, and just as dominated by technocratic thinking that gives little attention to our ethical and spiritual sensibilities. Instead of relying on someone else to do things for us, the idea is to create institutions in civil society that we fully control and in which we personally participate.

The only way in which some people can imagine my program in our current world, with its set of assumptions about human beings, is to imagine that I would impose my plan through coercion—precisely the opposite of my intentions. Coercion will seem to such people the necessary implementation of my plan, because they can envision no other world but one in which each individual is involved in the frenetic pursuit of self-interest. In such a world, cooperation can only be achieved through manipulation or coercion or some economic incentive. From such a paranoid perspective about what human beings are like, all my ideas would have to be written off as naive or fantastic, or (at least implicitly) as a plan for more government.

But this is not what I have in mind. My vision is based not on government, but on cooperation among people. That is what civil society is about. In civil society, people construct arrangements of mutual cooperation based on shared ideals and goals. Nobody forces them; they are free to participate to the extent that they choose.

I have one further caveat. Whatever government we leave in place will have to be dramatically restructured, democratized, and made accessible in a real way. One possible way to implement this is to ask every citizen to serve in the government for a period of time. Try to imagine a government whose major positions were filled by people doing a limited term of service, who were motivated by a true desire to serve the common good, and who felt joyful about the opportunity to do so. While there would be no guarantee that such people, too, might not develop a tendency to interfere, the fact that they would themselves soon be regular citizens again would act as a counterbalance. A reconstructed government should present itself as a vehicle through which all of us show our collective caring for one another.

Envisioning a Different Society

Envision a society in which people typically act as though they care about one another—not only about the people in their immediate families, but also about neighbors, coworkers, and even passersby.

I do not expect people to care *equally* about everyone else. In my view, this is impossible. People always will have hierarchies of caring, because we have a limited amount of energy, of which it will be appropriate to give more to our families, friends, and neighbors, and somewhat less to anonymous people, strangers, and others with whom we have less of an ongoing, face-to-face relationship. I have met people who are in love with the entire human race—and all too often, I have found that those who "love everyone equally" actually are incapable of loving someone in particular.

All this caring and loving sought by a meaning-oriented society could seem like a burden, especially if it were being done as a result of people constantly reminding themselves, "I ought to be caring for others, so I'd better give up what I really want to do and sacrifice myself for them, because that is the right thing to do." I reject this model. Instead, the kind of ethical life I envision would flow from our natural attraction to one another—that is, from the immediate recognition that we have of one another as beings deserving of our caring and respect, and from the desire that we have to connect with one another in loving and caring ways.

The French philosopher Emmanuel Levinas has talked about this recognition as something that flows immediately from our capacity to see the face of the other. In my book *Jewish Renewal*, I argue that it is precisely this capacity to recognize the sanctity of the other that generates this sense of caring and ethical obligation, and that constitutes in part the meaning of the Bible when it says that we are created in the image of God. So instead of thinking of a politics-of-meaning society as one in which people are going to be excessively focused on wondering about their duty, we can picture it as one in which people will be so excited to be meeting one another and having the opportunity to spend time together, that we will resemble playful puppies, joyfully exploring and celebrating one another's existence.

Loving and caring about one another will flow from human beings who have not been systematically denied the recognition and caring that they need, and whose capacity for *giving* love to others has not been systematically stymied by living in a society where such giving is seen as naive and potentially dangerous.

Imagine ourselves in a society in which people regularly detach themselves from other activities to reconnect to their deepest inner selves and to the spiritual dimension of the universe. Imagine people who are spiritually attuned in ways that make them continually reconnect with their own appreciation of nature and of other human beings, and with their sense of awe, wonder, and radical amazement at the grandeur and mystery of being. Imagine these same people being filled with joy and delight, without pollyannishly denying or avoiding life's inevitable sorrows.

The energy that is pulsating through these beings is more than what Freud called erotic energy, though it includes that as well—it is the life force, or what religious people call God-energy. Social theorist Sharon Welch has suggested thinking of our energy as analagous to a horse running freely through the fields. That horse does not need to be given incentives to run—it runs out of the sheer, joyful life energy that pulsates through its being. The question that we ought to be asking is not, "How do we create this in human beings?" but, "How do we dismantle the psychological and social structures that have managed to shape human beings who are no longer in touch with this life energy?"

The vision of a new society is not another form of social engineering. The task of social policy is to clear away all the destructive processes that have kept human beings from living fully and from staying in touch with *Being*—not to reshape us according to someone else's plan. Of course, unlike earlier romantic, Rousseauesque visions of a new society, which expected an easy liberation of our fundamental capacities, I anticipate that it might take generations of living in a different way and with different values—plus intensive, society-wide therapy processes—before we clear ourselves of the psychological, spiritual, and social debris that limits our development. As a therapist, I have often witnessed how difficult it can be for people to unpeel the layers of internalized obstacles. It is for good reason that the Bible talks of the sins of the fathers being visited upon the children for the third or fourth generation, and it may take that long after we have created a politics-of-meaning society before people can fully live up to their loving capacities. So I am as deeply suspicious of those who think utopia is around the corner as of those who spend their energies trying to convince us to narrow our vision and despair of fundamental transformation.

Notions such as "Love your neighbor," or "Love the stranger," are not utopian, nor are they newfangled, post-Enlightenment hubris, to be tacked on to human beings whose natural instincts lie in a different direction. Rather, they are ideas that appear, in various forms, in most of the world's great religious traditions. These ideas have roots deep in our unconscious and in the accumulated history and traditions of the human race, and have only been discounted as "unrealistic" for a relatively brief period in human history.

In a politics-of-meaning society, there will be millions of subtle acts of caring and mutual nurturing every day. It is these small acts, done on the individual level, that capture what a politics of meaning really is about. One reason I am optimistic is that we are already living in a society where there daily are millions of such acts of caring and joy. But when a politics of meaning becomes the norm, those little acts will be in constant interaction with societal institutions that nurture and sustain them. And this continual support will give each of these acts a different meaning and significance for all those engaged in them.

So follows, for the policy-oriented reader, a description of some of those new institutional arrangements.

THE ECONOMY

Economic Development

Our world faces accelerating social and environmental disintegration. The official soothsayers for the American economy proclaim its powerful triumph and the decline of all alternative systems. They celebrate the array of attractive new products and advances in electronics and computer technology. Yet they are unwilling to notice that the very corporations which have brought us these new products may leave many of us without jobs, unable to afford to buy the products. Nor do they notice that there have been dramatic increases worldwide in poverty, unemployment, violent crime, and environmental destruction.

The current way that we organize our economy cannot be sustained. Our children or grandchildren may become environmental refugees, seeking some safe place to live that has not yet been devastated by the destructive economic policies that we claim today to be "working." While some of the media owned by the conglomerates that are destroying the earth's resources do their best to focus our attention away from the tragic consequences of corporate environmental irresponsibility, the dimensions of our folly will become clearer in the twenty-first century. At that point, people will become aware of the need to make fundamental transformations in our economic system. Until then, the concerns raised by so many environmental economists will seem utopian. Once we allow ourselves to become more fully aware of what our economy is actually doing, fundamental economic change will seem like common sense.

It has been my argument throughout this book that the kinds of changes needed cannot be merely technocratic, but require a fundamental transformation of our notion of productivity and efficiency.

The basic idea for a politics-of-meaning economy is this: build an economy that rewards acts of caring and that encourages people and corporations to be ecologically and spiritually sensitive.

Today, our economy does almost the exact opposite of this politics-of-meaning goal. The globalization of the economy has significantly increased the power of huge multinational corporations to shape a world that increasingly ignores caring behavior or ecological responsibility. While a few hundred corporations have made significant moves toward addressing the meaning-needs (some even argue that a meaning-oriented focus will eventually increase corporate profits), many of the most powerful corporations are moving in just the opposite direction. They are downsizing their firms without regard to the fate of their employees, they are using their resources to support candidates for office who oppose any societal demands for corporate social and ecological responsibility, and they are exploring ways to take advantage of global possibilities that allow them to increase profits by eliminating environmental restrictions and reducing the amount they pay their workers.

Globalization allows corporations to play communities off against one another. If any given community or country is not willing to lower wages and environmental-responsibility demands, a corporation can easily threaten to move elsewhere, leaving communities or even entire countries with decreased employment and increased social unrest. Ten years ago it was communities or states that were fighting to attract corporate investment away from each other; today it is whole countries. Globalization of capital makes it much harder for democratically governed nation states to exercise significant control over the economic forces that shape their own lives.

Many people, faced with this situation, imagine that they can deal with their fear of job loss by working out private solutions ("I'll get myself job training for new skills, and let everyone else worry about himself or herself."). Such consciousness makes it impossible to build a social movement that could conceivably stop the irresponsible movement of capital. Yet much of this book has detailed how destructive it is for our personal lives when we live in a society where this consciousness becomes the dominant way people think about their lives.

Counter to this, a politics-of-meaning economy would seek to build strong neighborhoods and communities that would be the locus of economic activity. Investments would be aimed at strengthening the local community and allowing for the creation of productive processes that allowed people to experience genuine power and control over their circumstances. In addition, we would seek to build economic life in ways that were consistent with our understanding of the sanctity of every human being, the importance of allowing every person to develop his or her capacities, and this would encourage us to relate to our economic life as part of the process by which we come to experience our connection to all of Being. That recognition, in turn, would help us reorient our priorities and recenter our spiritual lives as we face the inevitable reduction in consumption that will be imposed on us willy-nilly by a planet that cannot sustain for much longer the profligacy of contemporary selfishness.

Neighborhood and regional economic planning will replace the huge national and international arrangements that dominate much of our contemporary society. Economic units will seek to diversify their production, and counter the tendency of the world capitalist market to push entire regions into a narrower and more specialized form of production.

I reject the two major models for economic life that dominated the twentieth century: huge and largely uncontrolled multinational corporations whose interests often shaped the agenda of governments that competed to please and woo these multinationals, on the one hand; or huge government bureaucracies that were equally out of touch with most of their own constituency, on the other hand. To put it in crude terms, neither capitalism nor socialism in the forms that they have developed in the twentieth century seem particularly appealing to me. I'll leave for others to argue out whether what I'm rejecting is "real" capitalism or only its distorted version, or "real" socialism or only its distorted version. I want to see a world in which economic development is closely shaped to meet the specific needs of the people within a particular community, so that people become the subject and not the object of economic decisions.

The politics of meaning sets a direction for economic life. But people involved in this way of thinking about politics do not all agree with each other on the best way to achieve this goal. In the next few sections of this chapter I shall talk about some of my own views of how the economy might look, but one could easily disagree with my specifics and yet agree that the direction is a significant and new one, though its details remain to be worked out over the course of the next several decades.

One significant debate that is already emerging within the politics-of-meaning community is about how to achieve the localization I am calling for, and what kinds of decisions may need to be made on a global basis (and then, what kind of mechanism for democratic participation would work?). After all, even as we move toward decentralization and democratization of the economy, we will still have to face issues like this: what if a particular natural resource that is needed for production in one part of the world is being depleted very quickly by people in another part of the world? Some politics-of-meaning people (let's call them the globalists) have stressed the importance of creating an international mechanism to allow all people whose lives are going to be shaped by a particular economic decision to have some power over that decision. But others (let's call them localists) warn, quite reasonably, that when we create mechanisms for international control of the economy we simultaneously risk reducing democratic control.

Both sides agree that these decisions cannot be left to private corporations. In the current state of affairs, we are losing ecosystems and vital resources at a rate far exceeding the ability of our planet to replenish itself, and polluting the air, water, and ground with wastes at a level certain to accelerate environmentally based illnesses. The vast concentration of power in huge multinational conglomerates has undermined many of the self-corrective mechanisms of a market economy. In effect, there is no force capable of restraining corporations in the contemporary world, and so instead of having to respond to market forces, they often shape the market itself, generating wants for their products and using their vast resources to shape a corporate-friendly media that keeps most of us from recognizing the level of planetary destruction that is a daily occurrence.

This, argue the globalists, is precisely why a politics of meaning is going to have to favor some form of international democratic mechanisms that will have the power to place restrictions on corporations and allow for global planning of the planet's diminishing resources. A new ethos of respect for nature and for human limits must attend the creation of such an international plan.

When I envision how a globalist perspective might work, I imagine the election of a worldwide economic legislature whose sole task is to present a series of alternative economic plans to the world's population. It is not hard to imagine that within a generation or two we would have interactive technologies that will make it possible for every person on the planet to participate in the discussion of these alternative plans, and then to vote directly on which plan ought to be adopted. Alternatively, I can imagine a less direct democracy in which we elect representatives directly to a world economic body charged with making these decisions rather than submitting them to us. In either of these two globalist scenarios, there would have to be appropriate safeguards to prevent undue influence of corporate or national blocs using their resources to influence the voters, and there would have to be a constitution that reserved a certain amount of economic resources for the use of minorities who might disagree.

The localists respond to this by arguing that any such global economic plan is inevitably going to make people feel less powerful, not more, because the decisions will seem so far away and so huge. The only way to restore democratic participation in our system, they argue, is to move in exactly the opposite direction from that proposed by the globalists: toward local communities that are economically self-sustaining, ecologically in balance with their own local resources, and that promote reducing consumption to address the realities of a world in growing ecological crisis.

But now the globalists respond with the following argument: If corporations are as powerful as you say, how could any particular locale exercise control over them? The entire direction of economic life in the past forty years shows that the corporations are able to move their resources from one country to another as countries compete in offering them the best terms (low labor costs and rights to pollute). Moreover, in each country where capital moves, a significant and powerful section of the population actually gains when they get the multinationals to move in.

Globalization has big winners and big losers. Significant minorities face impoverishment and destruction of their communities, plus all the other consequences (discussed in this book) of living in a world governed by the ethos of selfishness. But there are also significant population groupings that are doing better economically, and they will fight to maintain the "freedom" of the corporations to continue to make these decisions independent of any external constraints (such as social responsibility).

Given this reality, the politics-of-meaning-oriented globalists argue, the only way that corporations could possibly be brought back into a condition of responsibility to the community would be to create some kind of governmental mechanisms on a worldscale. And if one wanted to get to the point where one could talk of breaking down the corporations into smaller entities that would have as their goal to serve the needs of a particular regional community, the only way to get that control over corporate life would be to create international mechanisms such as the election of an international economic legislature.

So, the ongoing question for a politics-of-meaning economy is going to be this: How do we get control of the economic scene sufficient to confront corporate power, without recreating the kind of social democratic mechanisms that have proved so alienating and bureaucratizing in Western Europe, not to mention how to avoid the even worse alternatives of state control that emerged for several decades in Eastern Europe.

One proposal that I find intriguing is to envision the globalist option as a transitional stage to the localization and redistribution of power to regions and neighborhoods. In this scenario, the first step is to reign in the corporations. The second step is to reign in the power of the institutions created to do this task by redistributing their power on a regional level. The problem with this, of course, is that we know how "transitional stages" or "interim solutions" tend to take on a life of their own and become hard to replace. The Communist Party of the Soviet Union saw itself as playing such a transitional role while the proletariat developed itself in readiness to exercise real power, but as often happens with transitional arrangements, the transition is resisted by those who have gained power.

So I think that we might want to look at an arrangement in which we would begin immediately to decentralize power and economic decision-making. One of the explicit goals of any such global arrangements would be to move immediately toward the reempowering of regional and local economic self-sufficiency. Globalization then would be seen as a strategy aimed at decentralization, not as a separate stage.

In this regard, it may be useful to consider some specific suggestions made by the Economics Working Group of the Tides Foundation, and its plan for environmental sustainability. Its plan for the creation of regional sustainability boards, aimed at preserving the environment while developing joint public and private processes to preserve jobs, is one of many worth considering. There should be federal tax on pollution and natural resource depletion, as well as on market speculation. In addition, a network of local and regional public development banks, directed by their respective sustainable development boards, should provide funds for investments in projects that contribute to the economic and environmental sustainability of each region.

We should develop a set of minimum environmental standards, which would be incorporated into all trade agreements, that would develop worldwide standards for sustainable agriculture, encourage waste reduction (including maximum durability, repairability, reuse, and recycling), and promote the harmonization of environmental regulations so that corporations could not gain pollution rights by moving from one country to another.

Federal policies and laws that encourage the relocating of jobs to other countries, such as the foreign-investment tax credit, should be repealed. I would also add to the Economics Working Group the following stipulation: corporations that relocate should first be required to clean up any damage they have done to the social environment of the communities they are leaving, including finding adequate employment with comparable salaries and skills utilization for those workers being displaced.

The preceding proposals are what the policy wonks think of as "real politics." The hard-edged crowd knows how to critique these ideas, how to assimilate them to established forms of discourse, how to absorb and ignore them—which is precisely why most of this book has not been about particular policies.

Policies that seek to restrict corporations from moving their resources and jobs abroad, or that seek to achieve full employment and reduced workweeks, will be ignored or ridiculed. Their proponents will be dismissed as left-wing crazies or as irrational fools. And few people will rally around these policies until we first develop a politics-of-meaning framework that is widely accepted. In short, it is not that I am unconcerned with economic globalization, but that I believe it cannot be effectively addressed without first building a process in which we learn to expand our circle of caring. No one in the media today takes seriously ideas that seek to impose global ethical responsibility on corporate decision-making, because no one believes that there is any serious sector of the American public that is ready to care about anything but its own narrowly defined self-interest. Nevertheless, as a politics-of-meaning consciousness grows, so too will people's willingness to involve themselves in these larger issues.

All of these are transitional steps in the process of regaining democratic control of the economy. To the extent that they are implemented in a transitional way, fine. But the emphasis should be on moving toward reconceptualizing corporations in ways that allow them to be organically connected to particular locations, functioning to serve the people in those locations, and reorganizing economic life around the primacy of neighborhoods, communities, and relatively small regional units.

But economic democratization, while a necessary condition for a caring society, is *not* the defining element of a meaning-oriented economy. I have seen how democracy itself can simply reinforce the tendencies toward selfishness and materialism in a society where selfishness runs amok. A meaning-oriented society must aim to create an economic life which reinforces and supports our deeper desire to relate to one another in a caring way, and which creates opportunities for us to nourish our spiritual sensibilities and our desire to celebrate the joy and wonder of life.

Concretely, I imagine that such an economy would provide spiritual and material incentives for individuals who acted cooperatively and for corporations which were environmentally sensitive. Corporations would reward people for acting in caring and sensitive ways toward one another, and those who were best at tapping the highest creativity, intelligence, and caring capacities of their coworkers would be elected as supervisors and representatives to a democratically elected board of trustees of the corporation. Workers would participate in decisions about what was being produced and how, and about how to distribute and market products in ways that made it possible for potential customers to learn of their availability, without being imposed upon or manipulated into buying goods that they really did not need. Production would be based on the best information available about how best to serve the common good. The work week could be shortened dramatically, because, after an initial catch-up period of a few generations in which the basic housing, clothing, and other essential needs of the world's poor had been addressed, the total amount of goods produced could decrease. Because workers would be guaranteed employment opportunities in work that served the common good, they would have no incentive to promote their corporate product beyond the actual needs of the population. Corporations and other workplaces would provide opportunities for people to nourish their souls, intellects, and emotional well-being—with the same enthusiasm that today drives some of the most enlightened companies to provide their employees with opportunities for daily physical exercise. Yet the deep respect for the God within each of us would be reflected in an atmosphere that encouraged ethnic, religious, and philosophical diversity, and promoted tolerance and mutual respect of those differences rather than a single shared corporate approach to ethics or spirituality.

Today it is difficult for people to even begin to imagine a world in which corporations were motivated to serve the common good, and individuals were willing to work without being forced into it or given the incentive of becoming richer than everyone else. Yet the whole point of the preceding economic policy experiment is to allow ourselves to imagine what it could be like if people really did adopt a different bottom line, and if their desire for loving relationships and a world based on ethical, spiritual, and ecological sensitivity actually became the motivating force for their everyday activity.

The organizing principle of public policy today is the notion that economic growth is the central demand of a democratic society. Whatever provides for that growth is to be valued. This growth is not measured in terms of the overall well-being of those who are supposedly its beneficiaries, but rather in terms of the aggregate wealth or productive capacities of the society. Thus, we get this startling picture of contemporary America: "the economy" is doing fine, occasional recessions aside, while many, many people feel that their lives are becoming worse and are deeply troubled. The problem here is that "growth" is defined in ways that have helped elites of wealth and power convince everyone else that our society is doing fine, and that if others do not experience it this way, it is because of personal problems that ought not to be brought up in public.

Rather than spin off more details of what a new society would look like, I want to concentrate more on some of the principles that might underlie this new kind of economic life. Through this discussion, some more details will emerge of what such an economy might look like and why I think it could work.

Changing the World of Work

If the goal of an economy is to help nurture ethically, spiritually, and ecologically sensitive human beings who are capable of sustaining long-term, loving relationships, the workplace needs to be reconceptualized as a primary locus for human development.

As the Israeli kibbutz experience shows, even the most boring work can be fulfilling to workers when it is experienced as part of a larger project that has a transcendent meaning and is democratically shaped. When I worked on a kibbutz, I used to marvel at the degree to which garbage collectors, manure shovelers, chicken pluckers, and machinists in the kibbutz factory all could revel in their work, because in it they saw an expression of their contribution to the kibbutz or to the building of Zionism. Three elements of the kibbutz experience seem, to me, relevant to building a sense of community in the American workplace: seeing work as relevant to the common good, governing work democratically, and having the possibility of job rotation and Sabbatical years.

THE COMMON GOOD

We all have experienced moments when people harness their energies to the common good, for example, in competitive sports or in a shared crisis, such as a power outage or the aftermath of an earthquake or flood. Yet that same spirit can be harnessed when people share other kinds of goals, for example, building a social movement. National or local units could be engaged in good-natured competition to see who could produce the most fully satisfying and meaningful work conditions. There is nothing intrinsically unrealistic about a society in which people are truly dedicating their energies to the common good, particularly if they understand how much they personally benefit from it.

It will not be easy, given workers' experience in *this* society, to get them to believe that the transition to a different society is really taking place. Workers have had lots of experience with people talking about "sacrifice for the common good," when what they really meant was that workers should sacrifice for the benefit of those with the greatest wealth and power.

One step in creating a genuine sense of working for the common good might be for each workplace to take a few days each year (possibly after Labor Day, when children return to school), during which normal work would stop. At this time, workers at each workplace could create a mission statement articulating their goals for their workplace, including an analysis of how it was serving the common good. Each year, working people would review and revise this statement, and if necessary, take steps to make changes in their workplace—including changes in what was being produced, and how—in order to ensure that this workplace was in fact doing something that served a larger good.

Of course, one useful way of showing that something serves the common good is the market's validation that people want the particular product being produced or service being rendered. For this reason, a market mechanism can and should remain part of the economy. However, we must keep in mind that there are also a number of distorting mechanisms in the market. First, to the extent that there is unequal wealth, the market reflects what people with disposable income want, and this may tilt production away from the common good toward the needs of a few. Second, the market reflects what people have been convinced to want through manipulative marketing and advertising techniques. Third, the market reflects what we want as individuals better than it reflects what we want as part of a community. So, for all three reasons, although the market should be regarded as a very important consultative force, it should not be the final arbiter of decisions about what can best serve the common good. For all these reasons, we will need to develop democratic mechanisms to balance the market.

DEMOCRATIC GOVERNANCE

The process by which workplaces decide how and what to produce must be democratized. Increased productivity and caring are possible only when workers themselves shape the conditions of their work and feel deeply invested in the outcomes.

The formal mechanism for this process could be the creation of occupational safety and health (OSH) committees, democratically elected at each workplace. Their goal would be to change working conditions as necessary to increase workers' safety and health, as well as opportunities for workers to use their intelligence, creativity, cooperative ability, empathy, and sensitivity (ethical, spiritual, and environmental).

In addition, every year, each worker should have the voluntary opportunity to participate in twelve two-hour sessions of an occupational stress group (OSG), in which workers could reflect on the degree to which their workplace offers them adequate opportunities to be more fully realized as human beings. These groups would discuss internal and external obstacles to taking advantage of those opportunities, or what must be done to make the workplace more humanly fulfilling.

OSGs should have no management personnel; the facilitators should be chosen by unions or other workers' organizations and trained by those committed first to workers' emotional and spiritual health. OSGs are *not* to become a version of Total Quality Management or similar schemes designed by management to manipulate worker consciousness, in order to create a more pliable or productive worker.

When the politics of meaning first caught public attention a few years ago, critics portrayed my proposed OSGs and OSH committees as instruments of either government or management control over workers. In fact, they are neither. Workers at every workplace would democratically decide whether or not they wanted to institute OSGs or OSH committees. The government's sole function would be to ensure that management establish the committees if workers chose to establish them.

Still, the concept of democratic control will hold little meaning for people who have grown up in a world in which democracy was often merely a choice between contending elites who shared the same fundamental worldview. Thus, workers may at first be skeptical about this idea, given their previous experience with supposedly democratic mechanisms, particularly in their unions.

Democratic structures are important, but they can be hollow unless they are accompanied by a genuine experience of community and solidarity. The creation of this sense of connectedness and mutual recognition at the workplace is fundamental. Democratic structures may be a necessary part of this process, but they are not sufficient unless we attend to the creation of real caring and real commitment to one another. Otherwise, there is no limit to how much the democratic structures can be manipulated, and how quickly people will lose interest in them.

JOB ROTATION AND THE SABBATICAL YEAR

No matter how fulfilling a work task may be, people stuck in it for forty or fifty years are likely to find themselves deadened, and will withdraw their creative and emotional energy. For this reason, the economy must provide as an option (not a requirement) that people be allowed to change their work rotations.

Building on the biblical idea of a guaranteed sabbatical year after six years of work (an idea that is already institutionalized in most contemporary universities), I propose that all working people be given a sabbatical year. They could elect to use it to consolidate new skills that they perhaps had been studying in evening classes during the previous six years, and which would make possible a job switch to a different area. They could choose to deepen their own knowledge of subjects which they might not yet have explored (intensively immersing themselves in literature, music, or filmmaking, for example), or to simply relax in an unstructured way, perhaps through travel or reading.

Each person on sabbatical would be encouraged to volunteer some portion of time each week to a social service or community self-help project so that vital caring services could continue.

We could use the most advanced electronic information-gathering techniques to assist people with job searches following their sabbatical year. As these techniques become more sophisticated in the decades ahead, career changes will become easier to plan.

One could even imagine the beneficial effects of extending this sabbatical idea to the biblical notion that the entire society takes the *same* year off. To some people, taking biblical ideas seriously will seem utopian, fanciful, and implausible. To others, taking the Bible seriously will liberate them to explore possibilities outside the framework of our contemporary reality. The impact of having the vast majority of people on a shared sabbatical would be enormous. It would reduce tensions, and produce the possibility for societal deliberation about common goals that may be more difficult or more anonymous when conducted as a supplement to a normal workweek.

It becomes possible to envision society-wide festivals and enjoyments that may have been part of the life of an elite in the ancient world, but which could now become part of the firsthand experience of most people on our planet. Using the latest technologies to ensure widespread participation, the world community could use this sabbatical opportunity to make decisions about how to use our environmental resources, how to allocate production priorities, and how to resolve some of our important disputes. We could also use this time for retooling our own spiritual energies. The collective energy of the human community, liberated to celebrate one year out of seven, would empower us and free up our creativity in unexpected ways. It probably could cause leaps forward in consciousness and in scientific experimentation that would make us feel that, far from losing time, we had together made unexpected advances. And on the personal level, the healing and pleasure fostered by the sabbatical year would eventually make it easier for many people to feel close to one another and to our own inner selves, from which we are now so estranged.

Here is yet another good reason for a shared sabbatical year: the possibility of giving the earth itself a sabbatical. Imagine, if we did follow the biblical notion: one out of every seven years, we could significantly reduce production so that the earth could rest from all our busy activity and frantic intent to exploit its resources. In so doing, we ourselves could experience a different tempo in which to reflect upon our relationship to the universe.

Agricultural experts have come to understand that the earth becomes more productive when it is given a chance to rest and replenish its biological resources. And some ecologists, recognizing the earth as a living being that needs to be treated with caring and not seen simply as an object of manipulation or control, are joining with spiritually attuned people to insist that our long-term survival on this planet requires an utterly different orientation toward the physical world. Indeed, we might eventually ask whether there really is such a thing as "the physical world," or whether that concept itself is merely an attempt to abstract reality from its essential spiritual, ethical, and material interconnectedness.

Of course, people would not be forced to take a sabbatical if they did not want to. My proposal will cause some people immense anxiety. They might ask themselves, "What would I do if I didn't *have* to do what I'm doing?" Doubtlessly, some of them will invest their energies trying to figure out what is wrong with the sabbatical year concept, and why "it can't work."

But it can! Some vital services will have to be retained and some people would elect to take a *different* year as their sabbatical. I have made no attempt to specify in detail how it could work, but I am certain that we could mobilize teams of economists, psychologists, and social change activists to devise alternative scenarios for *how* to make it work, in ways that respected our different wants and desires. Try it as a thought experiment with your friends: what services are vital and which of these could be run by people who do something else the other six years?

Respect for Work

One of the great failings of the social change movements of the 1960s was their inability to value work or workers. Unable to imagine that work could be anything but the alienating labor of the advanced industrial societies, it seemed obvious that anyone smart would try to avoid work, or do as little as possible. But if work is transformed into an activity in which people have greater opportunity to actualize their capacities as loving and creative human beings, they will have more respect for work and for one another as working people.

While the total amount of work time each week might be reduced to thirty hours, allowing more time for people to develop other capacities, workers' total productivity will increase as they use their fullest beings in the world of work. We will develop a pro-work ethic based not on sacrifice, but on seeing work as the activity through which we are able to externalize ourselves in the world and act together toward shared goals. One of the great indictments of this society is that it does not offer us enough opportunities to experience this kind of work.

Mainstream economists assume that no one will work unless motivated to do so by some extrinsic rewards, because work has been so distasteful. Certainly, in the world that they have constructed, they are entirely right. If overnight, without changing anything else, we were to institute the changes at the workplace that I have been describing here, they would almost certainly flop. In a system which has thoroughly indoctrinated people to distrust one another, and to assume that they would be harmed if they did not dedicate their energies to pursuing their self-interest, people would likely take advantage of the system that I have proposed and decrease their total amount of work. This action would be against their long-term economic interest, but most people would find it difficult to act on a different set of assumptions, unable to conceptualize the world from the standpoint of all being together in the same boat.

For this reason, no plan for the economy can ever be separated from a plan for the entire society. If we have organized our world in such a way that, from earliest childhood, people are encouraged to find ways to contribute to others, to see themselves as part of a common enterprise, and to recognize that work could be a mechanism for contributing toward the common good and not solely a means for self-advancement, then people will be far more likely to find fulfillment in the working world that I have proposed.

Being Agnostic about Capitalism

By now, the reader will have noticed that I have *not* called for redistributing wealth, or socializing the ownership of corporations, as a necessary ingredient in the economics of a progressive politics of meaning. On this question, I remain agnostic.

If it is possible to change the economy in ways that allow it to maximize the human capacities that I have been describing—which is the bottom line for a progressive politics of meaning—and to do that within the context of a capitalist ownership system, then capitalism is a viable economic form. But if private ownership of the means of production becomes too great an obstacle, if capitalists band together to use their power to prevent democratization of the workplace and transformation of production toward the goal of serving the common good, then perhaps another form of ownership will be necessary.

I have met many businesspeople who want to change the bottom line in the way that I am calling for. Yet, it is typical of the Left to make these people feel that they are unwelcome, or even the enemy. The need to dismiss progressive businesspeople, or people with high ethical and spiritual sensitivity who hold management positions in corporations, as "less than"—an extension of the desire to dichotomize between "us" and "them" at all times—gives some on the Left a feeling of moral superiority that helps compensate for their actual powerlessness.

From my standpoint, many people involved in the current economic system share the same desires for a more caring world as everyone else does. Likewise, they share the same fears and hesitations. In this sphere, too, it is important to stop demonizing. The question is not, "Are they capitalists, managers, or bureaucrats, who are working within an oppressive system?" but, "Are they willing to fight for a new bottom line that values ethical, spiritual, and ecological sensitivity and the ability of people to be loving and caring *over* the ability of their firm to maximize profits?" To the extent that people are willing to make that shift, and explicitly fight for it within their part of the corporate world, they become part of a progressive movement for a politics of meaning.

Critics on the Left who are about to write off the politics of meaning as a sellout should first ask themselves whether they believe that capitalist firms *can* reorganize to serve the common good and to produce in ways that maximize our positive human capacities. If people on the Left do not think so, then they should have no trouble recognizing that my criterion for the viability of capitalism actually fits their worldview. From within their own set of assumptions, what I am asking of corporations is impossible. But if it is impossible, then there is no sellout involved—and, from the Left's standpoint, I have restated progressive ideas in a way that will more effectively challenge the capitalist order. Accordingly, the politics of meaning should be embraced as a powerful way to advance a transformative consciousness among sections of the population that would not be willing to open themselves to this message if expressed in traditional leftist language. Some leftists who embrace the politics of meaning have even told me that, from their perspective, our willingness to really take biblical values seriously makes our approach the most sophisticated anticapitalist strategy to come down the pike in many decades.

Conversely, enthusiasts of capitalism should ask themselves whether capitalist production really can be organized to serve the common good and to produce more caring human beings. If so, capitalists should have no trouble accepting my criterion. From their perspective, I am proposing a way to make capitalism more consistent with the emerging spiritual and ethical awareness that it must address in order to survive in the twenty-first century. The politics of meaning, for capitalists, can be a powerful way to highlight the transformtive possibilities within the current system.

In either case, it is clear that the socialist/capitalist debate is a red-herring issue today. The key is not to ask, "Who owns?" but two other questions: "To what extent does the economy *really* serve the common good?" and "To what extent does the economy produce spiritually, ethically, and ecologically sensitive human beings who are capable of sustaining loving and caring relationships, and who feel themselves actualized and fulfilled in the world of work?" Using these criteria, we can move on from the endless debate about social and economic systems in the abstract, and move toward specific guidelines for reorganizing society and the economy according to plans aimed at promoting these spiritual goals. If, in so doing, we have to make changes in the economy, we will not be doing it for the sake of implementing our commitment to an ideology, but only out of necessity for achieving our morally and spiritually centered form of economic life. And if this goal really is consistent with capitalist ownership, let the most enlightened capitalists be in the vanguard of making the necessary changes.

By staying focused on the kinds of changes we need rather than on the way we label them ideologically, we may produce much greater progressive social change. In additon, we may get beyond the sterile Left/Right debate, which feels so stale and outdated.

Of course, creating a work world that really embodies this new bottom line is not just a matter of using a new way of talking, or hiring human-relationship experts to facilitate communication at work. A new bottom line would manifest itself in corporate practices. For example, a corporation adhering to a new bottom line would not transfer plants or equipment without first developing a strategy to ensure that those who had been previously employed could sustain themselves without significant downward mobility. Nor would it seek to relocate in order to pay lower wages or to take advantage of more lax environmental safeguards.

Those who think that these kinds of changes in corporations are impossible ignore the one vulnerable spot in the corporate world: the fact that it is peopled by human beings who have the same meaning-needs as everyone else, the same ability to understand how destructive the consequences of the ethos of selfishness have become, and the same anger about the way that the values of the corporate world may lead to ecological destruction and the further undermining of our connections to each other. Yet I have to also acknowledge the point made by the Left: that in the short run, corporate culture frequently (not always) marginalizes meaning-oriented demands and evaluates individuals on the basis of their ability to maximize the firm's profits. The huge concentration of corporate wealth often translates into power to shape public discussion through the media, and more indirectly but nevertheless importantly, through the educational system at every level. Given this power, it may take a significant struggle before corporations are willing to give serious attention to their own employees and before management may actually wish to move corporations in a meaning-oriented direction. These corporate insiders who might rally to a meaning-oriented politics may be aided by a powerful movement that insists on the centrality of this new direction.

Yet building that movement is more likely to succeed if it does not position itself as an anticapitalist enterprise. If the Left could allow itself that degree of flexibility, by focusing on a meaning-oriented bottom line, it might soon find itself with the support it needs to push for significant changes in the corporate world. At that point, the corporate insiders may or may not be able to deliver those changes. If they do, the Left will have achieved much of its goal anyway. If they don't, those on the Left who always doubted that corporations could show this kind of flexibility will be vindicated, and they can then mobilize against capitalism with much greater success.

All the more reason, then, to stay agnostic and focus on the real issue: getting corporations, and all other institutions of society, to adhere to a new bottom line of caring and respect for human beings and for the planet.

A Social Audit

A politics of meaning aims to shift the bottom line from a focus on profit or other material values to a focus on ethical, spiritual, social, and ecological values. Accordingly, the productivity or efficiency or rationality of any given program is to be judged by these criteria.

To ensure for ourselves that we are on this path, people in a meaning-oriented society will institute a "social audit"—a social and environmental impact report to accompany every annual investment plan, every project, and every proposed piece of legislation, regulation, or budget item. A social audit will be sought from every corporation; civic institution; community project; and local, state or federal agency and legislative body.

The underlying notion here is that every institution, and every proposed policy or piece of legislation, has a group of stakeholders. These are all the people who will be affected by the operations of the institution or the outcome of the policy or legislation, and who therefore have a stake in knowing and shaping these outcomes. For example, for a company producing infant formula, the stakeholders would include not only the shareholders, employees, and management of the firm, but all the families whose children consume the product, as well as the community in which the plant is located. Not everyone will be a stakeholder in every venture. But for stakeholders, the social audit will be an important tool of empowerment, and one for which a politics of meaning will fight.

The goal of the audit will be to determine the likely consequences of an institution or a policy or a piece of legislation on the psychological, spiritual, and ethical well-being of our society and of individuals within it. Requiring ourselves to think about these goals will help us renew on a daily basis the connection between our specific projects and our sense of the common good.

Liberal reforms have tended to focus largely on predictable, "objective" outcomes. A politics-of-meaning approach, by contrast, questions the predictable subjective outcomes as well: for example, whether the prevailing emotional climate that then takes hold throughout society makes it more or less likely that people will feel safe to trust one another more, and to act in mutually caring or morally sensitive ways. Over the course of the past thirty years, liberals have passed some fine pieces of legislation, but they rarely have challenged the prevailing emotional climate of our society— one that has become, under the influence of right-wing movements and ideologues, increasingly mean-spirited. Liberal reforms are now being undermined or rolled back by the conservative beneficiaries of that mean-spirited climate, swept to electoral victory on a tide of anger at liberals who have failed to address the crisis of meaning in the lives of middle-income Americans.

The Goal of the Economy

It is easy to have utopian fantasies, but who is going to pay for all these wonderful ideas, and how can an economy function that is committed to such "unrealistic" ideals?

Let's start by asking ourselves, in the instructive words of James Fallows, "What's an economy for?" It is easy here to fall back into the thought patterns of the old paradigm, to imagine that the only way to judge an economy is in terms of the degree to which it produces "hard" or externally measurable, material goods. However, there is nothing self-evident about this conceptualization.

From a politics-of-meaning standpoint, the goal of an economy is to reproduce what the philosopher Ludwig Wittgenstein called "a particularly human form of life." An economy must have mechanisms for producing food and other essential goods, such as clothing and housing. But an economy must also sustain human beings, both physically and socially, with all our complexities and desires. One of the component elements in reproducing "a particularly human form of life" is that the process of doing this must *itself* be a part of the life that we seek to reproduce. Therefore, the way that we reproduce human life—both in terms of creating food and essential goods, and in terms of sustaining human beings physically and socially—is part of our evaluation of an economy's success. If there were an economy that could produce more food and more essential goods, by harnessing human labor in such a way that each of us died at age seventeen after years of painful forced labor, we probably would not judge that economy to be a powerful success, despite its greater "productivity" according to one narrow standard.

The goal of the economy should be to help produce and sustain human beings who are capable of realizing their highest capacities for love; creativity; intelligence; mutual recognition; solidarity; productive work; freedom; caring and nurturing; intimacy; commitment; trust; vitality; and aesthetic, ethical, spiritual, and ecological sensitivity. The materialist conception that promoting these capacities is difficult when people face material deprivation is correct, but needs to be qualified. There are, and have been throughout human history, societies that more successfully actualize these capacities than some of our contemporary advanced industrial societies, even though these others produce less, materially speaking. In my view, these societies have had a stronger economy—one that we ought to deem more productive and generating a higher standard of living.

The way we organize the production and distribution of goods and services is linked intrinsically to the way we reproduce the human species, both physically and socially. For example, how we arrange for the care and nurturing of children is as much an economic question as how we arrange for the planting of seeds in the earth, or for the resulting harvest. However, the economic import of child-rearing appears to be invisible, which is a consequence of the success of patriarchy in having assigned this work to women, not paid for it, and then defined it as "not real work." Those same patriarchal assumptions have held throughout our economy, so that wherever we have work associated with caring and nurturing, it typically is devalued and underpaid, when paid for at all. Similarly, how we organize the world of work, and the consequences for human relationships, is as much an economic question as the consequences for the production of goods. Separating these issues only seems reasonable once we have adopted the materialist and individualist account of human reality that this book seeks to challenge.

An Economy of Caring

The dominant economic model in Western societies assumes the primacy of the isolated individual and then tries to work out how such a lone individual, in a hypothesized state of nature, could ever arrange with others to work together, produce goods and services, and build social and political arrangements. The answer is "the contract." Individuals freely enter into contractual arrangements for the sake of maximizing their own individual benefits.

Some of the "intuitive" quality of this explanation may derive from its approximation of behavior at a certain stage in the development of capitalist society. But this model already assumes a world in which the social fabric has been so irreparably torn that people perceive themselves as fundamentally alone and in competition with others. All forms of connection have been dissolved and need to be reconstructed.

Feminist theorists recently have pointed out that this way of construing the world could never have been completely true, because it totally ignores or belittles the centrality of caring and nurturing relationships in the reproduction of the human species. These relationships are an essential element in any economic theory. For example, if we were to look at the noncontractual realities of the mother-child relationship, we would have a very different understanding of how human beings come into relationship with one another.

We would have a more accurate picture of the world if we started from the assumption that relationships between caregivers (female or male) and children form a better basis for understanding human beings and their potential economic relationships. That this notion seems so foreign to us testifies to the degree to which the patriarchal separation of work from caring has become second nature to us, though it was not always the case, nor need it be the case.

The Nurturance Gap

As James Ronald Stanfield argued in his presidential address to the Association for Social Economics in 1994, part of the problem with American productivity is that it has failed to take account of the nurturance needs upon which an economy is necessarily based.

Economists like to abstract economic relationships from their human context in order to imagine that they are dealing with a science that does not require attention to these "soft" (or "feminine") issues. But Stanfield, citing Marshall Sahlins's *Stone Age Economics,* argues that reciprocity is a central ingredient in economic life. The most critical aspect of reciprocity is that the long-term social relationship is strong enough to allow indefinite reciprocation. A transaction that is embedded in a permanent relationship, in the perception of those involved, can contain a large measure of indefinite reciprocity.

When there is no expectation of reciprocal benefit, employers and employees bargain in adversarial ways. Employees do not develop much interest in the financial health of the enterprise, and employers have no sense of obligation to keep employees should the firm face downturns in the economy. Nor do employers feel any obligation to invest in worker training if employees may use these additional skills to find employment elsewhere. In general, employees are seen as costs to be minimized rather than as assets to be maintained and improved.

Concerns of this sort are purely economic, and are *not*, as cynics would have it, the imposition of moral concerns into an arena where they have no place. It turns out that even within the narrowest definitions of economics, the quality of moral commitments among the participants is central to determining how successful the economy will be. The ethos of caring, embedded in the program of the politics of meaning, is far from being a utopian imposition from left field. It indeed may be the most effective way to improve American economic productivity, however narrowly economists may construe what productivity is about.

Conversely, social deterioration (what I have been describing as the crisis of meaning) has dramatic economic consequences. Stanfield points to the economic effects of a decline in reciprocity in schools: when children don't know how to comport themselves, "their teachers must relinquish academic time to crowd-control activities." This creates "a chronic loss of efficiency in dealing with discourtesy, which falls well short of the acute problems associated with the intrusion of crime and violence into the school environment. Such displacement of teacher time allocation is economically significant, as is similar displacement of the time of employers, retailers, and those who would engage in buying or selling with others who lack conformity to certain basic rules of conduct."

Other economists bolster this observation by arguing that a significant portion of the American workforce is engaged in what could best be called policing work or guard labor: enforcing rules that are seen as constraints by people who have been conditioned to maximize their own short-term self-interest without regard to the welfare of others. Most visibly, we have the police and firefighters, much of whose time is spent cleaning up the mess generated by the ethos of selfishness (such as the failure of property owners to pay for adequately upgrading their property with respect to fire safety).

Next, we have the host of government personnel, from teachers to welfare workers, who increasingly must dedicate time and energy to various policing functions. Then we have the huge array of supervisory and managerial positions in retail, manufacturing, finance, and the professions (such as regulating hospital cost and restricting the delivery of medical procedures), whose job is often to extract labor that employees might not otherwise offer voluntarily within our social system.

The United States has a disproportionate amount of guard labor compared to other countries. Consider our supervisors: a vast number of people are essentially work cops, checking up on whether other people are working hard enough. Some economists estimate that we have thirteen million supervisory personnel nationwide, only half of whom do any kind of productive labor.

Teaching people to care about one another is a much more effective way to get work done. Caring produces cooperative rather than conflictive workplaces, and that means less use of guard labor. The energy that is required to police workers constitutes a huge drain on the economy. It might otherwise be devoted to productive labor, or to decreasing the total amount of necessary labor time (which might be reflected either in a shorter workweek or in sabbatical leaves, as described earlier).

When we look at these costs to our present system, we realize that the crisis of meaning is central to the problem of the economy. Because there is a nurturance gap, people are willing to act in narrowly self-interested ways that are destructive to the common good, and hence destructive to their own long-term interests.

The future economic success of the United States and other Western economies depends on their ability to create a climate of nurturing and caring. People need to see themselves as related to others in a much more trusting and spiritually significant way than current economic arrangements tend to foster.

Instead, the United States has taken just the opposite approach to the ongoing economic crisis. The social deterioration fostered by the ethos of selfishness has produced a serious problem for the American economy, which has led economic planners to support austerity in order to finance further economic progress. And this in turn has led to the restructuring of firms, in order to reduce costs, and to stringent governmental fiscal policies—all of which further erode the social process of nurturing and the ideology of caring.

The total package makes a politics of meaning seem unrealistic, and contributes to further debilitation of economic performance which, as I have shown, is closely related to levels of trust and caring.

Haven't Various Similar Schemes Been Tried and Failed?

Those who are interested in preserving the existing system make various unsuitable analogies, imagining that somehow the politics of meaning is reminiscent of the Soviet system or of various European social democracies. But there really is very little in common, except the willingness of these societies to invoke "the common good." But so, for that matter, have societies as varied as contemporary capitalist America, antebellum slave-owning America, pro-apartheid South Africa, fascist Germany, feudal Europe, and various communist regimes around the world. We would not dismiss democratic ideals as having been proved failures just because "democratic" has been used by various communist and totalitarian societies to describe their repressive regimes. Neither will we dismiss notions of serving the common good just because that term frequently has been misappropriated for nefarious ends.

If we look at the substance of East European communist regimes, we find that in no way did they try out any of the ideas being suggested here. They did not establish any procedure to allow working people to define the common good; they did not establish democracy in the workplace; and they did not allow job rotation, nor a spiritual and ethical orientation toward the world.

In communism's early days, some communists championed at least the first of these three ideas: the notion that work should be organized for the common good. But too many leaders distrusted ordinary working people, whom they imagined would make bad choices. Communists thought that the Party should decide what was for the common good, rather than allowing the rough-and-tumble of democracy to make these decisions. For a while, many ordinary people went along, particularly to the extent that they believed that some of the Party's decisions (for example, industrialization; literacy campaigns; equality for women; universal education, health care, and retirement benefits) were in fact serving the common good. The existence of a common external enemy (the fascists), who might impose horrific alternatives, also helped keep most ordinary people in line.

Nevertheless, it did not take too long for many people to recognize that all the rhetoric of "the common good" was a cover for the particular and narrow good of the ruling bureaucratic elite. At that point, the miracles of collective effort that had built the Moscow subway, and had made possible the rapid development of a military capacity that could defeat Germany's advanced industrial might, began to fade. Workers reverted to various forms of resistance and depressive withdrawal from the common enterprise, the favored method being alcoholism. Economic failure, then, was *not* the product of an unsuccessful attempt at "nonmaterial incentives," but of popular resistance to the manipulation of noble phrases to serve the ignoble and selfish goals of a ruling elite. The failure of the Soviet Union—a classic case of elite selfishness—bolsters rather than weakens my case. It shows that it will be insufficient for the American elite to adopt the language of the politics of meaning while avoiding its substance, and then to expect that it can produce the desired results (though this subterfuge undoubtedly will be tried in the coming decades).

Nor is the politics of meaning a form of European-style social democracy. In its primary incarnations, European social democracy has been more concerned about a series of economic entitlements and rights than it has been about the importance of meaning and purpose and spirituality in life. Consequently, this European system has rarely been able to establish social institutions or practices that provide mechanisms for working people to define the common good, to democratically control their workplaces, to rotate their work, or to address the spiritual dimensions of their relationship to the universe.

What about the Failure of the Kibbutz?

The death of the kibbutz movement is being prematurely hailed by the high priests of selfishness. In fact, though many kibbutzim are facing economic difficulties, many are alive and some are flourishing. One hundred and twenty thousand people live on kibbutzim in

Israel as of 1996, and they produce nine percent of the total Israeli agricultural product.

The economic difficulties of the kibbutz movement do not result from having followed politics-of-meaning principles, but from kibbutzniks having lost their nerve while trying to function within a predominantly selfish economy. Their economic decline is more a testimony to the truth of Trotsky's notion that one cannot build socialism in one country (and certainly not in one village) while leaving the rest of the world under the sway of a different and opposing system.

Many kibbutzniks understood this tension from the start, and realized the problematic nature of attempting to build a society based on caring within the confines of a society based on selfishness. But the only alternative would have been to try to build a social movement to change Israeli society as a whole. Kibbutzim were small, economically marginal units during the first half of the twentieth century. The resources of the collective were reasonably dedicated primarily to producing the bare necessities that could make the kibbutz an economically viable unit, with adequate housing and food for its members.

Some kibbutzniks argued that building local economic viability should be a second priority after working to build a larger social change movement. But to many kibbutzniks, this idea seemed "unrealistic," especially when faced with the challenge of Palestinian hostility and the need to defend the Yishuv (the pre-1948 Jewish community in Palestine) from Arab assault. On this matter, also, one group of kibbutzniks argued that what should come first was a broader view: a different attitude toward Palestinians. They believed in opening up the Israeli labor organization (the Histadrut) to Arabs rather than racially restricting it to Jews, and even advocated allowing Arabs to become members of the kibbutzim. But theirs was a minority voice, and the kibbutz movement became more deeply entwined with Zionist assumptions that cast the Arabs as enemies. This was in part a reasonable response to existing Arab hostility, and in part an entry into the self-fulfilling dance of hatred, for which both sides bear some responsibility.

Although, in my own view, the viciousness and implacable anti-Semitism of Arab leaders deserves more blame than reactive Jewish chauvinism or racism, the dynamics that caused the Arab-Israeli struggle are not my main concern here. Instead, I seek to illustrate that when one group becomes very invested in demeaning the other, it has a very difficult time building a society based on politics-of-meaning principles.

Once this destructive dynamic took root, it became increasingly difficult for kibbutzniks to imagine leading any struggle against Israeli capitalists or Israeli selfishness, because they themselves were so tied to these capitalists in the common nationalist struggle to retain and expand the Israeli hold on the land. (Some kibbutzim, too, benefited directly from the expropriation of Arab land.) So, in the decades after the establishment of the State of Israel, kibbutzniks did not give primary emphasis to building a transformative social movement, but to building their own economic units. And as their focus became increasingly narrow, the kibbutzniks focused on the economic "miracle" of having succeeded in building materially successful kibbutzim.

I remember my year on a Mapam (socialist) kibbutz in the 1960s. What people were most proud of was the concert hall ("See, we can have culture even though we are farmers working the land"), the swimming pool ("See, we don't have to be rich Americans to have life's comforts"), and the individual apartments in which each kibbutz member lived with her or his own family ("See, we don't impose collectivism on people, and yet we still share our economic resources"). I understood why people wanted these things, but from my perspective, if *that* was what kibbutzniks were *most* proud of, we had the same and better in the United States. I could find better concert halls, swimming pools, and housing—without having to pick green peppers.

This same realization led many in the next generation of kibbutz youth to leave the kibbutzim in search of greater material comforts and more fulfilling work in the cities. True, some felt guilty at leaving the collective-wealth–sharing aspect of the kibbutz. But the kibbutz movement had become increasingly oriented toward selfishness, though it was predominantly on a group basis rather than on an individual one. Devoid of any spiritual life (most kibbutzim were decidedly antispiritual, and heavily invested in materialist philosophies), or any serious sense of mission to heal or repair the larger Israeli society, the kibbutzniks could not provide their children with a sense of purpose sufficient to retain their loyalty.

Those kibbutzniks who proposed a change in direction were largely ignored or ridiculed. Spiritual or political transformation of the larger Israeli society? That seemed "unrealistic," and contrary to what an increasing number of kibbutzniks were beginning to believe was "human nature": namely, the interest in taking care of oneself.

Ironically, and just as we have seen in other societies, what really turned out to be "unrealistic" was the effort to live by some hybrid reality, which held the self-interest of the kibbutz as primary, but included other allegedly collective or communal goals as well. The kibbutz had incorporated democracy and job rotation, but it could not commit itself to the common good without having to dedicate its resources to a serious political struggle to change Israeli society. Instead, the larger society changed the kibbutz.

When, decades later, my son attended high school on another kibbutz, I asked the director of the educational program about its values and political, spiritual, or ideological orientation. He assured me not to worry, because "we have no ideology here; we just teach the same way you'd learn in the U.S." It was precisely such emptying of vision and goals that led to the kibbutz's economic decline, yet this was justified within the kibbutz movement as becoming "realistic" and avoiding all the "high-sounding idealism of the early kibbutz movement"—which, after all, "hadn't really worked." The "realists" sought to make the kibbutzim reflect the values of the larger society.

It was precisely this triumph of selfishness within the kibbutz, in the name of realism, that led many kibbutzim to borrow money from capitalist banks in order to expand their productive capacities and their potential wealth. This strategy led to economic hardships when changes in the capitalist market undermined their ventures and left them unable to repay their loans.

Had the larger society felt that the kibbutzim were centers of caring for others, it might have stepped in and generously bailed many of the kibbutzim out of debt. But to many Jews from Mediterranean and Asian countries (known as Sephardim or Oriental Jews), the kibbutz was a symbol of Ashkenazic (Northern and

Eastern European Jewish) selfishness and self-centeredness. The kibbutzim had rarely attempted to establish contact and common ground with the Sephardim, who were the most economically oppressed elements in Israeli society, next to the Arabs. So these Sephardim, who constituted the electoral majority by the 1980s, felt little reason to dip into communal coffers to help the kibbutzim. Had the kibbutzim earned a reputation as the vanguard of social change, or of struggles for economic and social justice, they might not have suffered economically, because other Israelis would have felt an obligation toward them.

The weakness of the kibbutz movement demonstrates that we cannot have narrowly nationalistic and chauvinistic goals in our larger society, compromise broader goals, and then expect to build ethical, spiritual, and transformative social movements. Roughly the same pattern happened with American labor movements, which accommodated to the Cold War and to various racist and sexist practices, and ultimately were weakened by their inability to sustain the support of a larger popular coalition. Realistically, to change society means to think more globally, not less so, and to strive for the largest changes, not the smallest.

Of course, the immediate situation sometimes limits the possibilities for change. I think that this may well have been the case in 1948 when Israel was created, just as it was at the time of the Russian Revolution. But things are not always so, and the kibbutz example is a warning to resist the immense pressure to scale down our vision to what is "realistic," to abandon our vision of what we really believe in. If the politics of meaning succeeds in getting people of the Western world to dream again—to ask the question, "What would we really want if we didn't have to be 'realistic'? What fits our highest vision?"—then it could make a significant contribution to positive change.

This is the essence of the philosophy of hope within the politics of meaning: to retain our vision of the possible and to refuse to bow to the actual. As long as the larger society does not succeed in fundamentally altering our vision, momentary accommodations are not necessarily destructive. There could be a positive version of realism: if being realistic means constantly making new assessments of how much we can embody our ideals, given the present reality, and making new assessments of how we can move beyond what *is* toward what *ought to be,* given the present reality, then realism would take on a dimension that has been lost in the contemporary world.

Worker Responsibility

I have described how work could be organized to give workers ongoing opportunities to actualize their human capacities. In addition, it is important to honor work and workers. American education should include the study of the culture of work—how it is organized and how it relates to society as a whole. Honoring work and appreciating the contributions that working people make every day should become a major focus of public attention. Similarly, Labor Day should be transformed back into a day that is really dedicated to honoring one another for the contributions we make to the societal good. Similarly, the contributions of the labor movement to the well-being of all working people is a history that deserves our attention and gratitude.

Nevertheless, worker empowerment entails a code of responsibilities as well. A progressive politics of meaning rejects the countercultural view that society is a bottomless cookie jar, with goodies for us whenever we want. We have to create wealth, not just spend it, and this means that at times we will have to work hard in ways that do not feel immediately gratifying. The test of nonalienating work is not that it is always easy or always fun, but that it makes sense to us. It makes us feel connected to others, and to a larger ethical or spiritual purpose.

Our commitment to one another will require that we give as well as take. But giving can feel very different in the context of a society in which others are giving too, and in which we no longer feel that in giving we are likely to be ripped off.

For this reason, I part company with the "responsibility crowd," which often uses the language of responsibility as a cover for its own punitive and repressive inclinations. Talking about responsibility when our society's wealth is being appropriated by a small, rich group for private purposes, without regard to the consequences for the rest of the world, is very different from talking about responsibility in a society whose dominant ethos is one of caring for one another. In this latter situation, we will not need so many sermons about responsibility, because caring for one another will feel more natural and less coerced by external societal demand. Yet, in our current society, with its ethos of ultra-selfishness, it is important for us to affirm a commitment to responsibility, as long as we can distinguish its tone and content from that of right-wing discourse. The Right likes to lecture the rest of us about working harder and giving more, although most of us know that if we follow their plans, the prime beneficiaries of our working and our giving will not be us, nor those we love.

One aspect of responsibility is that people must do a good job. If we care for others, and understand how our work is needed by them, then we must commit ourselves to doing our best. Concretely, this means that people cannot be allowed to keep a job no matter how poorly they do it. This would be permissible only if the job did not matter (which it should), or if we did not care about the consequences to others (which we do).

People must face the consequences of doing poor work. Even after they have created work that is meaningful for them, they may have to be disciplined in part by market forces, which may fail to reward their work, if what they produce is inadequate. Factories or workplaces may shut down if they do not produce enough to generate profits, and people may then have to relocate or retrain.

The trauma of losing a job is enough of a consequence; we do not need to punish people by putting them into financial danger. Adequate unemployment benefits must be available for people as long as they are seeking work. Conversely, they must be prepared to move, to learn new skills, and to do what it takes to make themselves into contributing members of society. This consciousness of responsibility will never be fostered by repression. It will never come about by making working people feel bad about themselves, nor by acting as though workers have failed society because the market no longer values what they produced.

An Ecologically Oriented Economic Plan

It might appear, on the face of it, that ecological change has nothing to do with meaning. After all, if we want to save the life-support system of our planet, all we have to do is stop using the world's resources in a destructive way, create a rational plan for how to allocate resources and what to produce, and create massive incentives for decreasing the total consumption of nonreplenishable resources.

If none of this is happening, leftists imagine that the reason is simple: corporate interests are able to dominate public discourse and electoral processes in such a way as to ensure that no one interested in creating rational ecological plans will be given a serious hearing. This interpretation is true enough, but it does not explain how we could live in a world in which people continually are unwilling to focus on the overwhelming evidence that we are extensively damaging the environment—and with it, the life of future generations.

The denial and inability to stay focused on the ecological crisis, one of the great historical instances of collective denial, is easier to understand if we recognize that most people are in such immediate pain in their lives (caused by the frustration of their meaning-needs) that they are unable to pay attention to this larger but less pressing problem. If people feel terrible about themselves and their lives, and they internalize those feelings in the form of self-blame, they develop what I call "surplus powerlessness." This is a sense of themselves as being even more powerless than they actually are (beyond the reality of "real powerlessness" in the face of powerful economic forces dedicated only to accumulating profits at all costs).

I often have heard people tell me that they cannot imagine trying to deal with the ecological crisis because it seems so overwhelming. Meanwhile, they would go on to say, "I can't even get my own personal life together; I've made such a mess of that. So until I get that together, don't expect me to deal with the big issues." People who say this would be helped by the politics of meaning: understanding that the ethos of selfishness and materialism has shaped a society that undermines loving relationships and impedes our ability to sustain meaning-oriented lives. Then they might not blame themselves, develop surplus powerlessness, and refrain from engaging in ecological struggles (even though, in their hearts, they would be on the side of the ecologists).

Ironically, it is precisely the de-meaning and the disenchanting of the world that has created the context for the ecological crisis in the first place. It is only because we have suppressed our natural tendency to respond to the world with awe, wonder, and radical amazement, that current environmentally destructive practices are tolerated. We have replaced these sentiments with a willingness to see the earth as a resource to be exploited for the benefit of anyone who has the economic or technological capacity to do so.

It is no wonder, then, that the environmental movement is divided between liberal reformers, who think that all they need do is pass specific pieces of legislation to stop specific environmental abuses, and meaning-oriented environmentalists, who understand that we need a totally different approach to reality if we are going to save the planet. We have seen the surprise of the liberals when conservatives cleverly manipulate the crisis of meaning into right-wing electoral victories, and then are able to dismantle significant portions of existing environmental protections. The meaning-oriented environmentalists understand that we need to roll back the atomistic conceptions of the world and learn to see ourselves as deeply interconnected with one another and with the universe.

As I argued earlier in this chapter, a progressive politics of meaning is agnostic on whether its goals can be achieved in the capitalist market. But assuming the continuation of the current mixed economy, there will certainly need to be a greater degree of rational planning, at least for the sake of preserving the earth's resources. The unfettered market does not have adequate mechanisms for taking into consideration the interests of future generations in having a pollution-free earth with sufficient resources. We will need a world plan that can ensure that resources are not depleted, and that the environment is preserved and defended against any plundering of resources that the market generates.

To some people, this may sound like the kind of human arrogance that has been tried and has led us to our current crisis. However, we have not approached nature with the combined wisdom of our creative intelligence, spiritual and ethical sensitivity, and ecological awareness. We have not attempted to develop policies that fit our highest understanding. In fact, "we" have not approached nature at all. For the past one hundred and fifty years, it has been mostly a small subset of corporations and wealthy individuals who have decided how to use the material world; the rest of us have ratified these choices either by consuming or not consuming what they have produced. There has been no communal process through which we could discuss these issues or participate in decision-making. We may vote by not consuming many products, but the corporations do not thereby conclude that they should produce fewer things—only different things, which they hope they can induce us to want. We have no way to convince them to produce less.

There is nothing inherently arrogant about human beings using our creative, spiritual, ethical, and ecological capacities to decide how to deal with the world. Rather, we ourselves are the product of nature (or, religiously speaking, of God). If nature had not wanted us to use these capacities, she would not have allowed us to have them. But in order to use them fully, we first need to develop the capacities we do have and be sure that it is they, not profit-seeking special interests, that guide us.

Second, we need democratic mechanisms to ensure that we all participate in deciding how best to secure the future of the planet, and in developing the corresponding guidelines and restraints on the use of the earth's resources.

Finally, we have to keep in mind what Zygmunt Bauman calls "the indeterminacy of unanticipated consequences." We need humility in approaching the planning process. This quality has often been absent from the minds of government bureaucrats, technocrats, and whiz-kids who are reluctant or unable to imagine the complexities of human responses, which can throw off the best plans. Humility ought not to be an excuse for inaction, as it is when invoked by conservatives to forestall attempts to save the environment, or redistribute the world's food supplies in equitable ways. Humility *should* bespeak a willingness to consider alternatives and to experiment with a variety of approaches to solving a problem. Humility reminds us of the sanctity of human beings, when developing plans for what we think will be in someone else's best interest. It thereby provides the rationale for democratic participation in planning: those who are affected by a plan have a real opportunity to shape it and to participate in the community process of affirming or rejecting it.

In this context, it is wise to acknowledge that market mechanisms can have a certain efficiency that ought not to be abandoned. Within an overall plan that protects the earth's resources, markets can sometimes allocate resources in effective ways and can allow smaller groups to get some of what they want, without convincing the majority of the population to validate those wants by putting them into the overall economic plan. Markets can spur creativity that might be frustrated by the longer time it takes to influence a democratic process.

Moreover, markets would be much less distorting if they functioned within the context of a society in which the sanctity of every other individual was a central aspect of our consciousness. We should also try to approach the consumption of resources and products with a passionate commitment to the environment, to our responsibility as stewards of the earth, and to a spiritual communion of all being. The current functioning of our competitive market society plays a major role in preventing us from ever developing or sustaining such a consciousness, but should we as a society succeed in achieving it, then market elements would take on a different significance and could play a valuable role in a politics-of-meaning economy.

Spiritually Oriented Work

An economy can be a vehicle not only for providing our basic material needs, but also for reconnecting to our highest selves. Our work can be a moment in which we express our concern for the common good, and appreciate all those around us who are doing the same. We can build an economy that functions to connect us to the spiritual dimension of reality, and encourages us to respond to the universe with awe and wonder. We can reexperience every day the ways in which we together seek to serve each other and serve some higher purpose. And we can experience all this in a community of people who similarly seek a spiritually- and morally-centered universe. The meaning of work, and hence the feeling of work, can be dramatically altered.

This is partly a question of how we organize society and the economy. But it is not only that. A spiritually-oriented workplace depends on human beings who are engaged in their own lives and in their communities in daily acts of celebration, developing their own spirituality, and connecting to others in loving and caring ways. As with every step in imagining a meaning-oriented society, each part depends upon and interacts with each other part, and none of it is likely unless all of it becomes necessary.

This is so far from the reality of the contemporary world that it must sound vacuous or stupid to many contemporary audiences. It is my contention that the reorientation of our economic life has become a practical necessity, both for ecological and psychological reasons, and that it may be far more practical to talk about visionary changes than to focus solely on fine-tuning the existing ways we organize our economic life. It may take many generations before people are willing to imagine an economy that really takes seriously their meaning needs. But once this idea catches on, it will liberate incredible levels of creativity that will allow people to spell out in considerable detail a vision that I've only been able to hint at in this book.

EDUCATION

In the sphere of education, liberals have traditionally focused their energies on how to improve instruction by raising teachers' salaries and lowering the student-teacher ratio. While I support these positions, I have noticed that many of my fellow citizens do not. They are too upset with the product that our schools turn out: students who seem to have no moral compass. Liberals will never win the mass support they need to accomplish their very important demands until they first give people a motive for *wanting* to support them.

All too often, the public perceives teachers as yet another special interest group, reaching deep into the community's pockets. Conversely, teachers who find themselves having to strike for higher wages sometimes develop an opposing stance toward the very communities whose children they are supposed to educate. In the long run, teachers would be smarter to try to create public awareness that they themselves were interested in serving the community, and were as worried as everyone else about the problems being faced—particularly crime, the decline in ethical standards, and the alienation and loneliness that accompany a society based on individualism and selfishness.

Educate for Values: Teach Empathy

Values clarification is important, but it is not enough. Its premise is that the school should help students (usually later in high school) learn about the implications of various values that they do or might hold. The school plays a neutral role.

But schools should not be neutral. They should be explicitly committed to inculcating certain core values: love, empathy, caring, cooperation, commitment to others, spiritual and ethical sensitivity, respect for difference, respect for learning, respect for hard work, responsibility, self-discipline, tolerance, and honesty. Why only these, when we have other values as well? Because the schools cannot teach all of our values—this is also the task of parents. What the schools can teach is what we value as a community.

Students should learn about the multiplicity of philosophical approaches for *how* best to actualize these values in the world. Our communities often have very diverse views on this process. But students should not be left uncertain that *these* are the values that the school seeks to engender.

Let me give an example of one kind of approach. I propose a core course, from kindergarten through high school, whose focus is teaching empathy. At various points, it might focus on the following: empathy for other ethnic, cultural, and religious groups; empathy for whomever is the stigmatized Other in our society at that time (for example, homosexuals, African-Americans, Asians, Jews, Latinos, or whatever foreigners the media are telling us to view as our current possible enemy); empathy for fellow students; empathy for parents and other family members.

Schools will be very innovative in coming up with strategies to teach empathy if they are evaluated on how well they are creating an empathic student body. Schools that do better might be rewarded in some appropriate way. In addition, college-entrance examinations ought to assess empathy; so, too, ought entry-level job examinations. If students knew that college and jobs depended upon their ability to exhibit this skill, they would have powerful incentives to take the subject seriously.

Imagine what a change we might have in our society if students were genuinely involved in learning empathic skills and felt they really needed to master such skills: recognizing other people, recognizing their pain and their concerns, and showing others that they matter to us.

There are those people who wonder whether this kind of "social engineering" is appropriate in school, but the truth is, there is no avoiding it. Schools already do shape character—only they shape it in a very destructive way. They are structured to encourage young people to see one another as rivals for scarce rewards (grades, approval, honors, and so on). No wonder that students learn to distrust others, to view them as antagonists who might hurt them, and then, upon emerging from school, to regard random people on the street in the same way.

Some very foolish critics of values education imagine that they can handle the resulting problems by cracking down on violence in schools (for example, by punishing students who bring weapons to school). I support such punishments, yet they do not address the social climate that generates the violence, and generates the alienated attitude toward others that lets us see them as our actual or potential enemies. Teaching empathy will address this larger issue, and must be treated just as seriously as math or reading.

The school system already does teach values—just not the ones that it ought to be teaching. We need to change: to move from unconsciously teaching the wrong values to consciously teaching the values that we want to have taught. It will take hard work—yes, perhaps many years of experimenting, researching, and analyzing—to figure out how we can be most effective in teaching these essential values.

Don't Teach Religion; Teach *about* Religions and Teach Spiritual Awareness

Growing up in an American Jewish family that was both proudly Jewish and eager to participate in the cultural and intellectual life of American society, I experienced early in life the vitality and nourishment that communities of meaning can provide. My parents were deeply involved in the Zionist movement and in a variety of Jewish communal institutions. I jumped into their world—loving the music, happily embracing Temple B'nai Abraham's after-school Hebrew school three times a week, and delighting in the customs and commandments that gave shape to Jewish life. During the same period, I was sent to a private school in which I was the only Jewish child. Far Brook Country Day combined progressive education with a rich commitment to an interdenominational Christianity. It found expression in the music we sang each morning when the entire school met in assembly for an hour before classes, and in the annual Christmas play, which retold the Nativity story.

Though my own religious beliefs made it increasingly difficult for me to sing the songs or participate in the play, I could see the immense beauty and wisdom in the Christianity to which I was being exposed. I had my own faith community, but I was happy that my schoolmates had theirs as well. Still, I felt uncomfortable being in a situation in which their religion was the officially sanctioned one. By seventh grade, I insisted on transferring to a public school in the heavily Jewish (Weequahic) neighborhood of Newark, New Jersey, where I finished my schooling.

There was a Christmas play at public school too, and although our school was eighty percent Jewish, all of the students participated. But this was a very different kind of play; it avoided everything that was deep and profound about Christianity, and instead celebrated Christmas as a Santa Claus–centered occasion for gift-giving. Similarly, instead of the songs that I had learned at Far Brook, which conveyed a sense of reverence for God and for other human beings, the public school began each day with an imposed recital of the Lord's Prayer. Here, too, I could not participate. I did not want to be forced to say a Christian prayer, nor did I want to participate in a Christmas-oriented observance—no matter how depleted of meaning, no matter how tame and secularized.

Yet, though I wanted school not to *impose* a particular religious tradition, I also felt the absence of spirituality and religious concerns in the public schools that I attended, and in the larger cultural and intellectual life of the society which they served.

My public-school friends, both Christian and Jewish, had, I felt, the worst of both worlds: they had been presented a watered-down form of religion, sanctified by the government, that could not possibly speak to whatever inner spiritual needs were awakening in them. Meanwhile, they were surrounded by a society that was proclaiming the virtues of wealth and power, that constantly patted itself on the back for having "the highest standard of living in the world"—defined solely in material terms. They had never encountered a sphere of life in which a different ethos prevailed. They were encouraged to learn science and math, so that they could develop the practical skills that would get them into a good college, and then on to a job that would produce a high standard of living. Intellectual skills would be the ticket to what the public school really valued: economic success.

These issues came into sharpest relief for me during the annual Thanksgiving plays that were presented in the public school. These plays inevitably focused on some aspect of killing and eating turkeys, or, in the upper grades, on the encounter between Pilgrims and Indians. At Far Brook there had been no play about turkeys or Pilgrims, but a deeper celebration of thanks. All children were asked to bring a fruit or vegetable to school. Then a processional was held in which each child, with accompanying music produced by the school orchestra, presented his or her offering at a makeshift altar (with no cross or other particular religious symbols). The food was later donated to a nearby orphanage. We were encouraged, through song and individual expression, to give thanks for whatever it was that we were thankful for—and *this* became the individual and collective focus of this shared ritual.

When I tried to describe this sense of reverence and thanks to many of my public-school classmates, they simply had no idea what I was talking about. It just did not compute, given their experiences in the schools and religious communities of the city.

I was only twelve when I began to be troubled by all this. When I raised the issue with my civil liberties–oriented rabbi, he responded by telling me how grateful I should be that meaning had been depleted from American life. Himself a refugee from the Holocaust, he reminded me that if non-Jews ever got back into a search for meaning, part of the historical tradition that they would draw upon would be so suffused with anti-Semitism that our people might once again be dragged back into concentration camps. Yet my own experience with young American Christians led me to believe that there was nothing inherent in their psyches that would necessarily lead them in that direction. It made more sense to me to trust non-Jews than to build a world based on the assumption that they would hurt us the moment they were allowed to do so. I did not blame my parent's generation for having that distrust—they had plenty of recent historical reasons for feeling that way. Yet it seemed to me that their understandable paranoia could be self-fulfilling, and this seemed to me a big mistake.

For my rabbi and my parents, it was not possible to imagine meaning-oriented societies that were not imposing a particular religious perspective, and this they quite rightly wanted to avoid. Yet my experience of Thanksgiving at Far Brook showed me that schools could teach a rich spirituality and reverence without imposing a particular religious tradition's symbols or ways of limiting our conception of what we were thankful for, or to what, or to whom.

I believe that we should teach children an attitude of joyous celebration of the grandeur of the universe, and that we can do this without imposing a particular religious language in the process. I saw this happen at Far Brook because of another element of their educational philosophy, which ought to be adopted in our public schools: free play.

Nearly half of every school day at Far Brook was dedicated to taking the first- through fourth-grade students to a wooded area, and then allowing us hours to devise our own forms of free play. The first impact of this activity was that we learned fewer skills than our counterparts in public school. When I transferred, I found myself—at first—with less specific skills-training than my fellow public-school students. But I came in with one huge advantage: I liked school, while most of my fellow seventh-graders hated it. Within a year, I had picked up the skills to rise to the top of my class, while the others were stumbling because of their resentment of school.

But the second impact of free play is what concerns me here: our ability at Far Brook to develop a personal relationship to nature and to the grandeur of the universe. Given the amount of time we were allowed to play in nature, and given the introduction by our teachers of concepts like wonder and gratitude, most of us quickly worked out our own private moments in which we celebrated the wonders among which we were allowed to play. I do not think that a school needs to be located in a woodsy area to offer this experience (though trying to build schools in beautiful natural settings that allow for unstructured free play would be a wonderful idea). What is necessary is a commitment to providing students with regular opportunities to develop their own relationship to the natural world.

Schools might also try to teach students to adopt some of the spiritual wisdom of a given tradition, without necessarily tying it to the specific religion from which the practice derives. For example, the Jewish holy days of repentance create an opportunity for people to collectively reflect on their experience during the past year and consider the degree to which they actualized their highest vision of who they could and should be. Imagine if high-school students were given a day each year to perform that kind of reflection on their own past year.

These are elements of spirituality that could and should be developed in school. They would provide a useful counterbalance to the allure of a mechanistic worldview that promises material abundance as its primary outcome.

One might object that in making a case for some kind of spirituality, I have contradicted my earlier warnings about the dangers of teaching religion in schools.

This concern is absolutely legitimate, particularly at a historical moment when the Christian Coalition is seeking to reintroduce precisely the kind of coercive religious experience in schools that I hated as a child and which I always felt to be intrusive and disrespectful to my minority community. As long as we live in a world in which some religious groups have a propensity to use the state's coercive apparatus to impose religion, there will be good reason to fight to defend the original intent of the First Amendment.

It is difficult to argue that a minute of silence for private meditation or prayer would function coercively in public schools, if each individual student were allowed to direct personal thoughts toward whatever she or he chose, and if teachers were fined or penalized for directing students toward a particular religious tradition.

Nevertheless, there are reasons to oppose the minute of silent prayer. This is not real prayer, but phony prayer: it does not give anyone enough time to get into a spiritually serious space. So it is unlikely to succeed in bringing greater sensitivity toward the sacred to young people. It is the worst kind of tokenism.

However, I share with many people on the Right a desire to increase our children's spiritual sensitivity, and I believe that a serious prayer experience can often be part of the way in which this is accomplished. Thus, I would like to see the various religious communities develop morning religious services, in locations near the schools, to which parents could take their children and pray as a family before going to school. This is precisely the kind of "taking responsibility" that is appropriate to expect of individual families. It is not an individualistic solution—it merely recognizes the plurality of responses in our communities to the issue of how best to initiate our children into a relationship with God.

Moreover, the *best* way to get our children to take spiritual and religious life seriously is for them to see adults taking it seriously. For this reason, the morning prayers should *not* be held in schools, where children are almost exclusively among their peers, but in communities, where their parents can join them. If, instead of using this issue as a political football, we were to concentrate on the question, "What is the best way to sensitize our children to God and to the spiritual realities of the universe?" our answer would not be, "a minute of silent prayer in schools," but, "regular exposure to a religious community that takes God and the spiritual universe seriously."

By foisting this responsibility onto the schools, we can be almost certain that little will happen to awaken children's spiritual sensitivity. Those who have been leading the charge in this direction are *not* advocates for children's spirituality; they are people who are trying to win a political and cultural struggle. In essence, I agree with their underlying presumption that our lives have become too devoid of spirituality and the sacred. But I believe that the kind of spiritual experience likely to emerge from the struggle for a moment of silent prayer will actually further secularize our children—by neutralizing what ought to be a powerful moment of encounter with the divine each morning. Having gone through years in which my entire class said the Lord's Prayer each morning, I feel confident that what happened in that context and in that way had little to do with a genuine experience of the sacred. The place for that encounter is within our religious communities.

Still, I am troubled by the way in which First Amendment absolutists have taken our society to the opposite extreme, so that today, a child goes through a public-school education and learns nothing about the great religious, spiritual, and philosophical systems that have shaped the experience of our human race. Instead, what they learn are the values and worldview of a particular version of empiricist materialism, taught as part of science and history courses. Despite claims to the contrary, there is nothing "neutral" about this approach—the metaphysical foundations of science are no less "religious" than the metaphysical foundations of any other religion.

Schools should teach about the religious, spiritual, and philosophical heritage of the world, which should include the traditions of Asia, Africa, and South America, as well as Europe and North America. Some schools do this already, but usually to fulfill a mandate to "teach diversity," rather than to attune children to the spiritual dimension of universal human existence.

The most effective way to let children know that there is something exciting and alive in these various traditions is to allow their adherents to advocate for their religious or spiritual worldview. But advocacy presents some problems for children in the early grades, where the very presence of an adult in front of a classroom creates the assumption that what is being taught is the truth. So, in the early grades, it makes more sense to have social-studies teachers introduce these traditions, and the only values they should try to instill are tolerance and respect for diversity.

By tenth grade, however, students are capable of hearing alternative views and making their own judgments. This is when it becomes appropriate to allow a certain level of well-regulated advocacy.

Here is a possible approach to teaching about religions in high school:

1. All major religious traditions currently operating within the United States should be taught, except any that specifically acknowledge a belief that certain other human beings are fundamentally inferior by virtue of some intrinsic feature (that is, groups that explicitly teach racist or sexist ideas). For example, one need not and should not teach any religion that says that African-Americans or Jews or women are inferior beings.

2. Given the strong influence that local religious groups are likely to have on the way in which given school districts or teachers present the material, religious traditions might end up being taught in accordance with the local community's majority tendencies. Therefore, the only way in which religious advocacy can be done fairly is to take it out of the hands of the teachers and the local districts. Instead, each major religious community should be given the opportunity to present its material on videotapes, tailored to the different grade levels. Each tape should begin and end with a warning that clearly states:

   "What you are about to hear (or have just heard) is being presented to you *not* because we at this school think that it is the truth. There are many different approaches to religious and spiritual reality, each of which claims to have the right approach, and we do not pretend to say which one is true or that any is true. But we believe that it would be inappropriate to grow up in this society and not learn about the rich religious, spiritual, and philosophical traditions that have contributed to the development of humanity. Some of the views that you are about to hear (or have just heard) may be offensive to you, and none of these views ought to be accepted blindly. But we want you to know what different groups of people believe today, and how they see the world. You are not expected necessarily to agree with any particular view, or with any of the views in this or any other video that you see about religion, spirituality, philosophical traditions, or any other worldview that is presented to you."

3. Within these restrictions, each major religious tradition and denomination should be allowed to present its approach to spirituality, but not with equal time for all. The reason: the majority religious traditions in the United States all are forms of Christianity, so that if each denomination were given equal time, students might be likely to hear repeatedly about Christianity while learning far less about Judaism, Islam, Buddhism, or other approaches.

4. There should also be presentations from advocates for philosophical and spiritual approaches that are *not* represented in major religious traditions, such as atheism and scientific materialism (the latter to clarify the point being made throughout: that the dominant empiricist tradition of our society is just one of many different and contending worldviews).

5. Local school districts should be free *not* to use the religious advocacy series, but they should be prohibited from teaching religion in some other, more one-sided way that offends members of minority religions or atheists.

I certainly do not want to see a school system that inadvertently forces children to conform to a given religious standard, and for this reason, I advocate scrupulous protection of minority rights. I think that this stance is appropriate when teaching a particular religious tradition.

Moreover, there are other values sometimes associated with religion that deserve public recognition and support. These ought to be taught in our schools, yet need not be taught as part of any specific spiritual or religious tradition. Consider again the example of Thanksgiving, with its values of gratitude and celebration. Or consider the values of humility, or of reverence for nature. These values ought to be part of a school curriculum, and teachers ought to be trained to teach them throughout the rest of the curriculum.

There has been a peculiar contradiction in the recent conservative educational agenda. On the one hand, its proponents sometimes talk about getting back to basics, and here they usually mean reading, writing, and arithmetic. On the other hand, they quite correctly complain about value-neutral school curricula. What they apparently neglect to notice is that they have determined what is "basic" in terms of what will help people succeed in the economic marketplace. Much of my argument in this book has been aimed to show that we ought to be fighting for other values, some of which conflict with those that are enshrined in the materialism and me-firstism of the competitive market. So when we get down to basics at school, we should be teaching values like gratitude, reverence for nature, and humility—along with the primary emphasis on empathy discussed earlier. If these kinds of values were taught in school, children would be much likelier to be receptive to religious and spiritual instruction at home, and it would remain in the parents' hands to determine which specific religious or spiritual tradition to teach.

Teach Family Coping Skills

A frequent reason why students have difficulty in school is that they face difficult problems in their families, but have no perspective on these problems and no one with whom to discuss them. They often cannot concentrate in class because they are upset about what is happening at home. Too emotionally distraught to concentrate, they shift their attention to daydreams, or become discipline problems. Even those students who are doing their best to concentrate sometimes are impaired because of family distress.

To help these children, we need to create a class at each grade level in which students are taught about family dynamics and are encouraged to talk freely about their own family lives. Students should be taught how to identify problem dynamics in families. In earlier grades, the focus could be on teaching students the different ways in which families are organized in different cultures, and the kinds of problems that tend to emerge. In later grades, the focus would be on students' own families. Students would learn to recognize and report systematic physical abuse, to recognize areas in which family communication skills could facilitate better understanding, and to not blame themselves for parental failure to provide them with adequate recognition or caring.

Students should also be given the chance to learn about the world of work and the competitive marketplace, and how the values frequently communicated in the media interact with these arenas to undermine the ethos of loving and caring that is central to family life. In earlier grades, students should be taught how to watch television critically and how to identify the messages that are conveyed about "common sense" or about family life. In later grades, schools should teach about the psychological impact of work and economic competition.

There may be some students whose problems are acute and who need special therapy. According to a 1991 federal survey of U.S. high school students, twenty-seven percent had "thought seriously" about committing suicide (including eight percent who had actually made an attempt). Emotional distress is a major factor in our classrooms. Since even the most successful students often face deep inner conflicts about family issues, virtually everyone would benefit from an opportunity to discuss what has been happening in his or her home life. Moreover, one of our goals in a politics of meaning is to strengthen family life. The opportunity for children and teenagers to think about these issues will create adults who are far better prepared to enter into lasting relationships, and to be sensitive to the needs and conflicts that their own children may face.

Programs to teach family coping skills must eschew any effort to identify one ideal family form or to impose any single ideal psychological style on family life. But every family will benefit if students learn certain basic communication skills, including the ability to articulate their feelings. On the other hand, some cultural traditions do not give high value to the articulation of feelings. Students from such backgrounds would still learn the skills, but would be encouraged to make their own assessments as to when and how those skills might be used.

Teach Responsibility and Self-Discipline

In order to foster a perpetual and ever-expanding market for America's products, our society has created human beings who think that our sole purpose in life is to take in and consume whatever we wish. Things are there to consume, and if we can get the money (however we can get it), then we should consume them. Many children grow up with the expectation that they are entitled to receive, but they are not taught to expect that they also ought to give back.

Schools need to challenge this attitude. They should value hard work and an ethos of responsibility that encourages students to understand how the world has been constituted, and how many people are contributing daily to make their world work. Schools could focus students' attention on how much the objects of one's physical and social world have been constructed through the energies of generations of people. Students should also learn that having been part of a group that was exploited, poor, or relatively powerless does not free them from responsibility to others or to society as a whole.

Moreover, schools should teach self-discipline. The major obstacles to self-discipline in schools today have to do with the level of psychological pain that students bring with them from home. I already have suggested some ways in which a politics-of-meaning–oriented school would deal with this pain. But there also ought to be an explicit focus in early grades on teaching students how to study, how to put distractions out of their mind, how to concentrate, how to let go of pain and hurtful memories, and how to control one's impulses. Impulse control need not always be authoritarian or repressive; sometimes it is the necessary precondition for learning or being with others.

Discipline should not mean getting students to blindly obey the rules of the institution. Rather, discipline should flow from a growing awareness of the needs and rights of others, which flows in turn from a growing ability to recognize others as self-creating, meaning-seeking beings who deserve to be cherished and respected. Discipline, then, is best taught when we generate in students a genuine concern for others, and when we foster the habit of seeing through and rejecting the cynicism, indifference, and selfishness that they have already come to recognize as the way "the real world" operates. Discipline, in this regard, is not blind submission to constituted authority.

Work-Study and Community Service

One of the more effective ways to teach about the value of hard work, the need for people to cooperate with one another, and the need for individuals to take responsibility, is to place children in work situations for some extended period of time. Structured learning programs could be built around the work situation, so that American students could be both learning and working during the same day. For example, if fifth- or sixth-grade students each spent three months picking vegetables or fruits and accompanying migrant laborers in the fields, they would have a very different and deeper understanding of how food comes to us and of the value of hard work. If once or twice more during the junior and senior high school years, students spent another three-month period in a work setting, they would learn things that no book could ever teach them.

It is also important to encourage students to develop a critical perspective, because their fresh eyes might help people at the workplace see ways in which things might be done differently. To inspire this kind of reflection, schools would provide workplace mentors for each student so that skills could be learned and mentors' wisdom and experience could be shared. Experiences could be analyzed at weekly discussion groups for students at various workplaces. The groups could help each member problem-solve, and a teacher could introduce ideas, moral instruction, and a historical perspective on related issues (such as how the forms of work and related technology have developed, what kinds of workers' struggles have taken place, and what possible workplace changes have been or might be considered).

Another way to teach responsibility is to include community service as an integral part of education. At every grade level, starting in fourth grade, students would spend a certain amount of time each week working in a community service program, doing something to benefit the general welfare of the community. Community service would not be spurious, makeshift work—it would have to be something that really was valued. Each community would need to have democratic mechanisms through which to make yearly decisions about what volunteer activities to present to students.

In our society, the desire to contribute to the common good is often constricted by the "common sense" feeling that, in order to do so, people must sacrifice their own personal self-interest. But in the world we envision in this chapter, the common sense of society would be one of valuing and desiring to serve one another. Teenagers, far from having to be coerced into community service, would feel that doing so was a mark of how grown-up they were. Service to others would be seen as the most valued activity of our society. Accordingly, at the end of high school, students who had demonstrated that they qualified as sensitive and caring would be allowed to participate in a high-prestige national service program. Being chosen for national service would be a great honor, and students throughout their high school career would be engaged in activity to show that they deserved to be given this kind of opportunity to serve.

Teach Respect for Learning

If the school system itself does not respect learning, why should we expect that the students will?

For this reason, teachers' pay must be made commensurate with that of other respected professionals. Classroom size also should be reduced. For the same reason, teachers themselves must visibly be involved not just in teaching, but in learning. Every school should have a daily period during which each teacher is involved in learning new material, in some area outside the one(s) in which they teach. Some schools might arrange to have visiting scholars from nearby universities come and give lectures on new developments in their areas of expertise. In other schools, the federal or state Department of Education might provide a video series of top-notch scholars presenting this kind of information. In still other schools, faculty might meet and study a challenging text together.

The school itself should strive to be a model of what it hopes for students to learn. This principle applies also to the maintenance of basic peace and order in the classroom, hallways, and parking lots of schools. There is a difference between youthful exuberance, which should be strongly encouraged in school systems, and lack of internal discipline, which should be challenged. In the transition to a new society, communities must give serious attention to ensuring that this kind of discipline and order is enforced—perhaps in part by people from the national service program.

Education for the Community, Not the Corporation

Parading under the banner of education reform in the recent past have been various attempts to orient schools more toward teaching the skills that corporations say job-seekers ought to have. The focus is on training the individual to be able to enter the job market with the specific talents that local corporations say they may need in the years ahead. The notion that education should focus on preparing children for the job market, currently being advanced by the Clinton administration (particularly by Secretary of Labor Robert B. Reich), has an obvious advantage: it shows that we as a nation care about whether young people can find a place in the world of work. But although we want students to get the training that they need in order to have jobs, the bottom line for education ought to be the fostering of loving; caring; and ethically, spiritually, and ecologically sensitive human beings.

Svi Shapiro, professor of education at the University of North Carolina, has made a persuasive case that there may not necessarily be a contradiction between these two goals, if we realize that the workplace of the future may need workers skilled in democratic decision-making, cooperation, creativity, and sensitivity to fellow workers. Shapiro writes, "Our schools need to educate individuals in cooperative work, collective responsibility, negotiation of priorities, and conflict resolution . . . [W]orkers will need to consider critical economic and human issues that include the environmental impact of particular production decisions, the effects on workers' security and labor conditions of the adoption of new technologies, or the consequences of investment decisions on employees and their decisions." In this situation, "work-related education becomes not simply job-training, but a genuine form of critical, cultural education where the broad human, social, economic, and environmental consequences of one's work" can be explored. Workers who have developed these skills are likely to be more effective in helping to shape firms that can effectively position themselves to survive in the limited markets envisioned by a politics-of-meaning economy.

To train this kind of a worker, we need what Pablo Freire called a "critical pedagogy." Students need to learn how to question the assumptions of each discipline, and of the organization of the larger society. But the questioning is not for its own sake, nor is it for assuming that no one can ever have justified authority. Rather, the questioning of assumptions must be done in the name of the core values, articulated above, to which education must be committed.

This questioning could be facilitated by a course that taught about the history of domination of consciousness. At least part of the history and English curriculum in high schools should be dedicated to teaching students how to recognize the cultural and political assumptions built into the dominant ideas of each age, how people have struggled against this domination in the past, and theories about how domination can be transcended.

Yet, the questioning of assumptions cannot only be about forms of political domination. The most powerful techniques of domination today depend upon emptying the world of ethical and spiritual content. So it is precisely here that students need to be encouraged to grow and develop. Each student should be asked to do a personally or communally oriented senior project in which she or he develops and demonstrates heightened ethical or spiritual awareness. Graduation ceremonies should focus on students presenting to family, friends, classmates, and community members some of what they have done in this project, individually and collectively with others who have participated in it, or who have benefited from it.

Honors awards at graduations from such schools should be based on moral achievement. The primary focus of ceremonies should go to those who, regardless of academic competence in other areas, have shown themselves most capable of sensitivity, caring for others, and commitment to the common good. Scholarships to college should be awarded not only for academic mastery, but also for excellence in having developed ethical or spiritual sensitivity, as demonstrated through acts of compassion and caring for others.

HEALTH CARE

Many contemporary physical health problems result directly from the deprivation of meaning. Human beings are fundamentally meaning-oriented, and our ability to flourish depends on our connection to and congruence with the spiritual/meaning dimension of the universe. Throughout history, much human sickness has been produced by the disruption of the spiritual and ethical ecology of the universe. When human beings are engaged in violent, hateful, corrupt, materialistic, individualistic, or immoral social orders, in which the ways we embody God are denied or misrecognized, we create societies that are physically unhealthy.

In Western medicine, health and illness have been construed as solely a function of what the atoms and molecules in our bodies happen to be doing at any given time, as they follow the meaning-blind laws of nature. Dr. Larry Dossey, writing in the journal *Alternative Therapies in Health and Medicine,* reports that he and many other physicians eventually discovered in their clinical practice that medicine badly needed to attend to the meaning-dimension. Dossey cites some recent clinical studies that show, for example, the potent effect on longevity of having a perceived meaning in life. Similarly, studies show that "the meaning of the relationship with one's spouse is a major factor in the clinical expression of heart disease; that the meaning of a job and one's level of job dissatisfaction can be major predictors of heart attack; that attention to the meanings surrounding heart disease, when combined with dietary discretion, exercise and stress management, can improve cardiac performance and reverse coronary artery obstructions; that the bereavement and mourning following a spouse's death are associated with severe immune dysfunctions; . . . and that for certain cancer patients, group therapy in which questions of meaning are addressed can double survival time following diagnosis."

Dossey argues that the systematic denial of purpose and meaning may take its place in a future Hall of Human Silliness. And he warns physicians that "no matter how technologically effective modern medicine may be, if it does not honor the place of meaning in illness it may lose the allegiance of those it serves."

The separation of meaning from medicine is only one of the many specific consequences of the triumph of a worldview that denigrated ethical and spiritual truths, saw these as "non-sense," and constructed a world based on mechanistic and materialistic principles. Our task in the coming generations is to rectify the consequences of this narrow way of understanding reality.

There are, however, two dangers in emphasizing the meaning-dimension. First, there are some New Age formulations that regard illness as having no physical causation whatsoever, attributing all disease solely to the patient's attitudes and beliefs. This philosophy can lead to disastrous consequences, such as the refusal to employ drugs and surgical procedures when they might be appropriate, and even lifesaving.

Moreover, a misunderstanding of a meaning-oriented approach can lead to blaming the victim: suggesting that any given sick person may be sick because of some personal immorality or spiritual depravity. But this is *not* what I am saying. We may each work on improving our individual ethical and spiritual lives, and this can have some limited impact in improving our health, but (as I have argued throughout this book), the impact of the macro on the micro aspects is immense.

It is impossible to live a spiritually and morally appropriate life in a world full of pain and oppression, materialism and selfishness. Withdrawal from such a world equates to turning our backs on the needs of others, and that is not a morally appropriate choice. But involvement in the world, even in struggles to change it, inevitably leads to being affected and shaped by the distortions of others. Thus, there is no possibility of anyone fully living a spiritually healthy life in a spiritually and morally degraded social reality. For this reason, although health is a function of spirituality and morality, and not some separate sphere, it *cannot* be dramatically improved on an individual basis without simultaneous improvements in the moral and spiritual health of our entire society. So any person's sickness in our social order is not a badge of individual shame, but a reflection of the health of the entire community.

There is a growing body of research that shows some salutary effects on health when people actively engage in communities of meaning and purpose, and even, to some extent, when people engage in a personal search for ethical and spiritual meaning. Meaning and health are intrinsically linked, both on the individual and communal level.

Once we recognize these connections, then we can also recognize how distorted the current debates about health care in the United States have become. On the one hand, we observe the moral insensitivity and perverseness of conservatives who do not even understand our obligations to our fellow creatures, obligations which they could have easily learned about by reading the Bible. On the other hand, some liberals seem to think that the content of what our medical system delivers is basically fine, and that the major problem is to make sure that more of it is available to more people. Both sides are very far from understanding the crisis of meaning and its relationship to health.

In another corner are some proponents of New Age views who understand that the meaning-dimension is central to health, but who focus exclusively on inner healing without recognizing that our entire social fabric is permeated with moral and spiritual disease.

Healing People Rather Than Just Fighting Disease

Our physical health problems are connected to the way we have abused our bodies and our environment in the pursuit of selfish and materialistic ends. Corporate opposition has effectively stymied research that could begin to show the relationship between environmental hazards and various forms of disease, such as cancer and Alzheimer's, though many scientists have speculated that those ties could eventually be demonstrated.

The dominant model of Western health care regards its primary task as healing a sick body. But the division between body and soul is mistaken. We are animated, enspirited bodies, and so the task is not to heal a body but to heal a person. Part of the healing, then, is to nurture the life energy of the individual, and this process can be done by an entire community. Health can be fostered by rituals and communal festivals as well as by life-cycle events that contribute to increasing the life energy in most who participate.

Physical healing is closely connected to psychological and spiritual well-being, so our approach to health care must serve the whole human being. Health professionals must set out to achieve the highest possible level of well-being for the patient, rather than simply to eradicate some germ or disease from a body. Every person is a physical/spiritual/ethical/psychological unity, embedded in a larger ethical/spiritual/ecological totality. The health of the individual is intrinsically linked to his or her well-being on all of these levels, and to the well-being of the totality in which he or she is embedded. We are most likely to make significant advances in healing when we reorient medicine on the basis of this understanding.

Illness is not solely a problem facing the individual. Family therapists have come to understand that when a particular child is acting out in some destructive way, that child is often indicating a problem in the entire family system. Many of our health problems may similarly have significance for a larger system, so it behooves us when approaching the healing enterprise to imagine what kinds of healing may be needed not only by the patient but by the hospital, the health-care profession, the family, the community, and even the country.

Training and Rewarding Health-Care Personnel

The primary reason for which people enter medicine and other health-care professions, is their desire to care for and protect other human beings. Yet this motive quickly is undermined in a society that places primary value on money and power. In the field of health care, these dynamics can be particularly destructive of the trust that is necessary between providers and their clients.

Accordingly, if we are to train medical professionals to serve in a caring society, then we must give priority to the development of their moral and spiritual sensitivity that is equal to the development of more narrowly defined skills. Starting with premedical training, and throughout medical school and residency, the practitioners should learn the full range of approaches to healing the soul, as well as the mind and body. The principles and techniques of chiropractic, holistic health, nutrition, and preventive health care should be fully integrated into training. Practicums for medical professionals should focus as much on how to develop one's own inner spirituality and healing capacities as on how to master various medical techniques. Interns and residents should spend at least one rotation per year at a spiritual healing center where they learn how to connect with healing energies not yet fully incorporated into Western medicine.

Because doctors, nurses, and other health-care workers are going to use their skills primarily to serve the common good, the cost of their training should be fully paid by the community. While in medical and other training, they should receive a stipend that is sufficient to support themselves and family. Moreover, the practice of staffing hospitals with overworked interns and residents in order to avoid hiring adequate medical staff must be forbidden. Instead, interns and residents should be given a humane workload, with adequate time off to compensate for night shifts, no consecutive day and night shifts, and enough vacation time to ensure that no one suffers from the sheer physical exhaustion that is so common today among medical trainees.

Medical trainees should be encouraged to take semesters or years off to broaden their knowledge in other fields so that their focus does not become too narrowly medical. Since they would be making a comfortable wage while preparing for their profession, they should no longer have a case for seeking excessive compensation afterwards on the basis of "having sacrificed so much," as the current argument goes.

After medical school, the differential between medical salaries and those of others who serve the common good would be reduced, and profiteering on health care would be abandoned. Some of the kinds of people who today enter medical schools would no longer be attracted there, because medicine would no longer be the royal road to disproportionately high incomes. Introduced as a reform in our own contemporary society, this policy could have disastrous consequences for the quality of care. But in a society that was simultaneously changing its values orientation in every sphere, this change would seem both natural and appropriate. There is every reason to believe that a society based on a different bottom line would soon produce many talented, highly skilled, motivated people who could supply as good—if not better—medical care and as good—if not better—medical technology, as that which is available at this moment in the United States. Better care could result from altering many of the practices that distort health care today—practices based on the primacy of profits rather than the primacy of care.

Rejecting Medical Arrogance

Much of what passes for "medical science" in hospitals is a conglomeration of guesses, traditional practices that have not always been confirmed to have healing effects, and chutzpah. In fact, if doctors and hospital personnel were able to be honest with themselves, they would acknowledge that they often have only limited knowledge of what to do in any given situation.

Faced with the distorting impact of years of indoctrination into the notion that medicine is a science, that there is a right and a wrong way to do things, and that they ought to know which is which, many medical personnel feel terror at their own lack of certainty. They compensate for the fear and self-blame that they might otherwise feel by leaping into the arrogance of a false certainty—backed by studies, journals, and endless encouragement from drug companies and medical/biological technology producers, who can play on these unconscious insecurities and purport to have scientifically validated remedies.

It would be far more humane for hospitals to be based on the principle that, in dealing with matters of life, human beings have only partial answers. Our lives are part of a mystical body/soul continuity whose healing is only partially in our hands. The healing that we can offer can only be partial, particularly to the extent that we live in a world that is itself off-kilter, and hence undermines the spiritual and ethical health that are important components of any healing process.

Once we abandon the notion of the doctor as omniscient expert with privileged access to medical science, we have good reason to challenge the hierarchical structure that dominates so many hospitals. Nurses and medical technicians may have more useful information and insights than many doctors, and they ought to be included in central roles on the team that plans the patient's health care. Nor should a healing environment be torn apart by the kind of class conflict that is inevitable when such vast disparities exist between the pay of orderlies and other so-called lower level hospital workers, and those who make the important decisions. Adequate pay and respect for all the workers in a hospital is an important part of the solution, but so, too, is including everyone in various daily hospital rituals which convene the entire staff to nurture its own healing energies. One idea would be a daily gathering of the healers to take some time for meditation, and for a ritual recommitment to the patients' health and to the nobility of the healing enterprise. This practice would reinvigorate spiritual energies, as long as it were not coerced or counterposed to good pay and an equalizing of power relationships.

To base health care on relationships is to dramatically shift from the individualism of the current contractual model, symbolized by the informed consent form that patients must sign to symbolize their role as autonomous buyer. But if we view each human being as infinitely precious and as fundamentally connected to us, then his or her vulnerability at the moment of seeking this care creates an obligation in those who would heal, which no contract can vitiate. This obligation extends to a point at which the healers should be doing everything they can (not pretending they can do more than they can) to bring to bear the greatest wisdom on how to heal, derived from medical science and other healing practices.

The Ethics of Allocating Scarce Resources

Critics of the individualism of the U.S. health-care system have sometimes noted that we each expect to be treated as though we were the center of the universe and no one else existed. Yet we actually belong to a community with limited resources, and we may have to make decisions soon about who will receive care and when we can no longer continue to keep a particular kind of patient alive, or no longer can afford to pay for extremely expensive but under-utilized medical technology.

The emphasis on restraint and recognition of others is an important counterweight to our entitlement society that assumes there are never any limits. There are.

It will be far easier for people to understand those restraints when the scarcity is shared equally. As long as it is possible for some people to buy better care or greater access to the latest medical technology (or even to the best advances in spiritual healing techniques, which today tend to be more affordable to the upper middle class), it is going to be very difficult to convince others that they ought not to struggle for the same access, and to insist on their "right" to that access.

In actual practice, however, the scarcity of health-care resources is closely tied to the profit-oriented nature of the current system. The ever-higher costs of medical care are *not* inevitable. They only seem so because doctors charge as much as they can get away with (just like everyone else in our society); since we entrust our lives to them, they tend to get away with quite a bit. So do medical technology suppliers and drug companies, and of course, the private owners of hospitals who benefit from the high fees for hospital visits.

Nevertheless, there may very well come moments when we must make the decision to take someone off a life-support system, or to withhold monies for certain extremely expensive forms of treatment. These decisions ought not to be made by a group of financial analysts or health-care professionals, but by the entire community, because all of us are implicated in a death that might have been avoided had we done more or spent more. At such a moment, it will be important once again to avoid the technocratic language of scarcity economics; instead, we should continually remind ourselves of the sanctity of human life. We should seek guidance in our own spiritual traditions, and proceed with caution, humility, and a refusal to allow moral and spiritual questions to be obscured by murky language, or by supposedly scientific or economic categories that mask underlying values.

Ultimately, of course, these questions lead us right up against the central issue that our culture tries to hide: our own mortality. Through the frantic consumption of goods and the pursuit of various life projects, we each pretend to ourselves that we are not really going to die. But we will.

One manifestation of our avoidance of death is our penchant for mystifying the potential of medical science. As a result, far too many people have taken few steps to prepare themselves spiritually for death, but imagine that some scientific miracle will emerge to protect them.

The hospice movement, spurred by the acceleration of AIDS-related death among young people, has sought to create contexts in which Americans might face death with a fuller awareness than is possible in many hospitals, where death is systematically denied and covered up, and where there is little preparation given to patients.

Can We Afford Caring?

No part of a progressive politics-of-meaning program can be considered in isolation, but only in relationship to the totality of transformations we seek to establish. With the totality of those societal changes, actual health-care costs would dramatically decrease, because health would increase.

There would be less stress-related disease as workplaces became democratized and ferocious competition subsided. As people felt less of a need to escape the pain of their isolation and alienation, drug and alcohol abuse and related illnesses would decrease, as would accidents on the job and on the highways, and random acts of violence. As people learned a higher level of empathy for others, for parents, and for children, there would be less family violence. As corporate practices were reformed to take more seriously the impact of their actions on the physical and psychological health of the community, health would improve. And as people paid more attention to caring for one another, demands for caring that got acted out through becoming sick would decrease.

Moreover, there would be a much higher level of volunteerism in hospitals and health-care services. Since health-care personnel would not fear that these volunteers would cut into their incomes, they would find rational ways to provide people with enough training so that their volunteer help became useful, and reduced the overall strain on the professionals and the total cost of the system. As patients were treated with greater respect by health-care professionals, and given a greater role in participating in shaping the actual plan for their recovery, demands for monetary compensation for negligence would decrease.

The general improvement in health that would accrue to people living in the kind of caring society that a progressive politics of meaning could create would far offset the increase in costs, and would liberate monies that could be used to help finance other needed social programs.

It is only in this context that we connect with the narrowly construed "health-care reform" issues currently being debated in the United States. Most of this debate misses the issues that I have been discussing, and focuses more narrowly on how to provide access to health care. Had this debate been framed in a larger ethical and spiritual context, its focus would have moved from plans devised to protect the profit interests of health-care providers and insurers to the issue of how to make access consistent with our highest moral vision. In such a context, I would have advocated a Canadian-style single-payer plan that provides coverage for all, but avoids the crushing bureaucracies that sometimes make socialized medicine seem unworkable.

Is That the Whole Program?

We have not even scratched the surface. I included this chapter to demonstrate that a progressive politics of meaning is not simply a rerun of liberalism, and to provide an idea of how taking spiritual and ethical concerns seriously would have real consequences for society. A progressive politics of meaning has implications in every sphere of life, and drawing them out will be the task of a movement that develops around these ideas in the coming decades.

In the coming centuries, as a spiritual and ethical framework such as the politics of meaning becomes widely accepted, different societies will likely choose different paths and experiment with different specific programmatic ideas. And part of building a politics-of-meaning movement in this country in the next decades will focus on engaging people in refining the program, in ways that will almost certainly improve upon or transcend the specific ideas that I have developed here.

But what will *not* be transcended is the criterion whereby programs are judged: do they in fact lead to a society in which people tend to be spiritually alive; ecologically and ethically sensitive, loving, and caring toward one another; trusted providers of mutual, genuine recognition; filled with life energy and hopefulness, and with awe and wonder at the grandeur of the universe? My examples in this chapter have demonstrated that using this criterion leads us to consider programmatic directions that differ from the typical Left/Right divisions, which must be transcended as we develop a politics for the twenty-first century.

8

—〰—

How Do We Get There?

....

The very idea that politics could be about creating a society based on ethical and spiritual sensitivity breaks the standard conception of politics. It allows all kinds of people who imagined themselves as isolated to see themselves as potentially powerful, and creates a significant counterweight to right-wing movements that use some of this language, but have never really asked their members to get involved in the details of making specific economic and social institutions more ethically and spiritually sensitive. Gaining visibility for these ideas, helping people recognize one another as potential allies, and encouraging those who already share this perspective to recognize that their principles are potentially transformative of the larger world, are among the first goals of a public campaign for a politics of meaning.

When all those people who *already* wish that they lived in a world based on the sensibilities discussed in this book begin to recognize their potential power as a social movement, we will reach a critical mass that will make it possible for others to take these ideas seriously.

To reach this critical mass will take many years of patient education. These are among the steps that need to be taken along the way:

1. *National and Regional Summits on Ethics and Meaning*

President Clinton began his presidency by assembling an economic summit. America's ethical and meaning problems deserve equal attention.

Annual public gatherings at the local and national level will bring together those who are ready to identify with a public campaign for change in the dominant discourse. The summits on ethics and meaning will include the following: opportunities for ordinary citizens to testify about the ethical conflicts that they face in daily life and in family life as a result of living in this society; opportunities for people to explore in small groups the ethical and spiritual conflicts that they face in their lives, and to learn from one another how they have been most successful in handling them; strategizing about how to bring various elements of the politics-of-meaning program into public discussion, and how to refine and extend the program ideas; and networking with potential allies.

2. *Networks of Meaning-Oriented Professionals*

In each city we will seek to create groupings of doctors, lawyers, scientists, engineers, architects, builders, psychotherapists, computer experts, financiers, and other professionals. Each group will discuss how it would restructure its own profession and the work it was doing if the bottom line were no longer money, but the politics-of-meaning bottom line (creating and sustaining ethically, spiritually, and environmentally sensitive human beings who are capable of sustaining long-term, loving, committed relationships). These groups would begin to engage in dialogue about these ideas with other members of their profession. They would also bring their ideas into the public arena and use the ethics summits to promote this new way of envisioning the world. Their ideas would become the basis for further refining of our program.

I have been at a few such gatherings, and the results are spiritually and emotionally invigorating to many of the participants. For example, I have witnessed a group of doctors, nurses, and hospital administrators discussing how they could reorganize the delivery of medical care. I have witnessed government workers imagining how they would reconstruct their offices, and scientists imagining how they would reconstruct their research goals. Many other groups can be similarly innovative and creative as they engage in these discussions, whose only ground rule is: "Go for your highest vision of how you could serve the common good if the bottom line in your profession were caring, and no one were there to tell you that any given path was unrealistic or ought not to be tried."

Among the most interesting sets of professional discussions have been those emerging from lawyers who have wondered what law might look like if it were reenvisioned within the context of a meaning-oriented society. Many of the lawyers involved have quickly come to the conclusion that the adversarial nature of our legal system, which is central to our current conception of how to provide protection from crime, would have to be scrapped in a society that was no longer driven by fear of others or of a government that had gotten out of control.

After the O. J. Simpson trial, many of these lawyers began to wonder what kinds of transitional demands might be made in order to advance our society toward a meaning-orientation. Some suggested the immediate adoption of a two-stage process in criminal proceedings. Stage One would continue to have the adversarial features of our current system, together with important civil liberties guarantees and protections. But following this process, in which a defendant's guilt or innocence had been established, Stage Two would begin, with entirely different evidentiary and procedural rules. This second stage would be a healing and repair process, in which the problems and pain that had been uncovered by the trial would be addressed. The jury would participate with the judge, the defending and prosecuting attorneys, and elected representatives from the general public, in a process aimed at formulating the best ways to address the larger familial, community, and societal issues that had become evident during the trial. Whereas during Stage One, the participation of those who had an interest in a particular outcome could be challenged (such as the victim, the defendant, and their families), during Stage Two, the involvement of such people would be actively sought.

In the second stage, the jury would function as a kind of grand jury, using subpoena powers and so forth. Some of the lawyers in this discussion group thought that the jury should have the power to actually impose fines or issue injunctions in order to rectify certain trial-related societal problems. These participants proposed, for example, that the Simpson jury should have had the power to require the accused to do community service work or face some other punishment for previous acts of spousal abuse, even though these were not the formal charges he faced during the trial. Other participants imagined that the jury ought to have had the power to require the Los Angeles Police Department to fire the detective whose racism had been uncovered during the trial, and to require the entire police force to undergo systematic retraining on issues concerning race. Still other participants theorized that a jury should not be able to impose any penalties during the second stage, but should be given societal resources that would enable it to mobilize public support for related recommendations (such as a recommendation that any corporation that employed Simpson should face public boycott, or a recommendation that voters pass a ballot initiative in Los Angeles decreasing funding for the police until their racist practices had been rooted out).

Many lawyers were unhappy with any solution that might create a situation of double jeopardy, or which might amount to the trial of crimes without safeguards. Yet, in light of the Simpson trial, an increasing number of these liberal lawyers were willing to consider that the legal system had strayed so far from concern with the common good that something dramatic had to be changed. Rather than abandon civil liberties protections for Stage One, these lawyers were beginning to imagine the creation of Stage Two as a possible programmatic element for a politics of meaning strategy. Many participants pointed out that unless we created some such device to immediately show genuine concern for the public interest, right-wing forces might easily mobilize public opposition against a judicial system that had let civil liberties run wild.

From my standpoint, this lawyers' discussion, while only in an exploratory stage, shows the possibilities for creative rethinking that might be undertaken by professionals within the framework of a politics of meaning.

3. *Public Intellectuals*

We will seek to redefine intellectual life, so that professional intellectuals see themselves not as lone individuals in search of an audience, but as people who should be working together with other intellectuals to serve the common good. This does not mean that intellectuals should ever limit the scope of their ideas or change the content of what they say in order to please others or to submit to a party line. However, it does mean that they should see themselves as responsible to the larger community beyond academia and the academic press. This responsibility will necessarily play itself out in different ways depending on one's own skills and inclinations. Among the elements involved in being a public intellectual will be:

- Using intellectual talents to help clarify for the public the important social and intellectual issues that we collectively face. This responsibility will require many intellectuals to expand beyond academic research, and perhaps even to learn whole new ways of thinking outside of their areas of intellectual expertise. Engaging in public education, participating in forums, and writing and speaking about vital social and political issues should be a part of the life of intellectuals, and success in these areas should become a criterion for tenure at every college or university.

- Writing about one's own work in language that makes it accessible to laypeople and that highlights what significant intellectual issues may be at stake.

4. *Public Journalism*

A growing number of journalists are beginning to understand that the way they serve the status quo is not by endorsing Right versus Left solutions, but by implicitly endorsing cynicism and materialism instead of idealism and spirituality. Journalists' bias and non-neutrality *already* surfaces in the way they seek to unveil self-interest but do not equally seek to reveal unexpected acts of caring and idealism, the way they assume economistic or power motivations but will not assume other-regarding or ethical motivations, and the way they seek a hard-nosed rather than a soft angle on reality, and discount what could be in favor of what is.

Many media people deeply hunger for a framework of meaning. They recognize that by undermining people's belief in the possibility of trusting one another, they are actually undermining people's interest in the public realm altogether, and hence in journalism itself. The shift toward tabloids and away from serious news coverage or analysis on television, like the decline in readership of books, newspapers, and magazines, is a function not of declining literacy but of declining involvement in a shared intellectual, political, or cultural undertaking. *Tikkun*'s media editor, Jay Rosen, has begun the Project on Public Life and the Press to involve media people in reconceptualizing their efforts and asking themselves how they might help reconstitute a community of shared meaning and purpose by promoting public deliberation and problem-solving.

At the same time, it will be useful for others to engage in more confrontational activities aimed at educating people to recognize the sustained indoctrination that we daily receive from the media, which puts forth as "common sense" the self-interested, competitive, and materialist underpinning of our contemporary world, and build those assumptions into movies and music, docudramas and sitcoms, talk shows and news reporting.

Decades from now, I suspect that the media will provide space for some politics-of-meaning voices. Eventually there will be a television evening-news show that reflects a meaning-oriented perspective, replete with serious analysis of the ethical implications of political decisions, which is willing to question the assumptions of selfishness and materialism that accompany other ways of reporting and framing what counts as news. There will be movies, talk shows, music festivals, and even sitcoms where a different set of values will be reflected (although long before these, there will be vulgarized versions like the current brand of Hollywood spirituality, which offers sloganeering in place of serious reflection, and trivializes morality and the life of the spirit).

5. Ethical Impact Reports (Social Audits)

This demand is straightforward: every major piece of legislation by a city council, state legislature, or Congress; every policy decision by the White House; every annual stockholders' report on the activities of major corporations, both for profit and nonprofit— each of these should be accompanied by an ethical impact report. As outlined in chapter 7, this report will describe the likely ethical, spiritual, and ecological consequences of specific legislation, policies or activities.

Nevertheless, we will need to watch out for a high level of obfuscation. Some corporations or government agencies might hire new grant writers ("ethical impact specialists") whose job would be to add words like "caring" or "ethically sensitive" without any corresponding change in what people actually were doing. There will have to be vigilant monitoring by self-constituted groups of citizens who are serious about a politics of meaning, and who challenge government and corporate entities to actually live up to their fine words and to reorganize themselves in ways that are sensitive to the ethical impact of their actions. This struggle can be part of the process of the transition to a different society. When public debate focuses on whether a policy really produces moral and spiritual awareness, rather than on whether it yields the biggest bang for the buck, we already will have made a start toward developing the consciousness necessary for building a very different kind of society.

6. Replace the GNP and the GDP

At the center of our current selfishness society lies a standard set of measures of communal well-being, such as the Gross National Product (GNP) and the Gross Domestic Product (GDP), which plays an important role in systematically misleading us. For example, when we think of the "high standard of living" in the United States, we tend to think of the average material income; we do not usually consider the level of social solidarity and caring, nor our ability to sustain loving relationships.

Hazel Henderson, a policy analyst, has pioneered a standard called Country Futures Indicators (CFI) that may point us in the right direction. Some of its measures include purchasing-power parity and income distribution (whether the poverty gap is widening or narrowing), informal household-sector production (measuring both paid and unpaid work done at home), depletion of nonrenewable resources, military-civilian budget ratio (measuring how military production depletes a country's wealth), and capital-asset account (measuring the value of public roads and other infrastructural resources).

Henderson also includes the following significant factors: birth and infant-mortality rates, population density, age distribution, health and nutrition (including calories consumed per day and protein-carbohydrate ratio), availability and quality of shelter (including degree of homelessness), crime rates, literacy rates, level of political participation and status of democratic processes (including impact of money on elections), status of minority and ethnic populations and of women (including protection of minority rights), levels of air and water quality and environmental pollution, degree of biodiversity and species loss, and level of cultural and recreational resources available.

And yet, we will probably need to move beyond the CFI measures to matters that may be much more difficult to quantify: the subjective experience of caring; the degree to which individuals and communities pay attention to spiritual and ethical issues; the level of gentleness, emotional openness, compassion, and mutual recognition in society.

By raising these issues in a systematic way, the campaign for a politics of meaning will seek to challenge the seemingly self-evident nature of a materialistic and egotistical consciousness, thus accelerating the tendency to question current forms of societal self-justification.

7. Consciousness-Raising Groups

Perhaps the most important step that the reader can take after finishing this book is to gather a small group of people who are interested in exploring the issues raised here. People should talk about their personal experiences—in relationships, the workplace, political life, encounters with the dominant culture—and get other people to talk about theirs. Just as the small consciousness-raising groups of the 1960s and 1970s produced a deeper analysis of the way sexism works in women's lives than was available through the original feminist texts, similar groups will help refine the ideas in this book as participants explore together the complex ways in which the denial of meaning daily shapes life and interactions with others.

The next step for such groups would be to challenge the dominant ethos of our society. They could organize protests against media cynicism and speak to individuals working in the media about the negative consequences of their approach, challenge elected representatives to begin to understand society's meaning-needs, and call upon local corporations to develop an ethical impact report. Friends and coworkers would be challenged to question "common sense" assumptions that nothing could be different and that the only possible bottom line is looking out for number one.

Not every consciousness-raising group will be the same. Some will feel more comfortable focusing on social activism, others on personal grappling with the ways in which the deprivation of meaning has affected their own lives. Some of these groups will be based in neighborhoods, others in workplaces or unions, others still in churches or synagogues or university campuses. Rather than waste much time struggling over which focus is the "right" focus, it usually is more productive when people who desire a particular focus create their own group, rather than try to convince others drawn to a meaning-oriented movement that their focus is wrong.

However they define their primary focus, all such groups should strive to encourage their participants to recognize the uniqueness and preciousness of every human being. One function of the consciousness-raising groups will be to teach us how to hone our skills at this kind of mutual recognition. Similarly, these groups should give us time and encouragement to develop our inner lives. Unlike most feminist consciousness-raising groups of the 1960s and 1970s, these politics-of-meaning groups should explicitly allow quiet time for people to meditate, check in with their own spiritual resources, or pray. They should encourage moments when the group can together experience, celebrate, and witness with amazement the grandeur of the universe. Moreover, these groups should initiate opportunities for group members, families, and friends to celebrate holidays together, to share major life occasions (births, marriages, deaths), and to take care of one another (as when people are sick).

A central point here is that the process of building a politics of meaning must be one that already seeks to embody the loving, caring, and spiritual sensitivity that we seek to develop in the world. On the one hand, we reject the view that all of this will come later, but now we have to do something else first (for example, gain power or achieve objective X or Y). On the other hand, as I have stressed consistently throughout this book, we must be compassionate and forgiving, expecting to be disappointed in ourselves and in one another for the ways in which we do not yet embody our movement's values. We also must be supportive of one another in a gentle and kind way as we each try to move forward to better embodying what we believe in. There can never be an abstract formula to tell us how to achieve this balance—yet it is the key to the success of our entire enterprise. If we must err, however, let it be on the side of compassion and kindness.

8. *Support and Democratization of the Nonprofit Sector*

Politics-of-meaning consciousness-raising groups might support a change in the tax code that would allow individuals to deduct $500 from what they owed in taxes to make a charitable donation. These donations, multiplied by one hundred million taxpayers, would dwarf what the wealthy donated, and thus would empower ordinary Americans to decide what kind of public caring they would like to see supported. Many nonprofits would begin to seek a constituency and would have to show how their activities actually contributed to the ethical or spiritual transformation of our society.

9. *Expanding National Service*

When President Clinton introduced his Americorps national service plan, he sold it to the American public in large measure as a method for young people to repay the federal government for student loans. This strategy may have made it politically more saleable in Congress, but it sent the wrong message. The right message is that people want to help one another and contribute to the common good, and our government should facilitate these goals by coordinating possible opportunities to serve. Politics-of-meaning groups could fight for this message.

Though every young person ought to give a year to national service, the program should *not* be focused on the young, but on providing a way for each of us to contribute at least five hours a week to a service project. A serious campaign of this sort might, after a number of years, mobilize tens of millions of people into activity that served the public interest. Most people would welcome an opportunity to be generous and giving to others, as long as doing so would not be interpreted as foolish, self-destructive, or naively idealistic by a cynical society.

10. *Family Day, Family Support Networks, and Occupational Stress Groups: A Strategy for Labor*

The labor movement could be fundamentally transformed and revitalized were it to take a politics-of-meaning approach and integrate this with its traditional bargaining and economic focus. If, for example, unions were to play a central role in the struggle for ethical impact reports and were to raise issues of corporate social responsibility in a serious and sustained way, they could have a profound impact not only on popularizing a politics-of-meaning perspective, but also on strengthening their own appeal. However, such a campaign would only make sense if the unions themselves were fundamentally democratized and their economistic focus was replaced with a broader understanding of human needs.

Politics-of-meaning activists would seek to transform meetings of union locals into opportunities for working people to discuss their actual experiences at work, their fears of globalization, and their ideas about how to change the larger society. Instead of insisting on a narrow and short-term pragmatic focus, these discussions could explicitly be dedicated to the "big picture" issues that have often been excluded from union meetings.

Unions could fight to get occupational stress groups as a worker benefit, so that each year some workers received some paid time off to participate in a twelve-session occupational stress group (OSG) run by personnel selected by the workers themselves. Such OSGs would provide an opportunity for workers to explore their own personal lives, and the interaction between workplace stress and family issues.

In addition, the labor movement could work with religious and community groups to initiate neighborhood family support networks and a yearly Family Day, as described in chapter 6.

Finally, the labor movement could create talk shows and television programming that reflected a sensitivity to the meaning-issues, exploring how these intersected with daily life and the experiences of most people in the economy. In place of hate radio and television, the labor movement could present commentators who validated people's anger at nonrecognition and lack of respect and caring in this society—but then would direct that anger more appropriately at the social and economic institutions that generate these problems, rather than at the minority groups and other typically demeaned targets of hate radio.

If all this proves too visionary for the labor movement, meaning-oriented activists should create community coalitions to spur the formation of neighborhood support groups, OSGs, and an annual Family Day. These activists would train local community people to become the organizers and leaders of such activities, embedding within them the ethical and spiritual consciousness that a politics of meaning seeks to encourage. These activities will be more valuable to the extent that people explicitly understand them to be linked to a larger social movement, because they will thereby see their own activities as being supported by and supporting a larger social transformation which publicly validates their own local efforts. The more explicit their connection with a politics-of-meaning strategy, the more these local activities will move beyond therapeutic groups and become agents of larger healing and transformation.

11. *Campaign for Full Employment, a Thirty-Hour Workweek, and Other Interim Policy Goals*

I am working with others to create the Foundation for Ethics and Meaning, a policy-oriented think tank that will coordinate efforts to build a progressive politics of meaning. I have hesitated to try to detail the kinds of interim political struggles that we would propose, for fear that they might become the focus of discussion. But I am well aware that the struggle for a politics of meaning must also engage in concrete, traditional political demands—while resisting attempts by others to reduce our vision to those interim demands.

Among the policy issues that would have high priority would be the struggle for full employment and the creation of what the Economics Working Group of the Tides Foundation calls "environmental sustainability."

A Major Caution

A politics-of-meaning strategy must be governed by a meaning-oriented consciousness: one that is constantly seeking to maximize human connection and mutual recognition, to break through the manipulated forms of mutual estrangement, and to allow us to recognize and rejoice in one another. This consciousness must encourage people to move beyond the mind-set of accomplishments and into the mind-set of celebrations of the grandeur of the universe and of one another. It must create quiet spaces for us to withdraw into ourselves, nourish our own souls, and connect ourselves to the totality of all being. And, simultaneously, it must move us beyond ourselves and into a sense of our potential power to reshape the world in accord with our highest vision of ethical and spiritual truth.

I have participated in movements that had a high ethical purpose, but nevertheless lost direction when they began to rely on technocratic assumptions in the course of winning struggles. For example, I have witnessed the contrast between civil rights and environmental movements when they were aiming to mobilize people into action, and those same movements when they were relying primarily on Washington lobbyists and courtroom lawyers.

Even a consciousness-raising group can become technocratic, dominated by the fastest talkers and those who are best at distancing themselves from their feelings. It can become waylaid by a focus on "issues," while avoiding any serious self-revelation of how those issues affect our own lives or how we might need one another for real caring and support.

We must remember that the goal of our work in civil society is to build a parallel meaning-center to the existing institutions, so that their emotional deadness can be challenged by people who insist on reintroducing the deepest ethical, spiritual, and ecological practices into daily life. Part of the reason we need the consciousness-raising groups is in order to support one another when we enter these struggles and attempt to introduce a meaning-dimension. But we need to be equally attuned to bringing the meaning-dimension into our own movement.

In the final analysis, the way we will win is not by any particular technique, but by bringing more and more meaning into our own lives together, and showing others what it might look like to do this in broader and broader contexts. Others may say, "Go for the gold," but our movement will say, "Go for the meaning."

Learning from Feminism

The best analogy to what we are trying to accomplish in a campaign for a progressive politics of meaning is the women's movement. It has sought nothing less than to change the way that our society talks and thinks about women. The scope of feminism's goals—to uproot patriarchy—once seemed as grandiose and unrealistic as our goal of changing the bottom line of our society. Yet in a scant thirty years, the women's movement has made unprecedented changes in the way that men and women relate to one another in their personal lives, as well as in the way that women are treated in the economy, in the media, and in politics. Similar changes are possible within the next thirty years in challenging the ethos of selfishness and materialism, and championing a meaning-orientation in every sphere of life.

There was no shared strategic consensus among women about the best strategy for changing societal attitudes toward them. For some feminists, the focus was small consciousness-raising groups, while others argued that this structure was too introspective, and that what was really necessary was the higher-profile social and political activism embodied in a structure like the National Organization of Women. There were factions in the women's movement whose primary focus was to empower women in their personal relations with men, while others saw the key in changing women's lot in the economic world. Among those who saw economics as crucial, some feminists argued that the goal should be to get women into positions of power, so that they could be on corporate boards or on the Supreme Court. Others insisted that feminism would require a transformation of our corporate and political system, based upon rethinking our understanding of power. Some argued that what was needed in the political realm was an equal rights amendment, while others argued that specific rights, such as legalized abortion or child care, were more suitable goals for a feminist agenda.

As it turned out, they were all correct. That is, it was precisely the pursuit of all these seemingly conflicting directions that eventually led to a broad societal questioning of the old ways of thinking about women.

Similarly, those of us pushing for a politics of meaning will use a variety of approaches to challenge the status quo and to establish a new language and a new paradigm for politics. Out of the cacophony of voices that will emerge, a fundamental transformation of consciousness will be forged in the course of the next several decades.

In the meantime, the central internal goal of a progressive politics of meaning must be to build a sense of mutual confidence, so that we will not be too disillusioned with one another when we encounter our faults, egos, and petty betrayals. Such disillusioning elements are inevitable. Nevertheless, without denying them, excusing them away, or avoiding our responsibility to find ways to encourage people to move beyond their own distortions, we need also to learn how to see enough of the God in ourselves and in one another that we can proceed in building communities of meaning in a compassionate and loving manner.

This process of building confidence in one another may take many decades, and there are likely to be moments when a movement for a politics of meaning will look like it is disappearing. But eventually we will develop a core leadership that has the skills and capacity to develop in others this sense of mutual confidence. The more this happens, the more others will feel safe to join the movement and experience its compassion. Confidence-building is the key to undermining surplus powerlessness. The more we believe that others will be there for us, sharing the same risks and caring about what happens to us, the more we will be willing to challenge our own internalized cynicism and despair, and will be willing to consider transformative possibilities that were dismissed previously as naive or counter to human nature.

Part of the process of building this compassion and mutual confidence can take place as people participate in occupational stress groups and family support networks. Each of us needs to be in some group context that is helping us rethink parts of our lives in which we have come to blame ourselves inordinately. One mechanism for ensuring that political meetings do not devolve into therapy groups is to make it possible for people to meet in another context for deeper and more personal exploration. For some, the small consciousness-raising group will serve this purpose. For others, we will need to develop groups that are specifically designed as adjuncts to political meetings. We must ensure that these groups are led by people who support the larger politics-of-meaning struggle, and who understand the deep connection between personal lives and social realities.

No process of overcoming selfishness can really work if it depends on people who feel a desperate sense of inadequacy. When people feel underrecognized, they grow so emotionally hungry and so pained that it is almost impossible for them to notice others or respond to their needs or their pain. Therefore, we should also encourage people to do some individual work in psychotherapy, recognizing that understanding one's own childhood and learning how to feel good about oneself, far from being an act of selfishness, can be a central step in the process of becoming the kind of person who can really be nurturing and caring to others.

Of course, in our society, many therapists conceptualize their work within the context of individualistic assumptions that place autonomy above commitment to others. They imagine that the essence of mental health is learning to care for oneself and to live a life free from obligations to others. Yet there are other therapists who understand that a healthy individual is one who has been freed to be fully loving and caring, and who can feel obligated to others precisely because she or he recognizes in them their beauty and their sanctity.

Spiritual Practices

While not endorsing any particular approach or practice, a campaign for a progressive politics of meaning will encourage people to participate in some form of daily meditation, prayer, aesthetic enterprise, or spiritual orientation. The goal of such spiritual practice will be to reconnect individuals to their own highest and most centered spiritual knowledge, and to create a moment during which they can leave the goal-directedness of daily life and focus on responding to the marvel of the world with joy, wonder, and radical amazement.

In isolation from a larger campaign for a politics of meaning, these activities are valuable but not likely to lead to social transformation. But a campaign for a politics of meaning that does not also encourage the development of an inner spiritual life will inevitably, over the many generations during which the struggle is fought, move in a technocratic direction. It will lose its spiritual center, becoming yet another reason for cynicism and despair as people watch the language of spirituality and caring used on behalf of power-hungry individuals or groups whose rhetoric has little to do with its actual reality. We have already seen this perversion at various times in various organized religions, and there can never be a formal guarantee that the same thing will not happen within our movement.

This is all the more reason why we need to constantly be seeking to maximize the spiritual and ethical dimensions of our movement, making sure that at least as much energy goes into building ethical relationships and spiritual centeredness as goes into struggles to spread the word or build meaning-oriented institutions. The danger comes from both sides. On the one hand, there is the temptation to abandon hope of larger transformation and withdraw into the "working on one's own head" approach. This tends to lead to New Age–style solipsistic distortions that eliminate the awareness of how much we are shaped by larger social realities and how much those realities need to be changed. On the other hand, we need to guard against the tendency to become conventional political beings and try to win respectability in the eyes of the powerful by playing their game: abandoning our ethical, spiritual, and ecological sensitivities and transforming meaning-politics into technocratic politics.

There are two handy guides for staying on course. First, we must ask ourselves always whether the experience of the movement feels spiritually alive, ethically sensitive, and filled with love. If it does not, we should not denounce it, but change it by bringing love, spirituality, and ethical sensitivity into the meaning-oriented activities that we shape. Second, we must ask whether the politics side or the meaning side seems to have a greater presence in the movement. If either side is greater, something is out of kilter, which will be possible to repair by introducing more of the other kind of energy.

A Concluding Unscientific Postscript

I feel confident that a politics of meaning will eventually become a central focus for American politics in the twenty-first century. The necessity is too great to be ignored for much longer.

However, I fear that we may first have to go through intense human suffering and yet another manifestation of mass psychosis. It is not difficult to imagine in the twenty-first century one more round of the crazy oscillations that have shaped the twentieth. The cycle begins with people so disillusioned by the emptiness, selfishness, and materialism of the competitive market that they willingly embrace xenophobic nationalism and fundamentalist religions to find the meaning and community that are denied in daily life. Subsequently, military conflicts are produced by these distorted communities as inevitable outgrowths of their technique of demeaning the Other. We then see the reemergence of a more robust liberalism, which *still* denies the meaning-needs—and feels justified in doing so because it can once again point to the irrationality and hatefulness of the latest array of distorted communities of meaning.

Eventually this cycle must be overcome through the creation of progressive communities of meaning that do *not* demean or scapegoat; that do not avoid (as so many religions do) the specific question of how to transform our economic, political, and social institutions so that meaning is not a mere compensation or distraction from our alienation, but a guide to overcoming it; and that do *not* create oppressive hierarchies, or perpetuate patriarchy, or insist that meaning can only be obtained by repressing pleasure and joy and individual freedoms. Sadly, if it takes another convulsive cycle before we are ready, the twenty-first century could see yet more of the violence and bloodshed that have so deeply stained modern life.

Equally dangerous, the world might not turn to a politics of meaning until its environmental destruction has advanced to a point beyond repair. The human race might spend the last half of the next century mourning the decline of our planet's life-support systems, and turning to a politics of meaning only at the moment when such a politics can no longer promise transformation quickly enough to save the world, but can only promise a rational and humanly dignified way to manage the decline of human life on earth.

Or, perhaps neither extreme scenario will happen. Instead, we may see only an escalation of what is already happening: more selfishness; more alcoholism, drug abuse, television addiction, and other forms of escapism; more disintegration of loving connections and more loneliness; more random violence; more frenetic pursuits as we desperately try to avoid looking at the world that we are creating; more manipulation of conscious and unconscious processes by the media and the corporate world; more decline in our capacity to remember or to provide a history for ourselves or our world; more willingness to embrace superficial spiritualities that quickly disappoint; more New Age self-help without substance; more divorce of spirituality from an ethical and political program; more psychotherapy that reconciles us to a crazy world; and more worship at the altar of cynicism and despair.

What happens to our world in the years to come is not independent of what we—you and I—actually do with our lives. We can help people understand that "seeing through" the craziness of the current world is *not enough*—that we need to be engaged, both individually and collectively, in the process of healing and transforming the world, and that we need to reject all those feelings and ideas that tell us that such change is impossible. The toughest part of building the politics-of-meaning movement will be to assemble and mobilize the first few million people to share this perspective. After them, tens of millions more will feel that it is safe enough to acknowledge similar hopes and dreams without appearing to be crazy, self-destructive, or utopian fantasizers. But for the first few generations, those people who insist on pioneering this perspective are likely to find that doing so costs them friendships, professional success, and credibility, even among people whom they respect. It is always this way when one pushes for a different paradigm.

Yet, the conditions for the emergence of this new direction for our political lives continue to grow stronger. More and more people are rejecting the one-dimensional technocratic thinking taught in most universities and regurgitated through think tanks, government, and the media. More and more people are already engaged in activities that involve a new way of thinking.

There are millions of people who are already involved in their daily lives in activities that are based on a progressive politics of meaning. They are involved in daily acts of caring in their churches, synagogues and mosques, or in community self-help organizations. They are involved in organizing projects and unions. They are involved in social change movements. They are involved as social workers, or nurses, or progressive lawyers, or in other helping professions.

There are "renewalists" in the religious communities who are insisting that the spiritual truths of those traditions must be made consistent with a fundamental respect and caring for others, including previously demeaned peoples (such as ethnic minorities, women, homosexuals, Jews) and then brought into the public arena.

There are environmentalists who are reframing their struggle in ways that transcend the scientific, technocratic language that dominates the thinking of some ecological circles, and are beginning to address the underlying spiritual and ethical issues. There are psychotherapists who are coming to understand that the problems that they see cannot be solved without making changes in the larger society. There are feminists who are embracing a spiritual and ethical agenda that transcends a narrow, rights-oriented focus. There is a growing number of people who identify with New Age or other spiritual concerns, and are becoming aware that spiritual transformation will remain extremely limited until it enters and challenges the dominant discourse in the economic and political arenas. There are people engaged in holistic medicine, or holistic approaches to other traditional professional enterprises, who are expanding their understanding of the fundamental interconnectedness of all being.

Many of these people have already made a commitment to a different paradigm but, by and large, perceive of themselves as isolated. They do not usually articulate the alternative paradigm from which their actions flow, and do not believe that it is really possible to change things much beyond the specific acts of caring in which they themselves are involved. Many have imbibed the larger societal skepticism and imagine that there are very few people like them, who would really want to live in a society whose economy and public life was organized to promote caring and nurture spiritual and ethical sensitivity.

Two necessary preconditions to building a progressive politics-of-meaning movement would be, first, to help people *name* the implicit politics that underlies their activities, and second, to help people recognize themselves as part of something larger—a potentially powerful movement that could transform and heal the world.

Whether it emerges now, or decades into the twenty-first century, a politics-of-meaning movement will energize people to fight for their highest ideals. They will do so out of an inner necessity, because they know that they personally need to live in a spiritually and ethically healthier and more loving world, and because they know it is the only way to save this planet. They will do so because they will understand that fighting for a world based on love and caring is an immediate practical necessity.

I often talk about "fighting" or "struggling" for a world based on love and caring and spiritual, ethical, and ecological sensibilities. I do that because I don't want to be naive about how easy it will be to have the ideas in this book taken seriously. For thousands of years, the religious and spiritual leaders of our planet have been honored while their teachings were simultaneously ignored or turned into their opposite. The call for love has so frequently been used to justify hate, the call for social justice so frequently used as a cover for totalitarianism, the call for ethics so frequently used as a cover for self-interest, that today there are millions of people who have become deeply cynical about any vision of change. Given that history, I believe that people are not being unreasonable to be cautious about what can be accomplished in a single step. So I've talked about a process that will take generations, that will be self-correcting, and that will insist on democracy and checks-and-balances along the way. Moreover, even when we get to a meaning-oriented and loving society, we will not have reached "the end of history." I imagine that there will be formidable new struggles that will open up to us. At higher levels of consciousness we will become aware of new tensions and problems.

Yet there is a danger that I've allowed the deep cynicism that reigns in public life and the media to overplay the difficulties and underplay the fun, the pleasure, and the joyfulness that can accompany us in the next few generations as we seek to actualize a politics of meaning. We are at a moment in our history when the highest ideals of the Bible and of the spiritual heritage of the human race can no longer be marginalized. Recognizing the God in each other, recognizing our place as part of the totality and unity of all being, is no longer a task for an enlightened minority—it is the practical survival requisite for our planet. Whether or not they use the language of "the politics of meaning," millions of people already know of this practical necessity and are already making important contributions to the development of a meaning-oriented consciousness.

Together, in the coming generations, we shall be experiencing the next stage in the evolution of Spirit, what some people call God-in-the-making, or what other traditions would call the full acceptance of our human role as partners with God in tikkun (in healing and transformation). The God energy in the universe, working through the human race, is realizing itself, becoming more aware of itself and its task, and is thus manifesting itself more fully. As Ken Wilber puts it, "Spirit is not some particular stage, or some favorite ideology, or some pet god or goddess, but rather the entire process of unfolding itself, an infinite process that is completely present at every finite stage, but becomes more available to itself with every evolutionary opening." We, human beings, created in the image of God, are one of the vehicles for this evolutionary process. And we are on the threshold of one of the major advances in self-understanding, as we fully realize that our survival depends on our ability to love and care for each other and our ability to respond to the universe with awe and wonder that incorporates and transcends the technocratic consciousness that has recently dominated the human enterprise.

The more we recognize that we are part of this evolutionary process, the more we can move beyond the "struggle" aspect and recognize also the joy of being able to see the God in each other. We are in at the beginning of a process in which human beings will recognize each other, rejoice in each other, and treat each other with the respect and caring that heretofore seemed only a distant ethical aspiration. There are millions of people already moving in that direction, and millions more ready to move the moment they see that they will not be alone (so that they can feel safe enough to withstand what will still be the dominant cynicism that reigns in the media and the larger society). We ought not be so focused on how far we have yet to travel that we neglect to take pleasure in the fact that there are so many of us already moving on the same road.

This is a wonderful moment in human history. I feel blessed to be living in the historical epoch in which so many people are beginning to recognize each other as part of the growing movement of healing and transformation for which our world so deeply yearns.

Epilogue

The Clintons and
Contemporary Politics

....

W*e are at a stage in history in which remolding society is one of the great challenges facing all of us in the West. If one looks around the Western world, one can see the rumblings of discontent, almost regardless of political systems, as we come face to face with the problems that the modern age has dealt us.*

And if we ask, why is it in a country as wealthy as we are, that there is this undercurrent of discontent, we realize that somehow economic growth and prosperity, political democracy and freedom, are not enough—that we lack meaning in our individual lives and meaning collectively; we lack a sense that our lives are part of some greater effort, that we are connected to one another.

All of us face a crisis of meaning. Coming off the last years when the ethos of selfishness and greed were given places of honor never before accorded them, it is certainly timely to ask about this problem.

This problem requires all of us to play a role in redefining what our lives are and what they should be.

—HILLARY RODHAM CLINTON, 1993

Many Americans had high hopes for the presidency of Bill Clinton. Yet by 1995, most had become deeply disappointed.

During the 1992 primary campaign and then during the fall election season, both Bill and Hillary Clinton had projected an understanding of human needs that seemed to transcend the old assumptions of liberal politics, and to embody a meaning-oriented approach.

True enough, the tactics of the campaign as summed up by Clinton strategist James Carville's phrase, "It's the economy, stupid," seemed far from a meaning-orientation. But candidate Clinton's understanding of economic issues was sensitive to the meaning-dimension. Rather than list a series of "rights" that his presidency might offer, Bill Clinton talked to people about the lack of community support available to people when they faced unemployment, health-care bills, or child-care problems.

While the media—imbued with the "what's in it for me" mentality—focused on the programmatic specifics of Clinton's campaign, and often complained that his speeches seemed repetitive because they were not breaking new policy ground, they continually missed the real story: Clinton's ability to connect to the fears and concerns that most deeply affected his listeners. Many who listened to Clinton heard a candidate who seemed to understand what they were going through and why they were so scared. Most importantly, Clinton seemed to be communicating a new message: you have these problems because we, the community, have not been adequately involved in taking care of one another. It was in this context that Clinton mounted his criticisms of the selfishness of the 1980s. His point was not that it was wrong for people to seek their own economic well-being, but that a narrow focus on self-advancement should not be allowed to cut us off from caring about others and using our collective resources to solve our shared problems.

Because Clinton assured people that he was interested in reconstituting a community of caring, the specifics seemed less important. Few people follow the policy details of election campaigns, in any case, and, given the horse race–style political coverage, it would be difficult even for motivated observers to figure these out from media reports. True, previous Democratic Party candidates had sometimes used words similar to Clinton's, but they had done it in a way that sounded transparently like a speechwriter's attempt to sound caring. By contrast, Clinton's caring language conveyed sincerity. Americans could envision that from his caring would flow the specifics of his policy.

Moreover, Clinton was explicitly talking about the common good, insisting that it ought to be our shared focus, and critiquing the very self-centeredness that conservatives had unfairly been able to pin onto liberals in the 1980s. Rather than presenting a laundry list of demands, and thereby replicating the image of the Democratic Party as a coalition of special interests, Clinton seemed to be concerned about the general interest and about the frustrations in the lives of the American majority. Nor was he content to allow existing realities to define what could be. Clinton made repeated appeals to what he perceived to be the shared idealism of the American people, rejecting the cynicism that had become dominant in the media and in contemporary American political discourse.

The "Politics of Meaning" Speech

The tilt toward a politics of meaning was made explicit when Hillary Clinton turned her first major speech on health care, on April 6 1993, into an explicit appeal for the country to adopt a politics-of-meaning approach. The speech was all the more powerful because it was delivered extemporaneously and seemed to reflect ideas that she had personally been grappling with (at the time, her father was on his deathbed).

> We are caught between two great political forces. On the one hand, we have our economy—the market economy—which knows the price of everything, but the value of nothing. That is

not its job. And then the state or government, which attempts to use its means of acquiring tax money, of making decisions to assist us in becoming a better, more equitable society. We have political and ideological struggle between those who think market economies are the answers to everything and those who think government programs are the answer to everything—but neither is adequate to address the challenge confronting us.

What we must do is break through the old thinking that has too long captured us politically and institutionally so that we can begin to devise new ways of thinking about not only what it means to have government that works again, not only what it means to have economies that don't discard people like they were excess baggage that we no longer need, but to define our institutional and personal responsibilities in ways that answer this lack of meaning.

We need a new politics of meaning. We need a new ethos of individual responsibility and caring. We need a new definition of civil society which answers the unanswerable questions posed by both the market forces and the governmental ones, as to how we can have a society that fills us up again and makes us feel that we are part of something bigger than ourselves . . .

Change will come whether we want it or not, and what we will have to do is to try to make change our friend, not our enemy. But probably most profoundly and importantly, the changes that will count the most are the millions of changes that take place on the individual level as people reject cynicism, as they are willing to be hopeful once again, as they are willing to take risks to meet the challenges they see around them, as they truly begin to try to see other people as they wish to be seen and to treat them as they wish to be treated, to overcome all of the obstacles we have erected around ourselves that keep us apart from one another, fearful and afraid, not willing to build the bridges necessary to fill our spiritual vacuum.

This was an extraordinary speech and it seemed to many to confirm the best hopes for what the Clinton administration could be. Here was the president's wife willing to challenge the market itself. Here was the president's wife acknowledging that the transformations needed in our society could not be accomplished by relying either on the market or on government—but on something deeper and more extensive.

The call for a politics of meaning drew instantaneous fire from the cynical press. Newspapers and columnists caricatured what Hillary Clinton was saying, or feigned inability to understand what was being said. What are these people talking about, wondered *The New Republic* aloud; what can they mean by this? If her ideas were literally unintelligible, of course, then nobody had to seriously consider them—nor the revolutionary challenge that they put to our normal ways of thinking about American politics.

The New Republic immediately attributed Hillary Clinton's ideas to me and to *Tikkun* magazine (which I edit). But none of those who claimed to be unable to understand what she was talking about bothered to read the fuller expositions of the politics-of-meaning perspective that had appeared in the magazine, which both of the Clintons said they had been reading. Hillary Clinton and the politics of meaning had touched and challenged the deepest wells of media cynicism. Unable to take ethical or spiritual issues seriously, and deeply convinced that human beings can never be motivated by anything beyond material self-interest, many reporters and editors felt that their most cherished beliefs were now being challenged by the president's wife and her connection to the politics of meaning. Their response was a no-holds-barred assault.

Consider, for example, the response of political columnist Jacob Weisberg. Writing in *The New Republic,* Weisberg suggested that Hillary Clinton, in backing *Tikkun* magazine's insistence that we face a communal moral and spiritual crisis, was really only making a revelation about her own internal failings during her own ascent to power: "If she wants to talk about the discontents of her own climb, and the spiritual emptiness *she* feels, congratulations to her for real candor. But that doesn't mean everyone else is a moral failure."

The *Wall Street Journal,* the *Washington Post,* and the *San Francisco Chronicle* took another tack, claiming that I had become Hillary Clinton's "guru," and that she had fallen under my sway. The point here was to suggest that in adopting the worldview that *Tikkun* magazine had advocated for the past seven years, she could not possibly have come to this opinion through her own rational decision; she must have had her mind taken over by a Svengali-like male. To these journalists, it seemed appropriate to portray Hillary

Clinton as susceptible to the power of some strong and mysterious outside influence.

I immediately and repeatedly demanded that the media retract this demeaning designation. In a press conference, I issued the following statement: "I am not now, nor have I ever been a guru, to Mrs. Clinton or to anyone else. The term 'guru' implies a power over others that I do not seek and would reject if proffered. And in this case, it is nothing short of ludicrous to suggest that a woman like Mrs. Clinton with an independent and powerful mind of her own could be intellectually subordinate to me or anyone else." My statement was never reported.

The gravest hatchet job was done by Michael Kelly, who profiled Hillary Clinton's new position in a *New York Times Magazine* cover story on May 23 1993, alternately titled "Saint Hillary" and "The Politics of Virtue." Kelly portrayed Mrs. Clinton as a crusader seeking "to make the world a better place—as she defines better." Saint Hillary, according to Kelly, was not seeking answers, but "The Answer . . . something in the Meaning of It All line." Her "politics of virtue" stemmed from "the conviction of her generation that it was destined (and equipped) to teach the world the error of its ways."

The word "virtue," never used by Hillary Clinton to refer to herself or her ideas, has had associations in American culture that suggest being on a higher moral plane than others—and was certain to bring to mind President Carter's emphasis on the need for virtue in his politically disastrous "Malaise" speech. Thus Kelly portrayed her as another reformer shaking her finger at the lowly state of Americans—the exact opposite of the actual intention of the politics of meaning, which argues that the problem is not within individuals but within the social system that ingrains and rewards selfishness.

Media Cynicism and the Worship of Savvy

The media attacks and distortions of the politics of meaning were ferocious. In part, they were motivated by a genuine antipathy toward the politics of meaning by many people in the media—an antipathy based on their own deep, almost religious commitment to the individualism and cynicism that form the "common sense" of contemporary American life. It would be an exaggeration to say that the media is the major culprit in the ethos of selfishness; in many respects, it merely reflects the dominant ethos. However, there is no denying the media's powerful and sustained impact on continually reframing our historical consciousness, so that the way in which people join together in social movements to change things becomes invisible. The refusal of the media to reflect back to us the moments in which people do in fact transcend their own fear, and begin to act in concert with their highest moral vision, tends to make it much harder to convince people that it is realistic to fight for their own highest values.

Yet there is no media conspiracy to undermine social change. From the standpoint of many reporters and editors, the idea that people might be motivated by something other than material self-interest sounds implausible, given their own experiences in a world of selfishness. So what the media see as "the story" is the unveiling of the part of people that is self-interested. And since all of us possess this part *as well,* the media can always find and highlight it, thus seeming to "prove" that any individual or movement claiming a higher purpose must necessarily be lying.

This deep cynicism accounts for the media's unrelenting attack on Bill Clinton from the moment that he took office. It was one thing to talk a politics of meaning while running for office; this, after all, could be analyzed as part of the typical use of idealism to manipulate people into voting for a particular candidate. But if Clinton intended to persist with this kind of idealism while holding office, the media saw its task as exposing an obvious attempt at deception, since they "knew" that the only possible motivation for Clinton or anyone else was self-interest.

Four months after Clinton was inaugurated, the *Washington Post* was already questioning whether Clinton's was "Another Failed Presidency?". But what exactly had failed in four months? Clinton had already convinced Congress to speed through the Family Leave Act, which ensured that no one would lose a job by taking time off from work to care for a newborn up to three months of age. Most of the president's program had not yet been submitted to

Congress. So Clinton's real failure was with the gatekeepers of public approval: the press. He had failed to convince them that he was "savvy"; hence, from their perspective, he was on the verge of losing everything else. As Anthony Lewis observed at the time, "The press is ravenous, ready to see scandal in a speck of dust."

Indeed, to many people in the media, that very fact proved that Clinton deserved to be criticized, since he had not figured out a way to appear savvy to the media crowd. R. W. Apple of the *New York Times* had already begun to question Clinton's "political savvy" as early as February 1993. Having withdrawn two candidates for the position of Attorney-General, the president was now being advised that he "desperately needs a victory as quickly as possible." Apple went on to suggest that "part of the problem may be the absence from Mr. Clinton's inner circle of most of the savvy crowd that surrounded him as a candidate."

Jay Rosen, *Tikkun*'s media editor, has pointed out: "As a political style—the only style admired by the press—savviness responds to our desire not to be fooled, to know how things really work in the corridors of power, to be disenchanted grown-ups rather than naive children . . . Savviness is a moral suasion, a propaganda of the uncommitted. It teaches us to favor detachment over enlistment, shrewd technique over strong belief, the apprehension of what is over the imagination of what might be . . . Politics becomes a game of power fought by clever insiders and master strategists, a running scorecard of winners and (mostly) losers, a theater of contempt, a nightly joke."

What Clinton was being told over and over by many voices in the media was that he was not playing the game correctly, that he was not showing that he could speak to them, and that they would make the politics-of-meaning perspective too costly for him to retain.

The point was driven home forcefully when Charles Krauthammer focused on Hillary Clinton's call for a politics of meaning in the May 14 1993 edition of the *Washington Post*. Mrs. Clinton, Krauthammer suggested, had been having an adolescent identity crisis: "Her speech carries the distinctive marks of adolescent self-discovery: the self-congratulatory didacticism; the belief, upon encountering some large universal truth, that one has uncovered the

THE CLINTONS AND CONTEMPORARY POLITICS / 317

wheel; the conviction, upon experiencing some spiritual transcendence, that no one has ever been there before; and the breathless need to instruct the whole unlettered world about it. All delivered with the knowing self-assurance, the superior air of a college student manifesto." Krauthammer concluded by wondering, "Aren't there any adults at home in the White House?"

Jay Rosen, a vigorous proponent of "public journalism" that would render media responsible to the communities they serve, responded in *Tikkun* that the same analysis might be directed to Krauthammer himself: "Krauthammer's column carries the distinctive marks of post-adolescent jeering: the self-satisfied smugness, the belief, after seeing through the illusions of others, that one has arrived at an adequate vision of the world; the conviction, upon ridiculing "naive" hopes, that intellectual maturity consists in just this act of ridicule; the breathless need to appear tough-minded and cynical. All delivered with the knowing smile of a board-score star, told too often how smart he is."

There were only two things that Bill Clinton could have done at this point, and he probably needed to do them both: First, he could have enthusiastically and publicly backed up his wife, embraced the politics of meaning *or some other coherent and unifying framework,* and explained to the country how his specific ideas flowed from this perspective. Second, he could have begun a public discussion about media cynicism, preparing his supporters for the possibility that much of what he would be saying and standing for in the years ahead would be misrepresented by a cynical media.

He did neither. Instead, he capitulated to his detractors and brought in a new director of communications, David Gergen, who had served in a similar position for the Reagan White House.

Some members of the press were momentarily cheered. Here, at last, Clinton was showing that he knew how to play the game the way the insiders played it. Some liberals feared that Gergen would bring a Reaganite ideology with him, but they were quickly reassured. A key characteristic for a technician, like one who could switch from packaging Reagan to packaging Clinton, is that one need not have any ideology. This was precisely what made Gergen seem so safe and familiar to the media. This man, they presumed, would lead Clinton away from any politics of meaning or any other guiding ideological framework, and make him practical, pragmatic, and non-ideological. Unable to see that that anti-ideology *was* their ideology, many reporters and columnists could portray Clinton as having finally gotten some savvy.

The Struggle over Ideology in the Clinton White House

Although the discussion was almost never framed explicitly in terms of the politics of meaning, there was a pervasive tension within the Clinton White House, and within the Clintons themselves. On the one hand, their instinct told them to strive for their own highest values; on the other hand, the "reality check" told them to be more pragmatic, and reframe the idealistic themes that had excited people during the campaign into more narrowly programmatic language and policies.

To understand the battle within the Clintons, we have to recognize that they—like all the rest of us—are constantly hearing two voices: the voice that says that we should fully commit ourselves to our highest ideals, and the voice that tells us that doing so would be self-destructive. Though we sometimes try to find middle ground, the allure of "being realistic" often wins out because we are so firmly convinced (for reasons I have detailed throughout this book) that everyone else is going to seek narrow, personal self-interest, and that we will be hurt should we follow our highest values.

So when Bill Clinton was elected, the issue of taking ideals seriously resurfaced, both for him and for many of his supporters. America felt a surge of hopefulness and excitement when the Clintons took office. Yet, to the very extent that Americans allowed themselves to be hopeful, they were simultaneously filled with intense anxiety. Having been disappointed so many times before after having invested hope in social movements, political leaders, religious leaders, or others who promise some form of significant transformation, most Americans feel tremendous wariness when confronted with another movement that evokes hope and possibility. "What if we are being taken for a ride once again? Am I once again being suckered by a cleverly manipulative politician? Should I really be allowing myself to hope, when I know how hurt I'm going to be if I get disappointed?" These were the questions that arose—not for those who opposed the Clinton presidency, but for the tens of millions of Americans who, between the fall of 1992 and the spring of 1993, allowed themselves to hope that it might work after all.

This is the irony of hopefulness in the modern world: it is so under siege that whenever we allow ourselves to hope, we are simultaneously flooded with fear. I have watched this dynamic play out on a smaller scale in the meetings of political movements, where people are so scared that their highest hopes might be realized that they immediately act out their fears by behaving in ways guaranteed to undermine whatever is happening. Some people will dominate the meeting, insisting that their cohorts prove their political correctness or strategic wisdom. Others will introduce fear by insisting that nothing has yet been accomplished, or nobody will ever pay attention or take them seriously. Still others will insist that the only way to have an impact is by narrowing the goals of the group to something more limited and realistic (usually, as it turns out, something that most people do not care strongly enough about to spend their evenings engaged in politics). Meanwhile, by the third or fourth such meeting, those people who have remained quiet have become discouraged at the irrationality or lack of direction in the group, and this experience has convinced them that nothing is going to change. They return to the comfort of their privatized lives, in which they can individually despair about the direction of the larger world while joining with the larger cynicism of the dominant societal mantra that "nothing significant can change."

A similar dynamic plays out in public life. We are so fearful that this might really be the moment that we have been hoping for, that we are supersensitive to the slightest indication that we are being tricked once again. This fear itself explains the rapidity with which Clinton's public approval rating rose and fell in the spring of 1993. As soon as he began to take steps toward political compromise around issues such as gays in the military (retreating to a "don't ask—don't tell" policy), affirmative action (abandoning Lani Guinier's nomination to Deputy Attorney General for Civil Rights), the environment (abandoning attempts to restrict the

misuse of federally owned grazing lands), and a morally guided foreign policy (particularly in Bosnia and China), many of us felt that
our fears were being confirmed. We quickly distanced ourselves, allowing ourselves to grow skeptical and disapproving. Our hopefulness quickly soured. But our cynicism about Clinton mirrored his
cynicism about us. Though he often wanted to believe the words his
wife had uttered, he saw no visible signs that his supporters were
willing to stand up for the politics of meaning, or any other principle. His supporters remained passive and quiet, except when we
were ready to abandon him. We felt he should lead. He felt he
needed more support. Our mutual cynicism reinforced the side of
Clinton that was prone to opportunism—a side that we all know,
since every one of us has a part with similar inclinations.

The media offered a quite opposite explanation of Clinton's declining popularity. It was, they insisted, because of his "lunge to the
Left."

On its face, this explanation was ludicrous. Consider Clinton's
actual agenda throughout his first two years in office, when his popularity faded most:

- Clinton's major issue in the spring of 1993 was a traditionally conservative one, reducing the federal budget deficit.
  This was hardly a lunge to the Left.

- After he had passed his deficit-reduction plan, Clinton put
  his focus on passing the North American Free Trade Act
  (NAFTA), which was so insensitive to workers' rights and
  to ecological concerns that it attracted the overwhelming
  support of conservatives and the opposition of a wide
  coalition of liberals and progressives. Newt Gingrich rejoiced
  and took much of the credit.

- A great deal of White House attention in 1994 was devoted
  to a crime bill that was based on traditional conservative assumptions. It focused on constructing more prisons, increasing the number of offenses subject to the death penalty, and
  training more police.

- Instead of filling the federal courts with liberal or progressive
  judges to counter twelve years during which Republican

courts were being packed by ideological conservatives, Clinton failed to fill many judicial positions, and tended to fill the rest with political centrists.

In short, the "lunge to the Left" hypothesis had little to do with most of the energy expended by the Clinton White House, and hence little to do with his decline in popularity.

Conservatives, reflecting on their electoral victory at the polls in 1994, wish to enshrine that election as a repudiation of traditional liberal politics. To do this, they must forget about the key conservative elements in Clinton's agenda during the first two years of his presidency (as I have just outlined), and focus instead on the one element that fits their picture: the much-heralded Clinton health-care program.

There is no doubt that his proposed health-care program *did* fit the stereotype of a large-scale bureaucratic monstrosity in which many Americans might lose control of some aspect of their lives. This presumably was the sacrifice that "we" would have to make in order to benefit the poor. Yet the health-care plan was a monstrosity precisely because it embodied the conservative assumptions of the Reagan and Bush years. Rather than propose a sensible and easy-to-understand program based on the Canadian single-payer system, the Clintons decided from the start that they would have to play to the economic interests of the insurance and hospital industries.

Under the plan, most patients would have found themselves in huge health maintenance organizations (HMOs), with payments administered by large insurance companies. Not only would patients have lost the ability to choose a doctor, but doctors would have seen the current tendency in managed care—that medical intervention needs prior approval from cost-cutting insurance company bureaucrats—dramatically accelerate. The result was a program whose *only* popular feature was that it would cover everyone, but which proposed subordinating individual health choices to a bureaucratic maze that confirmed Americans' worst suspicions about the dangers of governmental involvement in anything.

Lacking any politics-of-meaning sensitivity, the technocrats who framed this plan seemed unaware of the extent to which the welfare state felt alienating—not just to those who paid for its benefits, but also to those who received them. The bureaucratic rigidity, the primacy of logic over human feelings, and the creation of passive consumers dictated to by those with supposedly superior expertise—all these characteristics reappeared in the Clinton plan, recreating the sense of powerlessness among Americans that has frequently defined the experience of dealing with even the most well-intentioned governmental bureaucracy.

Still, the plan did offer universal coverage, which would have been an extension of the principle of caring for others. Had the Clintons been able to talk about their plan honestly and acknowledge what was legitimate in the public's fears, they might have gone a long way toward building public support. The Clintons could have shown that the so-called free market in health care was itself dramatically limiting consumer choices, as an increasing number of HMOs and private health insurance companies were imposing limits on medical services and requiring doctors to convince cost accountants that each particular procedure was cost-effective.

Unfortunately for the future of their health-care plan, the Clintons were not prepared to openly fight the ethos of profit-making around health care. They failed to truly confront the profiteers who have made the system so prohibitively expensive: the doctors, with their insistence on large salaries, whether in group practices or as high-priced individual specialists; the hospital owners, with their profit requirements; and the insurance companies, with their insistence on a guaranteed profit level. Accommodating these profiteers, while simultaneously trying to ensure maximum coverage for everyone not yet covered, produced a plan that seemed to fully manifest the worst fantasies of what big-government liberalism had become. People would be asked to pay more and meanwhile have less control. Some Clinton supporters might have been willing to fight for this, even, had they believed that there was no other way to expand health-care coverage to the uninsured. But this was obviously not true, as one organization of progressive doctors made clear when they began to argue against the Clinton plan and for a far more rational single-payer alternative like the Canadian system.

To rally people around higher costs was one thing, but to do so when these higher costs clearly were necessitated by the desire to appease the self-interest of health-care profiteers simply was impossible. By honoring the dynamic of self-interest, the Clinton plan allowed many people to assess its proposals mainly in terms of their own self-interest. And why should they be asked to sacrifice on behalf of the self-interest of profiteers?

It is far too simplistic to conclude from the repudiation of Clinton's health-care plan that Americans are far more conservative than liberals used to think or unwilling to sacrifice for others. What is true is that most people face an inner conflict about how much to trust their own instincts to make sacrifices for others. The more they think that others are willing to make similar sacrifices, the safer this path seems to be. But if the nature of contemporary events is such that everyone else is frantically pursuing self-interest, and they are going to be the only ones who are sacrificing for the sake of idealism, most people respond by abandoning their own idealism and embracing a more conservative politics.

Part of the reason why people became so disillusioned with Bill Clinton was his implicit promise that we could trust one another to pursue the common good, and transcend the selfishness and me-firstism of the Reagan and Bush years. Many people would have accepted temporary retreats from his campaign promises had he tried to explain them as part of an overall strategy, in which there was a "we" fighting for common goals. For example, Clinton could have said of gays in the military that he felt he had made a mistake to raise the issue when he did, that he still believed that the majority of Americans were wrong on this issue, and that he would try to raise it again later on during his presidency, after he had taken other steps to educate people more about the problem of homophobia. Few of his supporters would have felt betrayed, and even some of his critics might have been moved by his political courage. Similarly, had Clinton tried to explain his other policy retreats as part of a strategy aimed at achieving some shared idealistic goals, there would have been far less widespread disillusionment.

If Clinton had sought to make people feel they were part of some community of shared higher purpose, they might have disagreed with his strategy but they would not have felt so manipulated. Instead, Clinton's policy shifts were explained by White House insiders as a response to his keen awareness of the latest polls and focus groups. "After all, he has to worry about what people want if he is to keep his popularity, the necessary condition for his being effective politically," his apologists insisted. But this was simply a way of saying that his own perceived short-term self-interest had to be more important to him than his principles. This approach, of course, was precisely what people had imagined he would challenge when he and Mrs. Clinton embraced the politics of meaning.

If, instead, the very person who had promised to lead the challenge against the ethos of selfishness was now saying that it was no longer in his self-interest to do so, is it any wonder that those who had allowed themselves to feel hopeful would end up feeling manipulated, disillusioned, and newly attracted to the dominant notion that nothing but self-interest is possible in this world?

And if the president of the United States does not feel that he has the strength to fight for his highest ideals, many people reasoned, how could they personally be expected to fight for these ideals when they had so much less power than Clinton?

Many Americans whom my colleagues and I interviewed over the past two years said something like this:

> When I first heard Clinton, I thought maybe he would bring back the Kennedy era, when people were willing to sacrifice for the greater communal good, and then I would have been willing to do the same. But once I realized that he was going to be focused on his own self-interest, and that the selfishness of the Reagan and Bush years was going to continue, it seemed foolish to make myself more communal than everybody else. Why should I and my family have to pay higher taxes, or higher amounts to get health care, or make other sacrifices, if meanwhile everybody else is making out for themselves? No thanks. I may have idealistic parts, but I'm not a sucker. So if that's the nature of the Clinton years, I'm going to look out for myself.

To some of these people, looking out for themselves meant voting to lower their own tax burden by supporting conservatives in both political parties. To others, it meant simply not getting involved in anything besides themselves and their family issues— detaching from politics altogether, not voting, and not allowing themselves to care.

Consequently, framing American politics in terms of a Left/ Right spectrum is misleading. It makes much more sense to see the spectrum as having cynicism at one end and idealism at the other end. Viewed in this context, Clinton was being perceived by many Americans as having lunged toward cynicism, rather than toward the Left, and it was for this reason that they lost confidence in him. To be more precise, they gave up their hopefulness, decreased their involvement in what was happening in the political arena, and then assessed what was happening in the same "realistic" terms that they had momentarily allowed themselves to believe the Clintons were going to help everybody transcend. People who had sustained their hopefulness through the Reagan and Bush years on the supposition that eventually there would be a shift toward idealism were dealt a powerful blow by the Clinton betrayal.

Had the Clintons appeared to stand for something and been willing to fight for it, they might have lost various legislative battles, but they would have won growing respect and allegiance from an American public that had sought change from the ethos of self-ishness of the preceding years. It was not gridlock—but opportunism and ethical spinelessness—that sickened most Americans. When the Clintons seemed to frequently shift their policies to win momentary popular approval, when they could embrace a politics of meaning one day and forget what it meant the next, Americans felt betrayed. When, however, during the 1995 budget disputes with a Republican Congress, Clinton appeared willing to fight for principles, his popularity increased.

Some alleged political realists counter this analysis by arguing that the Clintons *had* to abandon their unifying theme and revert to a more politically conservative pragmatism because otherwise they would not have been able to accomplish anything. But this latter explanation already assumes that the key to political accomplishment is to pass this or that piece of legislation. I argue that the far more important accomplishment is to win the hearts and minds of the population to a coherent worldview.

We need only contrast the Clintons' behavior with that of Newt Gingrich and other principled conservatives. When these conservatives have lost elections, they have not sought to position themselves as born-again liberals who had been misunderstood by the press. Instead, they have insisted on the truth in their vision. And since winning power in 1994, they have stuck with their conservative vision and used their power to push many of their programs through Congress. It is this commitment to consistent vision and principles that has earned them respect and trust over many decades.

Why could the Clintons not do this? Why did they not fight for a politics of meaning, or, if that was the wrong choice for them, then for *some other unifying vision*? (Almost any such vision would have been better than the ideological incoherency with which they became identified.) The reason: the Clintons had long ago decided that this kind of idealism would make them too vulnerable. Following the mistaken "wisdom" of political centrists, they had come to believe that being pragmatic meant avoiding ideology except at the moment when one is actually running for office.

This last axiom helps explain why, as the 1996 election nears, Bill Clinton has begun to return to the kinds of issues that a politics of meaning highlights. In the election campaign of 1996, those themes will reappear and people will be urged to believe that Clinton has found himself and his principles once again. But when he actually had the opportunity to use his office to shape a coherent vision of what America needs, Clinton instead followed his (inaccurately) perceived narrow self-interest.

Fearing Feminization

Some people like to romanticize Hillary Clinton, arguing that because she is smarter than her husband, in their opinion, she is also more principled. I see no reason to believe this. Both partners share a genuine idealism, and both were unwilling to fight for their idealism when they thought it conflicted with their perceived short-term self-interest. Both partners surrounded themselves with staffers who opposed any ethical, spiritual, or ideological framework for politics, except as a source of reelection rhetoric.

Both Clintons were concerned that a politics-of-meaning orientation, with its call for a society based on love and caring, might make the president look too soft. As one White House aide explained to me in early May 1993, the insiders were worried about what some referred to as "the feminization of [Bill] Clinton."

White House staffers believed that the difference between Clinton's election in 1992 and Michael Dukakis's failed candidacy in 1988 was the swing vote of white working-class men who returned to the Democratic Party in 1992. In fact, it was the loss of these voters in 1994 that paved the way for the Republican House and Senate victories. From the standpoint of White House insiders, these were precisely the kinds of people who were most disenchanted by the "soft" issues that a politics of meaning represented, as opposed to the "hard" issues like jobs and deficits. These voters needed to see Clinton as a tough male leader, whereas the meaning-issues seemed to play to a feminine version of what is important.

I believed then, as I do now after analyzing the 1994 elections, that the White House staffers were deeply mistaken about what these white working-class men really wanted and were moved by. Unlike those sociologists and pollsters, who only knew these men from their responses to superficially drawn polls or unimaginative focus groups (of the sort being developed by Clinton's then-advisor, Stanley Greenberg), I had worked for ten years with this very sector of our population. I had seen firsthand what was happening beneath the surface—after these men had given the kinds of replies to pollsters that they imagined they were supposed to give.

In interviews I conducted after the election, I learned that it was precisely Clinton's softness in the primaries and election of 1992— his ability to legitimize an image of a man as someone who was both a leader *and* simultaneously someone who cared about the soft issues—that made him attractive to working-class men, who publicly would profess only their toughness and their disdain for those who were less tough. It was precisely their yearning for loving and caring relationships, for a society that encouraged people to take care of one another, and for meaning and higher purpose, that led many of these same "tough" men to sometimes attend church, and also led many of them to secretly feel relieved that there was a Bill Clinton to vote for.

Yet what these tough men really needed from Bill Clinton was someone who would to be tough in fighting for what he believed in. Surely, many of these voters would be skeptical or dismayed about

Clinton's support for gays in the military or for a variety of feminist concerns. But Clinton had publicly supported these issues during the election campaign of 1992, and had nevertheless managed to retain the support of these men.

What changed after the election was that Clinton's vacillations and backpedaling on his own promises made him look weak. It was one thing to articulate soft principles in a tough way; it was quite another matter to advocate soft principles in a soft way. What the tough men needed, then, was to believe that their move toward an ethos of caring (reflected, for example, in their willingness to pay higher health-care premiums in order to ensure coverage for the poor) was being led by a strong and self-assured leader: someone who knew what he was doing, could sustain some blows, would remain steadfast in his convictions and commitments, and would offer sound advice on how we might move together toward their realization. In contrast, faced with a nonleader, who continually sought to reposition himself in light of the latest shifts in popular opinion, the "tough" men's cynicism would grow about the possibility of reconstituting some shared community of values.

I know how tempting it will be for some people to reduce my analysis of the Clinton betrayal to sour grapes: here is a writer who felt disappointed that the Clintons did not stick with his vision, and so he has written a critique. But my concern is not whether Bill Clinton adopted the politics of meaning that I advocate, but whether he adopted *any* guiding principle and fought for it in a consistent enough manner that others would understand him to be doing so.

From a politics-of-meaning perspective, an important first step in the process of rebuilding community is to overcome cynicism and restore hope—and Clinton could have done this by fighting consistently for his principles, even if they were principles that I do not share.

Instead, by embracing pragmatism and the pursuit of popularity, Clinton managed to demobilize those who had hoped for community. Forced to once again view reality from the standpoint of passive individual consumers, many Americans became far less sympathetic to the very pragmatic programs that Clinton espoused. As he managed to further discredit the public realm, by demonstrating through his own behavior that it was just another arena in which people pursued narrow self-interest, many Americans became less enthusiastic about using this realm to pursue a higher purpose, and hence less supportive of those liberals who had been identified with that goal. Thus, liberal Democrats lost the next elections to more conservative opponents.

This dynamic flow of energy in politics has been systematically ignored by the media and misunderstood by many politicians. People hunger for meaning, and fear that it cannot be achieved. They reach out hopefully for a vision of meaning and purpose that is offered to them by liberals, but if that vision is undermined in some way (for example, because those who are offering it do not seriously intend to go the whole distance to establish a morally ordered society, or, worse, because they appear to be interested merely in themselves), then people retreat into the individualism and selfishness of the market. But since the market does not satisfy, voters soon seek out some other vision of meaning. Recently disappointed by the liberals, they are likely the next time to try the vision offered by the Right.

Unless the Clintons change their direction, and more fully and unequivocally adopt some version of a politics of meaning, we are likely to see many people attracted to the Far Right, as conservative groups offer their own late–twentieth-century versions of repressive communities of meaning. As fascistic or xenophobic nationalist movements reemerge, some people will point to them as proof that this is what people really have wanted all along. In fact, what people really want is *some* vision of community and connectedness. The one being offered by the Clintons, a momentary assertion of commitment to a politics of meaning, was so quickly abandoned that most people never even got a chance to hear anything more than the first caricatured version presented by the media.

The Clintons would have had an easier task awaiting them had there already existed a social movement pressing for a new ethos of caring and idealism. It was, to be sure, the existence of the labor movement that facilitated President Roosevelt's New Deal, and the existence of the civil rights movement that helped give President Kennedy more backbone. Though each of these presidents faced sustained assaults on their administrations from powerful corporate forces, they also faced pressure from these independent social movements. So, to be fair to the Clintons, I must acknowledge that they have faced a difficult circumstance. Yet it is also true that they could have easily sparked such a movement, had they given the public the slightest indication that they would support it.

Some Clintonites argue that no such movement could have been built recently, because people are more conservative today than they were in the past. But this alleged conservatism is not a fact; it is an outcome of a process. To the extent that public cynicism has increased, people will believe less in the possibility of some shared vision, and hence less in the possibility of acting together to accomplish shared goals. Bill Clinton, as president, became the most effective recruiter for this kind of cynicism and conservatism, precisely through his inability to stand up and fight for a moral vision after promising that he would do so.

It is always easy to conclude that all that can happen is what actually does happen. But this inference assumes that we are machines, not meaning-seeking ethical and spiritual beings who are capable of transcending that which is, and fighting for that which ought to be. No account of "how things are" can fully answer the question of "what is possible" until we take into account the degree to which each of us is willing to go for our own vision of hope, and how much we are able to support one another in the process.

I can make the same point from the perspective of my experience as an activist in the 1960s. Popular culture looks back on that decade as one of progressive activism, and often ontologizes the reality (as in, "Sure you could organize X, Y, or Z, because that was the sixties"!). But for us at that time, we did not *know* that it was "the sixties" in this activist sense. On the contrary, though there was a small civil rights and progressive student movement, there was also a powerful right-wing movement that culminated in the presidential nomination of Barry Goldwater in 1964. I attended a Young Americans for Freedom rally in the summer of 1964 at Madison Square Garden in New York, and watched as twenty thousand young people proclaimed intense allegiance to reactionary ideas. News magazines were filled with analyses proclaiming this "the lost generation" and commenting on the strong conservatism of youth!

If some of us had not taken steps to build a different kind of social movement, historians and sociologists later would have written books explaining why the triumph of conservatism in the 1960s was inevitable. Once we took those steps, and fought to win adherents—often against seemingly insuperable odds—the historians and sociologists rushed in to show why what had actually happened was the inevitable outgrowth of existing social conditions.

A president cannot single-handedly create a social movement. But just as Kennedy did for the 1960s and Reagan did for the 1980s, a president can set a moral tone and have a tremendous impact on legitimizing a dominant way of thinking and interpreting our situation.

So the Clintons could not have been expected to call the first meeting and set the agenda. But they could have clearly, consistently, and repeatedly articulated a politics of meaning; defended their perspective from the cynicism of the press; and ensured that within their own administration, policies would be shaped to reflect the concerns and goals that would flow from such a politics. It would not have been reasonable to judge the Clintons on the degree to which they succeeded in passing legislation. But it was reasonable to expect that they would dedicate a significant amount of their time, energy, and political capital to promoting a different discourse in America: a discourse of hopefulness, idealism, and caring that would have explicitly challenged the dominant discourse of selfishness, cynicism, and materialism. Had they done so, they would have fostered a powerful social change movement that would have energized significant sectors of the American public.

The ensuing debate would have been ferocious. The Clintons would have sustained many blows from the forces of cynicism and despair, but they simultaneously would have given sustenance to the part of us and tens of millions of other Americans that really wants something different, even as we fear that nothing can be different. Today, that optimistic and hopeful part of us has no champion in the public arena.

It was not in the hands of the Clintons to deliver legislation. It was not in their power to stop the fierce corporate assault on them. But it was in their power to promote a consistent politics-of-meaning discourse and to challenge the underlying assumptions of the dominant discourse. It was in their power to help people understand why this challenge to the dominant discourse of selfishness and cynicism would be a politically significant accomplishment. Of course, to make this goal a major presidential focus would have taken courage—the courage to stand up to those voices in our society who would predict that taking a principled stand was "unpresidential" and likely to lead to disastrous consequences.

To implement this strategy, the Clintons would have had to talk honestly about what they were trying to do. They would have had to explain their compromises rather than pretend to have really believed in these all along. They would have had to explain how what they were fighting for flowed from central principles, and explain what kind of support they needed from people and what form they hoped that support might take. To make a breakthrough, the Clintons would have had to discuss their own prior compromises more forthrightly, particularly in light of the scandal over their Whitewater development deal.

Whitewater would have offered the Clintons a perfect opportunity to level with the American public about how the tension between self-interest and higher values reflected itself in their lives and everyone else's, and how it was precisely the recognition of the ways in which the ethos of selfishness undermines *everyone* (themselves included) that had led them to a renewed commitment to public service.

Hillary Clinton did the opposite, however, asserting that she had merely been doing in the 1980s what she had learned from her parents: to take care of her own family and its needs. But this was precisely not what people needed to hear. They needed an honest discussion of the conflicts generated by looking after one's own needs in a society that counterposes us against one another, and makes one person's success depend on another's failure (or "getting ahead of the other"). Had the Clintons talked about the conflicts faced by all of us as we make choices between our impulse to look out for number one and our more idealistic impulses, they would have been able to challenge the media cynics effectively—particularly if they had been willing to show how the media's own self-interested mentality shapes how they cover the news.

By being willing to acknowledge the struggle within themselves, the Clintons could have made it safe for others to talk openly about their own struggles. This would have been a major setback to the cynics who try to convince us that *all* that exists under every idealist is a self-interested scoundrel.

People have often said to me something like this: "But this isn't who the Clintons are, Michael. Face it, you got taken in by a pair of salespeople who manipulated you like they manipulated everyone else—people who really believed what they were saying as they looked you in the eyes, but then forgot whatever that was when they faced the next person, telling him whatever they thought he wanted to hear." This reaction, I believe, is far too simplistic.

The more complex truth is that the Clintons are typical of many people in contemporary America who do not have the inner strength to fight for their ideals when they feel that doing so requires giving up something else they want or need (money, popularity, power, or esteem). These people will pursue their ideals when they feel that they can, but they systematically underestimate how much their own choices will affect the larger picture of what seems possible to everyone else.

The reality is that there are millions of us who are together recreating every day—by our own choices of how to live, and which values to articulate and publicly embrace—the world within which we live. This world that *we* have co-created then appears to each of us as "the facts" to which we are forced to accommodate. Like the Clintons, most of us are stuck in what I described above as surplus powerlessness: the tendency to see ourselves as less powerful than we actually are. And powerlessness corrupts!

When we perceive ourselves as less powerful than we are, we begin to accept aspects of our world that we actually all detest. This was one of the most striking discoveries that emerged in the therapeutic work I did with middle-income people: how much they hated living in a world based on selfishness and materialism, and how deeply they believed that nothing could be done to change it. They felt that they would be foolish and self-destructive if they lived by any other principle, given the expectation that everyone else would be doing the same thing. Thus, they went about reconstructing the very prison walls that locked them into a world which caused them pain.

It is within this framework, not within the framework of thinking of the Clintons as *nothing but* self-conscious manipulators, that we can best understand not only the Clintons, but the many who will come after them. They will disappoint us again and again unless we—you, reader, and I—create a social movement that makes politicians feel that it is not so risky to commit themselves to challenging the ethos of selfishness and materialism, in all its manifestations.

But creating such a movement is going to require a lot of compassion for all of us, including compassion for the ways in which we all become frightened and run away from our highest values. This compassion should be extended to the Clintons as well. In his first letter to me, Bill Clinton wrote, "You have helped me clarify my own thinking and to feel a little more convinced to say what I feel." It never occurred to me at the time to ask myself why he needed me to convince him to say what he feels. Now, in retrospect, I understand that he felt, and continues to feel, the same fear that many people experience about standing up for their own values. I wish that this were not the case. But I know that most of us have faced similar fears, and sometimes we have backed away from a full articulation of our highest values.

It is not inconceivable to me that Bill Clinton may win reelection in 1996, despite the broad disillusionment with the way he failed to fight for any coherent ethical vision. By standing his ground on affirmative action, budget cuts, and the sending of U.S. troops to enforce a Bosnian peace accord, Clinton has given indications that he might at least try to represent himself as having some principles for which he would fight. If he once again moves beyond traditional liberalism and returns to the meaning-oriented issues, and if he faces a Republican who does not appear to embody a sincere interest in the pain that most Americans face as a consequence of the crisis of meaning, Clinton has a credible shot at convincing people to give him a second chance. Similarly, I can easily imagine Democrats retaking control of Congress in 1996 and then mistakenly assuming that liberalism has been vindicated. They would be deeply mistaken. Liberals may still win some elections, but until they embrace a coherent ethical and spiritual vision, the profound American disillusionment with politics and/or the movement of political consciousness to the Right will deepen in the years ahead.

Practical Politics

If we are to have a movement that takes compassion seriously, it is going to have to have a place of compassion for the Clintons and liberal Democrats as well.

Compassion does not require that we soften our critique, nor our demand that politicians who win our support by articulating our values should fight for them more vigorously when they have won office. Compassion *does* require that we understand how very hard it is for anyone to stand behind his or her highest vision in a world where values like looking out for number one have so thoroughly dominated public space that anyone who talks a meaning-oriented language is demeaned and ridiculed.

Precisely because it is so difficult for individuals on their own to stand up to the dominant cynicism, materialism, and me-firstism, I reject the New Age approach that calls for each person making a revolution in her or his own head first, and then imagining that social change will follow from this. It is too easy for people to condemn Clinton's character flaws and the way he has succumbed to the pressures that surround him. But how many of us have not made similar accommodations in our own lives? The very forces that undermine Bill Clinton work to undermine all of us, undermine our families, undermine our friendships, and foster a world that is increasingly alienated and devoid of spiritual and ethical purpose. That is why we cannot do this job alone—we need to stick together and give one another support. Hence, the need for a movement, not just for a series of disconnected people trying to do the best they can on their own.

Unfortunately, the need for huge sums of money with which to buy advertising time on television, and pay for the other expenses of running for election, has distorted almost all political campaigns in the United States. To raise the kind of money necessary for a congressional or presidential election, candidates must appeal to people who have tremendous sums of disposable money—which only accrues to candidates who can show that they are "responsible," in other words, that they will refuse to hold corporations and the economy to the same high standard of social responsibility to which they hold ordinary people.

This is why a politics-of-meaning movement cannot focus its attention on elections, or hope that a Clinton or a Colin Powell or anyone else can be our savior. It is conceivable to me that if liberals were to adopt the stance and analysis of this book, they would likely become more effective in the electoral arena, even as early as 1996. The Democrats could, for example, organize large public gatherings on a "National Families Day" in October 1996. These events simultaneously would explore the problems we all face in families, and would champion a contract with American families based on the politics of meaning, as an alternative to the Christian Coalition's version. This focus might win the Democrats considerable support from people who, until now, have believed that liberals lack any understanding of the difficulties they face in keeping loving and committed relationships together. But the liberals seem unlikely to respond to this strategy, and in any case, the politics of meaning is not about winning elections or taking power. It poses a far more profound challenge to American society, and it would quickly lose its prophetic voice were it to shape its concerns around the narrowly defined politics of the electoral arena.

The Immediate Task

Our task is far more complicated and significant than to win a particular election. Our goal should be to bring together and mobilize all those who wish for a society that fosters ethical, spiritual, and ecological sensitivity; a society that is safe for love and intimacy; a society that encourages rather than undermines our highest vision of who we could be.

Such a movement would be badly needed by President Clinton, should he win a second term, if his administration is to achieve anything more than a rerun of the disastrous betrayals of his first four years. Just as Dwight Eisenhower's election as president in 1952, far from undermining the New Deal, actually consolidated it by demonstrating that even the Republicans were willing to support it in the 1950s, so a Clinton victory in 1996 might end up being interpreted as little more than a liberal endorsement of the conservative assumptions that have shaped much of his first term in office.

If his second term is to be anything more significant, he will need to feel the same pressure from the voices of those who believe in a politics of meaning as he today feels from the voices of cynicism.

One of the many down sides to having been identified as "the guru of the White House" is that the media conflates the politics of meaning I advocate with the empty slogans uttered by Clinton. I have tried to show in this book that an ethos of caring is not merely uttering that "I hear your pain," but actually doing something to relieve that pain. As the 1996 State of the Union speech showed, Clinton will revert to politics of meaning-sounding themes during the campaign—but he will avoid their substance. He talked about support for families—but not about the way the competitive market imbues selfishness and materialism. He talked about responsibility—but not the responsibility of corporations and how we as a people might use our power as consumers to require it. Let's see him use the "one strike and you're out" theme he applies to public housing thugs and apply that to corporate polluters or irresponsible corporate downsizing or exporting of jobs.

Clinton's psychobabbling may create an additional obstacle, because we may once again have to show that "love and caring," "hope and possibility," are not the empty words that he uses, and are not about new technocratic possibilities for a value-free concept of "progress" nor about protecting social programs that have proved inadequate, but rather that they have a very concrete meaning in the way we might reorganize our world. You cannot build a world alive with ethical, spiritual, and loving possibility unless you change the way we work, the way we evaluate productivity and efficiency, and stop the way we manipulate each other for personal advantage. In this sense, the struggle against psychobabbling Democrats will be similar to the struggle against right-wing religious people: it is our demand that the flowery ideals espoused by these groups be taken seriously and used to shape the nitty-gritty realities in the economic, political, and social institutions of daily life. Our campaign for a politics of meaning is going to have its hands full in opposing cynicism and the ethos of selfishness, on the one hand, while simultaneously opposing the cynical misuse of the language of love and possibility by politicians and religious opportunists on the other.

But, as the Talmudic scholar Rabbi Tarfon once said, "It is not required that you complete the task, but neither are you free to desist from it." This struggle has been going on for a long time. History is not over—and future generations will build on what we accomplish. What we must not do is abandon our highest hopes or relegate them to the sidelines while we become "practical" in ways that recreate the very world we want to change.

Even if conservatives come to power in 1996, there will be an equally strong need for a politics of meaning. The media will interpret such a victory as an endorsement of right-wing politics and a proof that our country "really is" conservative. We, on the other hand, will understand that their victory stems from their ability to speak to the meaning-needs that liberals have ignored. And we will understand that then, more than ever, our country needs a visionary voice that transcends the old Left/Right rhetoric and speaks to our deepest ethical and spiritual needs, lest politics move even further to the dangerous legitimization of anger at scapegoats, and the abandonment of hope.

All the more reason why we need to construct a movement now for a politics of meaning.

To begin to mobilize successfully, a movement for a politics of meaning must help people develop compassion for themselves and one another. It must avoid the "blame the people" elitism that leftists and liberals often fall into by erroneously assuming that the current materialism and selfishness result from the democratic choices of a corrupted majority. It must avoid the psychological reductionism that attributes our contemporary mean-spiritedness either to some intrinsic feature of the human mind, or to some peripheral distortions easily cured in therapy or spiritual growth activity. Instead, this movement must see us all as people who deeply yearn for the very human connections and higher purpose that we simultaneously fear, and from which we are constantly running.

A movement for a politics of meaning must encourage an atmosphere in which we can reassure one another about our dreams, giving one another confidence in our ability to achieve a more loving, spiritually- and ethically-centered world, even as this movement openly and compassionately acknowledges our current limitations and the ways in which we are likely to disappoint one another. It must encourage us to embody our spiritual and ethical values in our personal lives and to reject the counsel of those who tell us that nothing is real except the struggle for power, money, and ego gratification. It must help us reject the cynicism that surrounds us. It must affirm hope and possibility, even as it acknowledges our frailties and the great distance we must travel from where we are to where we can and ought to go.

Index